Takeoffs
Are Optional
Landings
Are Mandatory

Takeoffs
Are Optional
Landings
Are Mandatory

*Airline pilots talk about
deregulation, safety,
and the future of
commercial aviation*

PENELOPE GRENOBLE O'MALLEY

IOWA STATE UNIVERSITY PRESS / AMES

For A.

First Things First

Penelope Grenoble O'Malley, Ph.D., has served on the faculties of the University of Southern California and Antioch College West of Antioch University, where she was co-founder and director of the Master of Science Program in Professional Writing. Currently she is a partner in Templeton Biological Systems and Research Associate at the Santa Barbara Museum of Natural History. She is an Associate Fellow of the Society for Technical Communication.

♾ Printed on acid-free paper in the United States of America

First edition, 1993

Library of Congress Cataloging-in-Publication Data

O'Malley, Penelope Grenoble.
    Takeoffs are optional, landings are mandatory: airline pilots talk about deregulation, safety, and the future of commercial aviation / Penelope Grenoble O'Malley.—1st ed.
        p.   cm.
    Includes bibliographical references.
    ISBN 0-8138-2414-1 (acid-free paper)
    1. Aeronautics, Commercial—United States—Accidents. 2. Aeronautics, Commercial—United States—Safety measures. 3. Aeronautics, Commercial—United States—Deregulation. 4. Airlines—United States—Deregulation. I. Title.
HE9784.5.U5045 1993
363.12'4'0973—dc20   93-10889

CONTENTS

PREFACE

This collection of interviews with commercial airline pilots represents testimony of an important group of workers about what is happening in their industry at a particularly important time—maturation from government-regulated industry to competition in the open marketplace.

The deregulation of a service industry is a multifaceted problem. Theory holds that competition ensures broad distribution of goods and services at reasonable prices—in this case, transportation from one place to another. But in practice, the hopeful but somewhat naive thinking that led to the deregulation of the airline industry made insufficient allowance for the vagaries in the national economy or for increased competition from abroad. In 1978, the year Congress passed legislation deregularizing the commercial aviation industry, there were twenty-seven major airlines flying; today there are seven. This trend cannot continue without substantial cost to the airline work force.

Among aviation workers, pilots are the most highly trained and their skills the least transferable. Until deregulation, their relative nonreplaceability was acknowledged, and in many ways they were the darlings of the industry. Today many feel alienated and disenfranchised, an attitude that has the potential to affect job performance. Pilots have the intelligence, background, and experience to comment knowledgeably on the issues of deregulation. Their work cuts across all aspects of the industry, and their testimony describes how deregulation has affected questions of aviation safety and the effective delivery of deregulation's goal—cheap, available air transportation to the general consumer.

Although I applied some traditional sampling principles to this collection of oral histories, and was sensitive to issues of validity and reliability, I most wanted these accounts to have immediacy. I wanted the humanness of the people I spoke with to come through. I wanted to capture their emotions as well as their thoughts. I didn't want them to be reduced to statistics.

The words that the pilots represented here have been willing to share shed light on the everyday reality of pilots' lives, not so much the minute-by-minute drama, but how these individuals define their world and see themselves within it. Understanding the domestic pilot force requires awareness of the various characteristics that define individual pilots, including the airline they work for, the equipment they fly, their age, background and training, where they're based, and their education, marital status, and relative seniority. Some pilots whose views are presented here fly for the major airlines, such as American and United, some on long-haul international flights and others on short domestic "hops." Others fly or have flown for independent regional airlines or smaller commuter airlines that feed both the regionals and the majors—Air Cal, Republic, PSA. Pilots who are married and those with families have different concerns from those who are single, and although the majority of pilots are still men, women in the industry have specific interests and their own particular way of getting things accomplished. (In 1970, there were 88 licensed female air transport pilots; by 1980, the number had risen to 480; two years later it had almost doubled. These numbers are infinitesimal, however, considering that total air transport licenses during those periods were in the tens of thousands.)

Pilots flying out of the same base usually identify with each other, while pilots who live in one place and fly out of another may have different views. Pilots who have been through difficult contract negotiations or have been caught in a merger or an acquisition speak of different interests from those who have had an uneventful career with one carrier.

I spoke with and otherwise evaluated hundreds of pilots during this project; the individuals presented here represent a cross section of the types discussed above. A number of other factors were regarded in their selection, including their intellect, candor, emotional empathy, and self-knowledge; the degree to which their views were representative of those of other pilots; their overall knowledge of the industry; their capacity for understanding the larger context of what might seem to be only personal issues; and their ability to synthesize and articulate what they wanted to say.

The people quoted here, however, may not be representative of the "average" pilot in the sense of a scientifically selected sample, any more than it could be claimed that what they say stands for all pilots, but their remarks tell you what it is like to work in aviation today and how well the industry is functioning under the mandate of deregulation. Of course, not all the changes that have occurred are a direct result of deregulation, but a number of factors have combined within the deregulated environment to create perceptible trends that now appear to characterize the industry.

Let me briefly introduce the men and women whom you will hear from. Except for Earl L. Wiener, their names have been changed and some of the details of their lives altered in order to protect their privacy.

Ann Alexander (first officer, USAir) is one of a new breed of younger women flying. Trained in commercial aviation, Alexander gained experience flying for a regional freight airline.

Hank Barnes (captain, Trans World Airlines) is a Boeing 747 captain less than three years from retirement. Barnes trained in the military. He lives in a small town east of San Diego and commutes to New York, where he's based. From there he flies round trips to Europe.

Pete Browner (captain, Eastern Airlines) is a plain-speaking Southerner with strong opinions and a commitment to action. Browner trained in general aviation, and when he worked for Eastern Airlines he generally flew short-haul trips on the Eastern seaboard.

Rex Chamberlain (captain, United Airlines) is a former Pan Am pilot who is especially interested in aviation history. Chamberlain trained in general aviation and received his initial experience flying for Aloha Airlines.

Craig Donlevy (captain, United Airlines) received his training in general aviation. Although originally a line pilot, he is now a flight manager for an East Coast domicile.

Bill Fredericks (captain, United Airlines) is a former air force officer who is particularly interested in the physiological effects of flying and is an advocate of responsible duty time regulations.

Ted Goff (first officer, Delta Air Lines) is a former Western pilot and confirmed bachelor. Goff is a military-trained pilot who flew in Vietnam.

Lisa Johnson (second officer, United Airlines) is a former tennis pro turned pilot. Johnson is married and has a young daughter. She trained in general aviation and flew regional commuters in the Southwest.

Al Kellogg (former captain, TWA Express) is following in sister Sandra Luft's footsteps. He is currently accumulating flight time in the commuter airline industry in order to apply for a job with a major airline.

Joyce Kennedy and her husband, Jim Kennedy (first officers, Northwest Airlines) are both full-time pilots and are the parents of three young children. Although Jim Kennedy trained in general aviation, Joyce worked her way up as a corporate pilot. Joyce is currently on leave.

Bob Keystone (captain, United Airlines) is retired. He has been involved in a number of National Transportation Safety Board investigations.

Sandra Luft (captain, Continental Airlines) was one of the first women to break into the previously all-male world of the cockpit. Luft's training and experience are in general aviation. She worked as a flight instructor and flew air freight. Al Kellogg is her brother.

Patrick "Bud" McKenzie (captain, United Airlines) is a former navy pilot. Shy and soft-spoken, McKenzie is heavily involved in his airline's employee assistance program.

Max Neeland (first officer, American Airlines) fits the rigid pilot image, tempered somewhat by his youth. He trained in general aviation and flew for a commuter airline.

Stan Page (captain, Continental Airlines) is a scrappy ex-Marine who was active in the strike against Continental's Texas Air Corporation management.

Brad Prescott (first officer, American Airlines) is a former Air Cal pilot who joined American when the larger company bought the smaller carrier. Prescott accumulated time ferrying corporate jets from one coast to another.

Dick Riley (captain, United Airlines) is a former mechanic turned pilot who is active in union safety work.

Bob Scott (captain, United Airlines) is interested in all aspects of his industry. Scott trained in general aviation and flew freight in western Canada.

Greg Scott (second officer, United Airlines), Bob Scott's only son, is trying hard to follow in his father's footsteps. Greg Scott trained in general aviation and taught at a general aviation training center on the West Coast.

John Staitsman (first officer, United Airlines) is a veteran of Vietnam who works in pilot training, specializing in cockpit crew interaction.

Earl L. Wiener, Ph.D., is a former pilot who is now an acknowledged aviation human factors expert.

Jason Young (second officer, American Airlines) is a good friend of the Scott family who acts as a comic foil for his buddy Greg's activism. Trained in general aviation, Young accumulated his flying time piloting corporate jets.

The commentary contained in this book is divided into three parts. The first section is an introduction to the pilots who volunteered to share their experiences ("Who They Are and How They Got There"), their opinions on the theory of deregulation ("Deregulation as Pilots See It"), and fallout from its practice ("How They Get Ahead and Is it Safe?"). The middle chapters speak to distinct industry issues: "Training and Experience," "Pilot Error," "The FAA and Air Traffic Control," and "Technology and Air Safety." The last two chapters address what the industry calls human factors as they relate to safety issues, specifically the effects of life-style on work-place performance, ("Home and Life-style") and the challenges of cockpit relationships, ("Crew Interaction"). Included at the end of the book is a brief epilogue, a list of acronyms common to the aviation industry and a selected bibliography of sources for those who would like to investigate this topic further.

It's important to note that what pilots say here represents their ideas, feelings, and opinions at the time and doesn't necessarily reflect changes in the airline industry or circumstances such as the subsequent failure of Eastern Airlines and alterations in airline management such as at Continental Airlines.

Special thanks to all the pilots who gave their time and shared their stories. Obviously this book could not have been written without them. Thanks to John Mazor of the Air Line Pilots Association; to William Traub, former vice president of training at United Airlines, who introduced me to Cliff Lawson; and to Cliff for his efforts to teach me to fly. Also to Capt. S. M. "Marty" Shelton and Capt. Dick Russell for reading various drafts of the manuscript.

The woman wore a black silk dress of gold and bronze flowers trimmed in gold braid. The dress had a high collar and a wide sash at the waist, which gave it an Oriental look. High heels made her seem taller than she was, and smokey gray stockings outlined the pleasant curve of her legs. She wore diamond-studded earrings in her ears and gold-and-black bracelets on her wrists. Over her right shoulder she had slung a beaded black purse that fell across the front of her dress and rested on her left hip. On one arm she carried a plastic bag covering something that from the shape of it appeared to be a man's suit. In her other hand she carried a small canvas tote. She looked elegant and self-assured and ready for a good time. She also looked out of place in the United Airlines terminal at Los Angeles International Airport.

She was late and she hurried through the lines of travelers to the monitors that announced flight arrivals. Flight 181 from Chicago was on time. Gate 46. She moved quickly up the escalator to the security check. "Damn," she thought, "I forgot I'm carrying scissors." The young Latino woman on the other side of the X-ray device grabbed at the canvas bag as it emerged from the machine. She rummaged among the thread and masking tape and safety pins.

"Scissors," she said triumphantly, holding aloft a battered pair of shears.

"Yes, scissors," the other woman answered, wondering how to explain it. The minutes ticked by. If she missed him at the gate, the whole thing was ruined; he'd head for the tram and then she'd never find him. She had less than five minutes to spare.

"I'm not going on a plane. I'm just going to meet somebody."

The Latino woman looked at her carefully. "Not going on plane," she repeated.

"Yes, not going on plane, just meeting someone."

"Okay, you go."

Relieved, the woman scooped up the canvas bag, replaced the scissors, and headed quickly down the long corridor to the gate. The high heels were a liability. "Not meant for walking," she thought to herself as she moved along awkwardly. She got to the gate just as the flight was scheduled to arrive. She moved closer and looked through the heavy floor-to-ceiling windows behind the customer service desk at the same time the nose of the big DC-10 came into sight. She remembered what he'd said about coming into the gate, about the effort to see past the bright spotlight, and she moved quickly toward the window. The cockpit in the DC-10 was larger than she expected, and at first she couldn't see anyone in the left seat. "Maybe the copilot made the landing," she thought and then caught herself, "but they still wouldn't change seats." Her mind raced through other obstacles: it was the wrong trip; he had missed the pick-up; the equipment hadn't shown up. Then she looked back, this time closer to the cockpit's front window, and this time she saw him. She recognized his mannerisms, the solid way he held his torso, the controlled movement of his hands. She saw that his shirt collar was unbuttoned and his tie loose, and she remembered how, after almost thirty years, he disliked the uniform.

The plane began spilling its passengers. She set

herself the task of watching cautiously in case he headed directly to the employee bus that would take him
out to the lot where his car was parked. Finally the
stream of people diminished to a trickle. Three men in
uniform came off together. One was tall, thin, and
stooped. He wore his rumpled uniform jacket like a
college professor late for class. The second was of
medium height, well filled out, and jolly-looking—the
counterman at an all-night coffee shop. The third was
the one she was waiting for. He was the same height as
the second man, but even in the uniform, his body
showed signs of care—athletics, perhaps.

His hair was curly and long under his hat. She noticed the four stars and the scrambled eggs on the
visor. As he walked toward her, his flight bag in one
hand, the airline suitcase in the other, she was aware
that a woman off to her right was watching them. He
came up to her, controlling his surprise. He put his
bags down and reached for her. It was a short, perfunc-
tory kiss. He was in uniform and had to be aware of
what he doing. "What are you doing here?" he asked,
his mouth slowly expanding into a grin. The woman to
their right still stared. They embraced again, this time
more softly, but still restrained.

"We're going to a formal dinner, black-tie," she
explained, her eyes shining. "I decided at the last minute, and you had already left Philadelphia, and the
flight office thought you wouldn't stop by in Chicago
and I . . ."

"So where's my black tie?" he interrupted.

"Right here," she answered, beaming, holding up
the plastic bag. I didn't know your size, but I took in
some of your clothes, and the man in the store measured them."

He didn't say anything; he just stood looking at
her. He had pushed his hat back off his forehead, and
she thought he looked more natural that way. Embar-

rassed now by what she had done, she picked at the jacket and the shirt. "If it doesn't fit," she began, "I have all this stuff . . . ," she gestured at the small canvas bag.

"Where did you get it?" he asked, and she started to explain, stopped herself, and said instead, "We only have half an hour; see if it fits." The woman to their right still stared.

Ten minutes later, the tired uniform pants and shirt had been swapped for the softer lines of a midnight blue tuxedo. She had bought a silk tie and cummerbund with tropical flowers that broke up the somber effect of the dark jacket. He wrapped his clothes in the plastic and picked up his suitcase and heavy flight bag. She carried his hat for him.

They took the escalator down and edged onto the moving sidewalk. He wasn't in uniform now. He put his bags down and moved toward her. The dress was soft to his touch, her body warm and gentle against the wool of the new jacket. An old man walked by, ignored their kiss, and kicked the black flight bag out of his way as he passed. They embraced, leaning against the moving rail, oblivious to the bright light. He could feel the special place in the small of her back; she leaned against him with her smile, her hair brushing softly across his cheek. He was home.

• • •

Capt. Bud McKenzie, a DC-10 pilot for United Airlines, grins as he tells the story. "Isn't that dramatic? I laugh whenever I think about how that happened. It coincides with all the stereotypes people have about pilots—adventure, romance, our affluent life-style. I could see it in the reaction of the woman who was standing there watching us as I came off the airplane. It was the first time Karen had come to the airport to meet me. We had just started dating, and she didn't like doing that so I knew the circumstances had to be pretty dramatic. And it was fun for a moment to live out the drama. Now when we tell the story to other people, we kind of elaborate."

McKenzie stops, thinks a moment. "I get tired of being kidded about being a pilot, about the money and the time off, because that apparently is what a lot of people think about us. I also think that people see us as aloof and arrogant and that all we care about is big homes and fancy cars. Or that we're cynical and chauvinistic and we drink and party a lot. But just because that's the image doesn't mean it's true."

Watching a pilot board an airplane, buttons sparkling, gold braid on his sleeve, it's easy to evoke the stereotypes Bud McKenzie refers to, difficult to think that the individual carrying a suitcase and heavy flight bag is only doing a job, not unlike many others in its challenges and pressures, some of which he or she doesn't like very much. Or that the quasi-official voice that comes at us over the plane's public address system belongs to a person who has concerns similar to our own, from job security to home life, and that these can affect the performance of flying an airplane.

The world of commercial aviation has changed dramatically since 1978 when the government deregulated the airlines and forced competition among carriers. Before deregulation, the management and administration of the air transportation industry was the responsibility of a progression of federal departments, culminating in the Civil Aeronautics Board (CAB), a government agency that controlled air carrier routes, set fares, and oversaw standards of service. If an airline wanted to open a new route or close one down, it had to apply to the CAB for approval. Ticket prices were likewise regulated, and any increase in fares had to be endorsed by the CAB. Once a route was granted, an airline was bound to serve it; a company couldn't arbitrarily discontinue service because the market wasn't as anticipated or business fell off or fluctuated. The thought was that the public's interests were being adequately served, but the reality was that in this comfortable regulated atmosphere the airlines actually catered to a small segment of travelers who, in turn, seemed to accept that increases in the cost of doing business would be passed along in the price of a ticket. By the midseventies, these costs began to rise due to a number of factors, including fuel shortages, inflation, and the higher cost of borrowing money. These conditions provided impetus to those who were already lobbying for a more egalitarian air transportation system. Suggestions and opinions were referred to Sen. Edward Kennedy's judiciary subcommittee on administrative practices and procedures, which recommended the government end forty years of airline regulation. The committee's position was that the move would increase competition, thereby making air travel more available, and eventually affordable, to customers previously priced out of the market.

Congress accepted the committee's advice and voted for deregulation in 1978, putting the Department of Transportation in charge of overseeing the airline industry. Pres. Jimmy Carter, who was himself a strong advocate of deregulation, signed the bill, with the proviso that it would be gradually implemented beginning the following year. Most travelers didn't begin to feel the effects until almost two years later. In defending the committee's 1975 report that provided the basis for the legislation, Senator Kennedy maintained, "I have become convinced . . . less economic regulation and increased reliance on market forces will mean lower fares and increased protection for the consumer."

The reality of the deregulated airline industry has been manifested in a variety of ways. Revenue passenger miles on domestic routes increased steadily in the first ten years of deregulation, from just over 200 million in 1979 to almost 330 million in 1988. During this period, per passenger revenue also increased from 8.93 cents to 12.31 cents. On another front, the airline industry has come of age in an increasingly hostile business environment, striving to move from its former role as a publicly regulated service to participation in open market competition, with its demands and opportunities. It is probably not unfair to assume that revenue increases during this time resulted in part from new cost-cutting measures implemented by airlines competing under deregulation.

In 1987, one year short of the tenth anniversary of deregulation, almost half a billion Americans flew on regularly scheduled flights. Even with departure delays, overcrowded airplanes, lost luggage, and missed connections, the large percentage made it to their destination. Two hundred and thirty-one of them did not.

Nineteen eighty-seven was one of the worst years for commercial aviation since deregulation. Primary among the thirty-one accidents that occurred that year was the well-publicized crash of Northwest Airlines flight 255, which hit the ground on August 16 shortly after takeoff from Detroit's Wayne County Airport. All of the 154 people aboard were killed except one—a small child—making it the third worst accident in U.S. aviation history. Twenty-eight other people died when Continental Airlines flight 1713 crashed in a heavy snowstorm at Denver's Stapleton International Airport on November 15, and 43 more lost their lives in the suicide-sabotage of PSA flight 1410, which crashed near San Luis Obispo, California, on December 10. Without doubt, 1987 was a very bad year. In fact, it was one of the worst years for commercial aviation of the fifteen that have passed since Congress voted for deregulation.

In terms of fatalities, 1988 wasn't much better. In September a Pan Am 747 exploded over Lockerbie, Scotland, leaving 270 dead: 244 passengers, 15 crew members, and 11 people on the ground. Among other considerations, the incident provoked widespread speculation as to whether the airline industry was capable of protecting itself against sabotage. Nineteen eighty-eight was also the year the top blew off an Aloha Airlines Boeing 737 during an otherwise routine flight between Hilo and Honolulu, Hawaii, raising questions about maintenance on older high-time aircraft.

Two years earlier, in 1986, the worst midair collision since deregulation occurred over the heavily populated suburb of Cerritos, California. A small Piper PA-181 collided with a Aeronaves de Mexico DC-9, killing 58 of the DC-9's passengers, its 6 crew members, the pilot of the small plane and his family, and 15 people on the ground. The incident called attention to the limitations of the see-and-avoid concept for aircraft flying under visual flight rules. Before Cerritos, in 1985, Delta Air Lines flight 191 was forced down by wind shear 6,000 feet north of runway 17L at Dallas–Fort Worth International Airport. That incident, which killed 134 passengers and crew members, led to questions about Delta's training relative to procedures for dealing with wind shear.

In 1982, a Boeing 737 operated by Air Florida, one of the first airlines to take advantage of deregulation, slammed into the Fourteenth Street bridge in Washington, D.C, killing all but 4 of its 74 passengers. Before the Air Florida incident, in the first major accident since deregulation—the crash of American Airlines flight 191—a DC-10—lost an engine on takeoff from Chicago's O'Hare Airport. Two hundred seventy-one passengers were killed along with 2 people on the ground. The accident raised the issue of the DC-10's airworthiness and led to inspection of the domestic DC-10 fleet. Finally in 1978, the year deregulation legislation was signed, a PSA jet collided with a Cessna 172 near Lindberg Field in San Diego, killing 144 people, including those on both aircraft, and destroying twenty-two homes in the residential neighborhood where the planes struck the ground.

An airplane accident is a compelling event, and most of us at one time or another have been drawn to reports of fatal air crashes. We have seen TV accounts of airplanes skidding off runways, listened perhaps to charges of pilot error, sloppy procedures, and inadequate training and experience of airline personnel, and probably even attempted to understand the implications of National Transportation Safety Board (NTSB) investigations. In all of this, however, one voice has been conspicuously absent—that of the people who are the most responsible if something goes wrong in an airplane and most vulnerable to name-calling and scapegoating when it does—the men and women who actually do the flying.

Pilots have a unique vantage point. They have a clear view of airplane maintenance, scheduling, air traffic control, safety procedures, advances in technology and aircraft design, the functioning of government agencies that regulate the business, labor disputes, and the economics of getting an airplane from one point to another. The fact that we haven't heard much from them as a group regarding the issues that affect their profession is curious, especially given the changes that have occurred in commercial aviation during the last fifteen or so years.

One explanation for this silence that comes to mind is the possibility of a self-inflicted gag rule. Although contract regulations generally prohibit pilots from speaking out immediately after an accident (most particularly those who are directly involved) and generally until the NTSB completes its investigation and issues its report, pilots do not necessarily feel formally inhibited from talking about their profession. As a group, however, they appear generally disinclined to discuss such things and tend to leave the public statements to representatives of their union. For its part the Air Line Pilots Association (ALPA) has generally adopted a relatively low media profile regarding issues in commercial aviation, a position with which most pilots appear to concur.

Many myths have evolved around pilots and their life-style: high salaries, short work hours, the adventure of travel, and freedom from the constraining routine of nine-to-five. Likewise, commercial pilots are often characterized in stereotypes inherited from the military, images that portray them as presumptuous and unapproachable, loners more comfortable with their flying machines than with people. Nonetheless, it doesn't take much to imagine the downside of this, and to develop some comprehension of what a commercial airline pilot's life is really about. High salaries for what appear to be short working hours can be a liability, particularly when much of the workday is undertaken in relative isolation, with little direct supervision and practically nonexistent management feedback. The observation that flight time may be limited to eighty or so hours a month does not take into account layover hours, which keep pilots away from home and family and which are less an energizing experience than a vacuum between trips. And when pilots finally do return home, they more often than not find themselves engaged in a game of catch-up as they try to reintegrate themselves into the household's routine and reestablish what they see as their rightful emotional place in family life. In these days of deregulation, life for commercial pilots can also mean longer and longer duty times and schedules that change erratically from month to month. Furthermore, the rugged individualist with nerves of steel who was once a symbol of the profession is not as vital to this era of advanced, technologically sophisticated airplanes, when many facets of a pilot's job are actually controlled from the ground.

In point of fact, commercial airline pilots are something of an anomaly; members of the most highly paid union, they identify less with traditional blue collar labor than with college-educated professionals—although they themselves may not have a degree. The scope of their personal on-the-job responsibilities is such that the consequences of faulty decision making can be extreme, their mistakes highly evident. For all of this they are paid not a salary but an hourly wage, computed according to a complicated formula dependent on the equipment they fly and their position in the crew. Unlike many industries, accrued service alone is of little value.

Commercial transportation is likewise unique in that direct responsibility for the safety, satisfaction, and well-being of both passengers and co-workers is attributed to one individual or a group of individuals loosely referred to as a *crew*. In the airline business, captains in command of an aircraft are considered to be the final authority, responsible for the plane, its personnel, and its passengers for the duration of the flight. If something happens, they are personally liable to explain the conduct of their own actions and those working with them, which they hope they can do according to industry regulations and their own personal standards. Given the state of the industry today, this seems to add up to significant responsibility without much real power, a condition that undermines self-esteem and respect. Added to this is the flight deck crew's customary isolation from supervision and the fact that their fundamental accountability is whether they deliver the plane from one place to another without incident.

As might be expected, the deregulation of the airline industry has amplified the inherent liabilities of the piloting profession. A more competitive industry has inevitably induced a more cost-conscious, bottom-line management. Unfortunately for pilots, who are accustomed to an elite position among airline workers, this philosophy tends to minimize their value as a corporate asset. Although such circumstances are not exclusive to the commercial airline industry, airline management has shown itself ready to meet the challenge of developing cost-cutting strategies that may seem to devalue its labor force. Perhaps the best example of this is the two-tiered B-scale developed and implemented in 1980 by Robert Crandall, chairman of American Airlines. Pilot compensation has traditionally been figured on the basis of an individual's "seat" in the cockpit (captain on the left, copilot on the right) and the equipment flown—the bigger the plane and the more advanced the pilot is in the chain of command, the larger the income. The B-scale has had the effect of creating two different pay schedules by lowering the amount beginning pilots are paid and freezing their compensation for a particular period of time as specified by their union contract. Combined with mandatory retirement at age sixty, this practice means substantial corporate savings. As older, higher-paid pilots retire, they are replaced by younger, less-experienced but also less-expensive recruits. (It's interesting to note that the B-scale began at American, where pilots are represented not by the independent Air Line Pilots Association but an in-house union.)

Another effect of deregulation has been significant revision in aircraft and manpower scheduling to reflect the foreign route acquisitions that have become important to the industry, as well as a more productive use of resources. Often this means longer duty times for pilots and more trips flown on the wrong side of the clock when biorhythms are off, which in turn requires more off-duty recovery time and results in what many feel is a general disregard for "pilots as people," as one old-timer describes it. In fact, the Federal Aviation Administration (FAA) has been slow to develop and mandate standards for duty times on international routes. Additionally, as in many other industries, the mergers and acquisitions that have recently come to typify the airline business have further distanced management from the rank and file, and in some cases from what labor sees as crucial industry concerns.

A related fallout from the trend of takeover-merger-acquire-absorb is what might well be described as the dehumanization of the workplace. Instead of courting and developing labor, in many cases postmerger corporations have introduced practices that have alienated management from workers and from questions that affect them. In the airline industry, specifically at Continental and Eastern airlines, for example, pilots have felt that postmerger management seemed to view labor as an adversary and treated workers accordingly, a trend that some media observers have described as an evolving characteristic of the industry. On one hand, this antagonistic relationship has left pilots and other airline workers feeling devalued, while on the other it has provided them with people they love to hate. In most accounts, the prime player in these developments was Texas Air Corporation chairman Francis J. "Frank" Lorenzo. Texas Air once owned Continental, Eastern, People's Express, New York Air, and Frontier, making it briefly the largest airline in the free world and the much-touted example of what a postregulation airline should be about. In a 1990 retrospective on Lorenzo's career, the *Wall Street Journal* observed that the Harvard MBA had the dubious distinction of mounting the first hostile takeover in the business (Continental, 1981–1982) and was responsible for many of the innovations that now characterize the commercial airline industry, including merged carriers, fare cuts, and use of bankruptcy laws to reorganize and break up high-cost airlines. The article also noted, however, that there turns out to be a considerable downside to these innovations, what the *Journal* labeled, "debilitating labor strife, crippling debt loads, and service problems."

The maneuvering and consolidation of domestic-based air carriers that has characterized the industry since deregulation began more than twenty years ago. In February 1978, Pan American purchased an 18.9 percent interest in National Airlines. At that time Pan Am served seventy-three cities in fifty-eight foreign countries and only nineteen cities in the United States. National, on the other hand, provided service to forty-nine U.S. cities in fifteen states. The same year, Air Florida, a carrier providing passenger and cargo service on various Florida routes, bought A.A.T. Airlines, which served the Florida Keys. The next year Air Florida went on to purchase a small interest in Piedmont Aviation (which eventually went on to be bought lock, stock, and barrel by USAir.) In 1980 Pan Am bought up more of National Airlines, and Allegis, the holding company for United Airlines, bought a big chunk of real estate to add to its Hawaiian holdings, which included other tourist hotels. TWA World Corporation, the parent of Trans World Airlines, also dabbled in diversity—apparently the dominant strategy of the time—owning hotels and food service and real estate franchises. In the airline business, however, the practice of diversification tended to backfire. In 1985 an ailing TWA was taken over by corporate raider Carl Ichan after a bitter fight, and United's president Richard Ferris resigned in the face of allegations that he had stretched the company's assets too thin.

In 1981 Bass Brothers Enterprises, Inc. (a privately owned development company) bought and sold a chunk of TWA holdings as well as eight percent of Western Airlines. Air Florida also bought into Western, and Norfolk and Western Railway Co. bought into Piedmont. In 1981, Texas International Airlines, a little-known regional airline specializing in half-price "peanut fares" increased its holdings in Continental Airlines, a conservative, full-service carrier, to 50.3 percent, and in 1982 Continental and Texas International merged. Also in 1981 Republic Airlines, a mostly eastern and mid-Atlantic carrier, bought out Hughes Airwest, primarily a regional western carrier. Republic itself was bought out by Northwest Airlines in 1986, and in turn British Overseas Airways bought into Northwest. In 1985 Texas International, now reorganized as Texas Air Corporation, bought out a greatly weakened Eastern Airlines.

Even the commuter airlines got into the buying mood. Provincetown Boston Airways (PBA), a large commuter airline serving nineteen airports, mostly on the East coast, acquired Marco Island Airways, serving Miami and the Marco Islands. Cut-rate People's Express, flush with success, bought Britt Airways in 1986, and United Airlines finalized the purchase of Pan Am's Pacific routes for $750 million, while Pan Am, struggling to increase its domestic fleet, bought Ransome Airways and renamed it Pan Am Express. In 1986, USAir acquired Pacific Southwest Airlines (PSA), adding that pioneering California aviation company to its expanding network, and in 1987 American Airlines absorbed Air Cal, another California regional airline. In 1987 Delta Air Lines bought ailing Western, in one step transforming itself from a regional to a national carrier, while USAir bought Piedmont. In 1989 American Airlines bought

Eastern Airlines' South American routes, and in 1990 Pan Am's London routes were sold to United. In 1991, TWA sold its London slots to American, and Delta took over the Pan Am shuttle and the airline's European routes, while United bought most of Pan Am's South American operation. The first fifteen years of deregulation were very busy indeed.

Pilots accustomed to being courted in the tradition of respected aviators have rebelled at being caught in this increasingly volatile business environment, sometimes to positive effect, sometimes to no avail. The latter was the case when Continental pilots struck in 1983 after having first agreed to salary concessions to help save the ailing airline. The strike provided the opportunity determined entrepreneur Frank Lorenzo was looking for, and in a complicated transaction widely reported in the media, he and his management team were able to use the federal courts to force out the airline's unions. Five years later, United Airlines pilots struck over the issue of United's proposed implementation of the B-scale. The strike, which lasted longer than anyone had projected, further hardened the line between labor and management. Even after top management was replaced, United pilots began to move toward an employee buyout of the company, an operation that was finally abandoned after five years of struggle.

The reality of a commercial pilot's life appears to be a complex of conflicting elements, particularly regarding the factors of job status, responsibility, pay, occupational prestige, satisfaction, and integration of job with personal life. Since these factors have been modified to some degree by the effects of deregulation, what pilots think about all of this is particularly relevant. Very little information currently exists on the reaction of aviation workers to changes brought about by deregulation as well as any insights into what they may have done to adjust. Among pilots, air safety has always been a rallying cry that many feel has now been made more significant in an industry increasingly dominated by the bottom line. In this age of deregulation, pilots have rallied around this traditional cause.

"The history of aviation safety is written in blood," says Rex Chamberlain, a veteran Pan Am pilot who now works for United Airlines. "Every single thing we've done in the past has been done only after a major accident. There's not going to be a dramatic, sudden, obvious, demonstrable upheaval of air safety, but we're eating away at the limits."

Bob Scott, a long-time Boeing 747 captain, is less dramatic than

Chamberlain but no less emphatic. "They [airline management] want us to do tricks in the airplanes, and some of these tricks are scaring people. Professional pilots don't want to scare people; they don't want to scare themselves either. But they're doing both."

"How far do you want to go with air safety?" Chamberlain demands sharply. "What are you willing to pay? We're gnawing away at the little bits and pieces. Each little piece by itself is not catastrophic. But every time we eat away at fewer safety exits, fewer engines, more delayed maintenance items; every time we add longer duty periods and decrease the number of dispatchers, we add to our potential for catastrophe."

The frustration behind Scott's and Chamberlain's remarks results from the devaluation pilots—and no doubt other airline workers—feel under current airline management. As the industry's highest-paid workers, pilots have typically been thought to be immune from the concerns of everyday labor, concerned only with take the money and run. They have been seen as an elite class of workers who have manipulated airline administrations for their own gain, thinking, "the hell with the rest of them." If the pilots who speak here are an example, however, the opposite is true. Highly trained and highly focused, these pilots are seeing their working conditions deteriorating, the rewards of their work eroding (even their very jobs disappearing, as the failure of Eastern and Pan Am indicates), and their authority undermined. They believe the current business climate minimizes the skills on which they once so much prided themselves: independence, self-reliance, dependability, quick thinking, and on-your-feet problem-solving capabilities.

Pilots maintain that routine matters of decision making that were once essential to the responsibility of command are being assumed by supervisors in company offices on the ground, that automation has affected the way cockpit crews interact with their equipment and with other crew members, that flight schedules are making it difficult for them to maintain what they see as high-level proficiency on the job. And perhaps most important for us, the flying public, many pilots feel their input in regard to safety is being minimized or ignored.

Takeoffs
Are Optional
Landings
Are Mandatory

CHAPTER 1

Who They Are and How They Got There

When you go for an interview on an airline, all they do is flash in front of you how exciting it is, all the travel and that sort of thing.

—BRAD PRESCOTT, American Airlines
727 copilot

Building flight time is the common thread that binds together most every general aviation pilot who finds himself addicted to flying and can't get enough of it, ever.

—SANDRA LUFT, Continental Airlines
DC-10 captain

The Continental DC-10 was flying smoothly over the Midwest on the first leg of its scheduled trip to Honolulu with an intermediate stop in Los Angeles. Flight attendants in gaudy muumuus and short-sleeved Hawaiian shirts were serving the 200-plus passengers, doing their best to stimulate a vacation mood. Up front in the cockpit, however, the atmosphere was tense. Capt. Richard Deverson, a twenty-year veteran of Continental Airlines, who had crossed the picket line during the historic 1983 pilot strike, and copilot Sandra Luft, with almost eleven years in commercial aviation and a striker newly returned to work, were calculating how long it was likely to take to get the happy vacationers to their island destination. The issue being debated was the advisability of continuing the flight to Hawaii with one of the airplane's two Inertial Navigation Systems (INS) malfunctioning.

According to Continental's minimum-equipment list, both systems were required to be in full operation for the plane to be legal to fly. The difficulty was that the ailing INS in this particular instance was not completely out of whack. Although it couldn't navigate, it *could* fix its position. Captain Deverson was satisfied with the situation as it was; copilot Luft was not so sure. She was concerned that the system's inability to navigate could spell bigger trouble, that it might ultimately fail and they would find themselves without a backup—a violation of basic aviation principles and a legitimate concern, especially since a good part of the Hawaii flight was over water and out of reach of land-based navigation aids.

So when Captain Deverson asked Luft if she had any trouble taking the plane to Honolulu with one inertial navigation system "acting up," Luft indicated she did, adding that she wanted the repairs made on their scheduled stop in L.A. With over three hours of flight time left before they reached Los Angeles, Luft reasoned there was ample time for Continental maintenance to fly in the needed part. That way the situation could be addressed before it deteriorated completely and at a location where the work could easily be handled. Luft told Deverson, "I see no reason to take this airplane with that thing being iffy. Sure it will navigate fine on one

INS, but what's it going to look like if something does go wrong and some investigator says, 'Miss Luft, how long did you know that this particular INS didn't work well?' And I say, 'As a matter of fact, I knew about it since yesterday, because I flew over on this airplane, and I watched it really screw up.' "

Luft's position reflected what she calls old Continental policy, and she worried that Captain Deverson's reasoning might reflect a more bottom-line mentality of Continental's new management. She explained later, "The captain wanted to save the company money, and my theory was no. Perhaps his wasn't an unsafe decision; it's just that the margin of safety he wanted to allow is not what I wanted. I didn't think there was any reason *not* to get the INS fixed. Why were we even bothering to discuss it? By not requiring repairs that should be made, you condition management to ignore things that should be done. This encourages the philosophy that they can let things go until the complaints mount up. My theory is if it doesn't work, you write it up. That's the reason they pay me—to make those decisions. And if I'm not comfortable with it, I'm going to have to assume that the guy with me probably isn't comfortable either; at least he shouldn't be."

In the end, Luft won out. The Hawaii-bound flight stopped in Los Angeles, the faulty INS was replaced, and the trip continued on to Honolulu without incident. Recounting the story, Luft considers that she was simply doing what was expected of her as any responsible pilot would, given the circumstances.

The model for commercial pilots comes from the military. In the days following World War II, when commercial aviation began to gear up to meet the increased demand for air travel, ties between the airlines and military aviation were tight. With pension or reserve commission in hand, military pilots, many of them decorated combat veterans, presented themselves to postwar airlines and were welcomed with open arms. In addition to top-notch training and experience, these veterans also brought with them the beliefs and values of military aviators, which in many ways continue to typify airline pilots today. Today, however, the statistics are reversed, and the majority of air transport pilots come from general aviation, a development of concern to some.

Does the military provide a more thorough training? "Certainly," says Ted Goff, a military-trained pilot who now flies as a first officer for Delta Air Lines. "You can't match the money they spend on a military pilot, and the washout rate is horrendous—about sixty percent. In civilian aviation they don't do that. You pay your money and you get your private license and you fly. And then it might take you two or three tries to get through the commercial test."

Although today the peacetime military trains fewer pilots than previously, the myth of the combat-hardened aviator continues to be attractive to all pilots. "I can spot a pilot anywhere," says Brad Prescott, former first officer for Air Cal who now flies for American Airlines as a result of the 1986 American–Air Cal merger. "It's the way they carry themselves. They never get out of the take-charge mode. You never see them laid back, kicked back, even if they're not a captain. Because throughout our whole career, we're trained for emergencies and to be in charge."

"In aviation, from birth up into the 1940s, the stick-and-rudder skills were preeminent," says Capt. John Staitsman, a former helicopter pilot who flew ground support in Vietnam and now trains pilots. "You needed that guy with the white scarf—the rugged individualist with the crooked smile and straight teeth who was willing to go off and have the adventures and take the risk."

Staitsman says he's always wanted to fly, and the military made it happen. "I remember when I was about five or six, my dad took me to the South Bend airport to pick up my uncle. I heard this blimp, blimp, blimp, and over came this DC-3 with the spotlight shining on its silver propellers. When the thing pulled up, and I saw these guys up in the cockpit, I thought, 'Wow, where did they come from? Where will they go from here? How do they *do* that?'"

Staitsman went to college, joined ROTC, got his fixed wing and multiengine licenses and figured the army would send him to school for more training. Instead he was assigned to helicopters, which he eventually grew to love. "It fascinated me to pull up on the stick and lift that thing three feet in the air with one hand, to be able to back up and go sideways," Staitsman says, his eyes bright. After the service, he looked for an airline job and joined United Airlines in 1969.

"The navy was really the model for aviation," Staitsman continues. "It started out that the ship's captain was the only guy that had any education to speak of, with the possible exception of the first mate. The crew was a bunch of scum, and those two guys were the boss. That carried through with the captain as supreme commander, a man whose word you didn't question." Relating the theory to modern aviation, Staitsman says, "It isn't always a bad system really. If the guy's pretty sharp, it often works out all right."

When it comes to personal life, however, pilots may not be as well-served by this mentality. "When the pilot, the supreme commander, comes home after being gone for stretches at a time," says Staitsman as he continues his description, "the very first thing he does is reassert control in the house. Does he tell his kids he loves them when he comes home? Of course not, he gives them a check ride—'Did you do this? Did you do that?' He probably won't have sex with his wife the first night home from his trip because he hasn't reestablished the pecking order. This doesn't mean he doesn't love his kids. It doesn't mean he doesn't love his wife. All this posturing has to do with the fact that the guy is frustrated that the household can run without him. The captain's been gone, and yet the house is still standing. He thinks to himself, 'How can that be? I'll get things shaped up.'

"And part of what I call a pilot's obsessive personality, which dictates the way he deals with life, is the fact that he will never complain. He will *never* complain. He will get the job done. He will complete the mission, strapped though he may be."

Air Force veteran Capt. Bill Fredericks, an Air Line Pilots Association safety representative who has become an authority on the effects of fatigue and other physiological effects on pilot performance, thinks the precision thinking associated with military training and operations is essential to a good pilot. Of middle age and medium height, Fredericks moves with the intent and purpose of a young man given to causes. When he isn't flying, he can often be found heading full tilt toward the ALPA office at Denver's Stapleton International Airport, lugging a beaten-up leather briefcase full of photocopied briefs that describe accidents in which sleep deprivation, improper diet, and lack of exercise may be contributing factors.

"Individuals like us, who are in the flying business, are a special breed of cat," says Fredericks, "not special, actually, but different. We're very precise about what we do. We're very controlled. If we're not controlled, there's something wrong. Fighter pilots are the ultimate example. The other thing is that we are extremely honest about what we do; this is also part and parcel of our personality. If you're not honest in this business, you're going to die."

Bob Keystone, a retired 747 captain with 28,000 hours of flight time, acknowledges the precision and forthrightness Fredericks calls honesty but expresses it differently. "Every pilot double-checks and triple-checks everything. That's part of his nature or he doesn't last in the business. His motto is never leave anything to chance."

Patrick "Bud" McKenzie, currently a United Airlines DC-10 captain, is another military-trained pilot, a navy reserve veteran who flew carrier-based A-4s during the Berlin crisis in the 1960s when Western Europe appeared under threat of attack from the Communist block. Now in his early fifties with almost thirty years of commercial flying experience, McKenzie belies the military stereotype. His voice is soft and his manner somewhat withdrawn. When questioned, he takes his time thinking about what he will say in response and then speaks slowly and chooses his words carefully. This, and the way he cocks his head and looks directly at you as he listens to a question, fosters an impression of reflection that is unusual among pilots. McKenzie also appears to have a genuine sensitivity about his effect on other people, another unpilotlike characteristic. Married for a short time fourteen years ago, McKenzie spends much of his off-duty time with his two teenage children, camping and fishing in the summertime, cross-country skiing in winter. "When Joanie and I split up," says McKenzie, "Michael and Rachel were quite young. I decided to make it a point to spend as much time as I could with them. Sometimes it was difficult, getting home late from a flight only to have to drive back into town to pick the kids up so we could spend the weekend together. All and all, however, it has been worth it."

McKenzie began his aviation career in 1957 when he joined the Aviation Cadet Program after a congenital spinal condition disqualified him from his appointment to Annapolis. As a navy trainee, McKenzie started out on what he calls "air knockers," Piper Cub look-alikes that flew all of 60 miles per hour. Even at eighteen, however, and right out of high school, it didn't take McKenzie long to pick up on what was expected of him.

"After six months in primary flight training, you go directly into jets, and for the first three or four weeks you're just buzzing, because it's a whole new series of experiences, very invigorating, very exciting. Your mind is racing to catch up; your reactions have been geared to airplanes going at the most 180 miles an hour, and suddenly you're going 300 or 400 miles an hour. A fighter pilot's mentality is ego. It's the insistence that you're going to do it alone. Single-seat fighters have always been the greatest kick going. But you have to realize they can kill you, too. I was one of those who always went just to the edge, never beyond, because I just intuitively knew that going beyond would kill me.

"Some people are perpetual fighter pilots, and that's not how we operate in commercial aviation. I had a copilot the other day who was flying an approach to Denver way too fast, and we had to extend the speed brakes, which I don't like to do because it makes a lot of noise in the back. When I reprimanded him, he started to argue with me." The look in McKenzie's quiet eyes suggests wonderment that a fellow pilot would even consider such a thing. "In his mind, he was just trying to have a little fun, playing with the airplane, but you don't do that when you're hauling people."

"Aviation is a business of tremendous egos," says Brad Prescott, agreeing with McKenzie. Prescott received his training in civilian aviation and began his career flying small corporate jets. "At one place I worked, the chief pilot had such an ego I used to say when we checked into a hotel I had to get three rooms—one for him, one for me, and one for his ego. I think it dates backs to the old military days—the fighter pilot, oh my God, he walks on water! Did you know that when some pilots get their license, they also get Jesus shoes?" Prescott stops, turns his head from side to side as if he's looking for something. "Where's my Jesus shoes? God, I was cheated. . . . Especially the minute they become captain, they change totally. Come on, gimme a break."

Aside from training, a primary advantage of military experience is that it provides the opportunity for would-be commercial pilots like Ted Goff to accumulate the flight hours required by the major carriers.

"I got interested in flying when my high school geography class chartered an airplane on a field trip to Colorado," says Goff. "That's when I said to myself, 'Hey, this is the life for me.' I enrolled in the junior college where I was living. I was a business minor with an aeronautic major, and I started taking private flying lessons at the same time. Actually I started lessons two or three different times and ran out of money each time before I could even get a private license. So I decided to go to a school that had an aeronautics department, and get a bachelor of science in aeronautics with a business minor. Then I went into the navy, and the navy traded me five and a half years for a lot of hours."

Like Bud McKenzie, Goff was married once, is now divorced, and has two children. Unlike McKenzie, he cultivates his bachelor image with a kind of devil-may-care attitude. Goff's laugh gives him away. It starts slowly and unfolds across his face; then the eyes light up, he looks at you with a shy, sideways glance, and you know if you're not careful, you can be had. It is obvious, however, that Goff also has a serious side.

"I got out of the navy in December of '71, and there were no jobs. After three or four months of not working, I got a job with a charter service. One of the things that I did while I was there was fly 727s out of Okinawa. We'd go over there and work and then come back over here and have our time off. After Okinawa, I flew Air Vietnam out of Saigon. I had been in Vietnam in the navy, but it was real different being over there as a civilian. In the navy, when the shooting started, you ran to the base and got behind a wall. But when you were a civilian and the shooting started, the only thing you could do was run to your hotel and have a beer." Goff laughs and pours himself another cup of coffee from his expensive European-made coffee pot.

"After my nine months with the charter service, Western hired me, and that's where I was when Delta took us over. Right now I'm flying copilot on the 727, which is a great airplane. I've been on others, the 737, the DC-10, but I like the 727. It's a super stable aircraft. A fantastic airplane—it just never conks out."

Although Capt. Rex Chamberlain came out of commercial aviation, he has adopted the looks and demeanor of the stereotypical military commander—a man of straight posture and strong bearing, a man of quick mind and honest thought, and a man, like many others in uniform, who always has time for a wink at the ladies. Chamberlain originally flew 747s in the Pacific for Pan Am. He now flies the old routes for United, which bought the once-celebrated Pan American Airlines Pacific operation in 1985. Pan Am was the first American airline to initiate scheduled international passenger air service, the first to offer flights across the Pacific, and the first to utilize jet aircraft. It was Chamberlain's experience with the legendary carrier that sparked his interest in aviation history.

Born in northern California, but raised around Los Angeles, Chamberlain learned to fly from his father, a military aviator, and began a college career as a math and science student. Sometime in his first year of college, however, an old family friend who was then a senior captain for Aloha Airlines stopped by for a visit and lured the young man to the islands to fly.

"I went out there in spring of 1960," Chamberlain remembers. "I signed on and they taught me to fly a DC-3. I was nineteen years old, and I was somewhat in shock. It was not at all what I had expected because the airplanes were so old-fashioned. It was flying in the earliest sense of air transportation. I was also studying how to do what the older guys called 'chat up the birds'—how to play games with the stewardesses and so on. I had signed on as an apprentice aviator, and I soon learned that a good part of that was learning how to talk a good line. I was fascinated by that.

"I was going to be in on the ground floor of what obviously was the opportunity of a lifetime, so I put my education on hold and beamingly showed up everyday to engage in this wonderful new opportunity. My father didn't appreciate what I had learned at nineteen about the seniority system, that you don't go off to college and then come back five years later and expect to pick up where you left off. During the next twenty years, fellows from the military would see their friends going to the airlines, and they would decide to finish their tour, re-up, and do it later. They didn't know what happened to me and my eventual career at Pan American, where I made 747 captain after sixteen years, and the fellows who joined the airline two years later had not yet even made first officer on anything we had."

While Chamberlain is sober, serious, and buttoned down, Dick Riley, a midcareer captain in his early forties, is affable and easygoing. Riley is a big man, unpretentious in a plaid short-sleeved sport shirt worn outside drab olive pants. Sliding behind the steering wheel of his 1966 Dodge convertible, he laughs, "This is the airport car; my other car's a 300ZX." Riley is that rare kind of individual who is forthright and responsible about what he does, but nevertheless manages not to take himself too seriously. He is a strongly moral man but he is also practical, and his beliefs and expectations are expressed without self-righteousness.

Riley came to airline piloting through maintenance. After graduating from college with a degree in aeronautics and turning down a job with an aircraft manufacturer, Riley decided what he really wanted was to fly. "Driving home from college in the summertime, I stopped at United and they needed mechanics. They were going to pay me more as a mechanic than I would have gotten as an aeronautical engineer, and they also let me take all the pilot tests. I worked as a mechanic for four years, and when a big hiring spree started in the midsixties, I moved over and started flying.

"I've been flying for United twenty-two years. I'm currently a 737 captain and I fly up and down the East Coast simply because I like the hours. I don't even like going as far west as Chicago. I stay on Eastern Standard Time and fly short legs. Sooner or later that's going to come to an end, simply from a pay aspect. I probably will take a DC-8 or DC-10 bid as soon as I'm senior enough to do it. But the 737 is so nice to fly. It flies like an F-86."

For individuals like Riley, who don't have the option of military flying, building flight time can be a considerable challenge. Although all airlines have rigid minimum flying requirements and the various ratings needed by a commercial air transport pilot are fundamentally related to flight hours, there are no officially sanctioned procedures for acquiring the necessary flight time or experience. As one general aviation veteran remembers, this means, "You do it any way you can."

Brad Prescott began flying lessons when he was twenty-five. "I joined an aero club and I got my private license. And then it mushroomed. I thought to myself, 'Well, this wouldn't be bad.'" Working as an airline ticket agent, Prescott built flight time ferrying Lear jets from Florida to California at night. Although Prescott's neatly pressed slacks and well-polished cowboy boots suggest a happy, casual guy, somewhere back behind the clear gray eyes lurks an impression of a deeply felt sorrow or perhaps a lingering fear of not measuring up, a result perhaps of how he came to fly-ing—working full-time to support his young family and flying in his off hours. The fist-pounding and expletives that typify Prescott's conversation are his way of emphasizing what he considers important points. Despite his emotional gestures, Prescott's thoughts are well-considered and his intelligence is obvious.

"I did go insane after a while flying airplanes. I can remember one time being so sick—I had the flu. It was gross. I had a bucket; I was puking and flying. I can remember that like it happened yesterday. The Lear distributor told me he couldn't pay me but he'd give me all the time I wanted and pay all my expenses. I was young and nuts. I flew in weather I shouldn't have flown in—thunder-storms, ice. . . . I knew I had a fixed amount of time to do the job. And I just did it."

Working full-time and flying part-time wasn't providing Prescott enough experience or money, however, and he decided he needed an alternative. "I went to the bank and tried to borrow some money to get all my ratings, but they wouldn't give me a loan, so I talked to Dick Mazi, a man who had a ranch outside Houston. I used to help take care of his airplane—I'd do the mechanical stuff and keep it clean. Dick was on the board of the local bank, and he told me to go down to see the president and that he would put in a word for me. So I borrowed the money and got my ratings and then I couldn't find a job because I was still low on time. So I went back to Dick, and he sent me over for an interview for a corporate flying job with the chief pilot of a big company in L.A., who took my resume and told me they didn't have anything but if something came up, he'd give me first shot at it. He told me to call him every month. I knew that Sunday night he was always home, so I'd call him. Finally he called me back on a Thursday night, the first week of March, and asked me if I could be there the next day to take a physical.

"I'll never forget it. They were going to start me out at $750 a month; I was making $600 as a ticket agent. I thought I was going to be rich. Unfortunately in corporate flying, they start you out pretty good, but it doesn't progress much from there. When I was a captain on a G-2 [Gulfstream II], flying for an oil company in Texas, I was making $57,000 a year; to me that was about $30,000 less than I should have been making. You're on call seven days a week. You have to be ready to fly anywhere in the world. I can remember coming from Europe all the way back to L.A., being up for goddamn thirty hours. I don't care what the story is, you should not be flying that kind of duty time.

"I don't understand these corporate people. If I was in charge of a big corporation and making half a million or a million a year, I'd fly first class on a regularly scheduled airline. The fatigue factor in corporate flying is phenomenal. I've come from Nice straight through to Los Angeles; that's fourteen or fifteen hours. You make stops but just for fuel. You're a zombie. And I think that was my biggest fear—being so tired. The fatigue is made worse by the fact that on a small jet there isn't much to do. You keep looking at the guy next to you, and you say to each other, 'Oh God, another six hours of you!' The FAA doesn't have any duty-time rules for corporate flying. You can do anything you want to do. Seven days a week, twenty-four hours a day. They don't care if you ever come out of the cockpit."

Brad Prescott and Max Neeland are buddies. Before they ended up at American Airlines together, they worked for a time on the same private jet charter service. Today they see each other when Brad drops by Max's fishing boat, which is moored at a marina in San Francisco Bay—Prescott in cut-off blue jeans, sweatshirt, and a baseball hat, Neeland neat in tan shorts, designer polo shirt, and sandals. Neeland is cool, detached, quietly driven, a man who believes there's a place for everything and who spends considerable time putting everything in its place. It's a trait that could account for the thin strain of tension that surfaces from time to time, cracking Neeland's usual casual demeanor. In his early thirties, Neeland is probably a good ten years younger than his buddy Prescott.

Max Neeland fought the battle of accumulating flight time working for an East Coast commuter airline. "I was about twenty-five and this was a period of rapid expansion for the airline. They bought a few more airplanes, and they needed more crews. I think I only flew as a copilot for about nine months when I was allowed to skip over a couple of guys and upgrade to captain. The seniority system was a little less formal there than it is with the major carriers. So was the duty time. I can remember during times when we were short on pilots and I would sometimes fly 150 hours a month, which is twice what we're scheduled for now on American."

Neeland is referring to federal regulations that specify the number of hours a pilot is allowed to fly during expressed time intervals, as well as the amount of rest time required between flights. Utilizing FAA standards, airlines are allowed some leeway in constructing their schedules, which must also factor in the terms of their pilot contracts, which for the most part are negotiated by the Air Line Pilots Association. There are different regulations for commuter airlines such as Neeland is speaking of, however, and often younger pilots eager for flight time are anxious to fly the extra hours.

"Commuter flying is much more difficult flying in terms of the stress on your body," says Neeland. "The turbo props are noisy; they vibrate and you're constantly operating at a lower altitude. And it's not uncommon for commuter airline pilots to fly six or seven legs in a day and make maybe six or seven landings, whereas the way I fly now, we're lucky if we have one landing on a two-day trip. So in the course of just a couple of years doing that, I went from being hopelessly underqualified for a major airline job to suddenly meeting the time requirements."

Greg Scott is another young pilot, the only son of an aviation family, who currently flies as a DC-10 second officer. Like Neeland and Prescott, Scott is a graduate of civil aviation. He accumulated his hours flying freight back and forth across the country. When he got his chance, he joined a general aviation training facility on corporate-size jet aircraft, figuring that as an instructor he'd be able to add to his flight time. Interestingly, Scott is not particularly impressed with military-trained pilots. "One thing that you'll find with a lot of military pilots is that they're set up to fly by themselves; they don't rely on anybody else. And in my opinion, that can cause problems. Your copilot or your engineer may have a great idea, but if you're not willing to listen, that idea doesn't do anybody any good. Delta is a big military-hiring company, and they have trouble with this."

Jason Young is the same age as Greg Scott and the two are friends, but while Scott assumes industry stereotypes—short hair, stern look, quick handshake—Young slumps along like a disinterested graduate student late for class. The story is that after a number of years of flying as a corporate pilot, Young applied to United where Scott was already working. Although a good pilot, Young was a little too cocky, didn't pass muster in the simulator and later ended up at American. He and Scott maintain a friendly rivalry—Scott fervent and excited by ideas about how things should be, Young baiting him then shrugging his shoulders and feigning nonchalance.

The demand for pilots that sent young men like Young and Neeland and Scott into general aviation to collect the hours they needed for their air transport certificate also helped open doors for women interested in flying. Women who decide to make their career in commercial aviation, however, are a special group. Although female pilots have made some inroads in the industry, the cockpit remains a male world dominated by male values, where the lingo is male, the jokes are male, and the traditions of behavior are male. To succeed women must walk a tightrope of tact. They must be able to assert themselves without being threatening. They must appear to accept traditional macho stereotypes while conveying a strong sense of their own confidence, independence, and self-worth.

A particularly noticeable difference between male and female pilots is that the women appear substantially more aware of who they are and how they project themselves. In a world of homogeneous values where standards of appearance hover between neutral and bland, reflecting the kind of detached mind-set that exemplifies the commercial pilot's world view, women pilots appear to be more outer-directed—more citizens of the world, so to speak—alert to larger issues and much more sensitive to subtleties of social interaction.

With her red hair pulled back in a ponytail and bright green eyes, Joyce Kennedy, for example, looks more like a young suburban housewife than a DC-9 copilot. Dressed in white shorts and a pale-pink sweatshirt, her rather feminine appearance does not suggest the vision and perseverance she needed to make herself a place in contemporary aviation. Kennedy originally planned to become a pediatric nurse and fly as a hobby. Her father was a pilot—a barnstormer who carried the mail in the dangerous times when, without navigational aides, pilots flew across the country from one water tower to another or followed railroad tracks. Retired from flying, he took to taking people up for Sunday afternoon plane rides at a small South Carolina airport. Sometimes Joyce and her brother would go along. Joyce kept up the interest in flying, borrowed the money to get her ratings, and eventually went on to become a commercial pilot. Conflicted about her love of flying and the nursing career she had planned for herself, Kennedy took a year off from college to consider what she should do. She decided that what she really wanted to do was fly.

"The ultimate goal was to fly for the airlines. That was what I wanted. I knew that there would be stepping-stones through that, and my plan of action was to be an instructor and then do work toward charter and then whatever I had to do to build time." Kennedy followed her plan, got her ratings, flew in a variety of small operations, and landed her first major flying job in corporate aviation, which gave her the opportunity to accumulate the multi-engine experience she needed in order to apply to the major carriers. From there she went to a small midwest commuter airline where, in addition to accumulating commercial flying experience, she also met the man who would become her husband. When Republic Airlines bought the small regional carrier, Jim and Joyce Kennedy—married by then—joined the ranks of Republic pilots who in turn went to work for Northwest when it absorbed Republic in 1986. Both have flown as first officers. Joyce is senior to her husband, and before she left on leave she had considered checking out as captain. "Jim says he wants to fly with me on my first flight," she laughs. "The other guys rib him about my being senior, but he's real secure. Not many men would do that."

Lisa Johnson was a tennis pro before she decided that piloting would be a more interesting way to earn a living. Making the transition, she had to overcome an initial fear of flying. "Back then there were so few women flying, even in civil aviation. I started applying to the major carriers in '75, when I did not have the qualifications. I still needed more ratings, but I just kept applying. They said to update every six or twelve months, and I updated every three months. I bugged them like crazy. Monday was my day off, and

I called them all, the ones I wanted to get on—United, Delta, American, TWA, Continental." Johnson was eventually hired by United; she is now a DC-10 second officer and is married and has a small daughter.

Ann Alexander, who flies for USAir, studied forestry in college and then, encouraged by her father who was a commercial pilot, went on to get her commercial ticket. Alexander is younger than Johnson and Kennedy and flies as copilot on the MD-80. She accumulated her hours flying for a small freight airline based near Phoenix. Her casual manner and two-seconds-in-front-of-the-mirror informality reflect her life-style as a young single woman. Her relatively easy access to an airline career was paved for her, however, by pioneers like Sandra Luft.

Luft headed for college before she knew she wanted to be a pilot. She says she was quickly bored and left long before graduation. "I didn't want to sit there and spend my parents' money on something I hated. I wanted to go out and get some experience. So I quit college and went to work as a freelance copy editor, just to have something to do. In San Francisco I met a guy who flew and was kind of a soldier of fortune. He said to me, 'If you want to know how to fly, go out to the airport and give them your five dollars and see what it's like.' Which I did, and I liked it. I kept at it and got the bug like everybody and wanted to stay in it.

"After I got my private pilot's license, I went back to the same school and got a flight instructor's license. In those days they didn't have any experience requirements; you could teach as soon as you got a teaching license, and you were teaching exactly what you had just learned. My first student was a guy who was trying to get his flight instructor's license. I had learned to fly at a small airport that had no control tower, and there I was, just starting to instruct at a big city airport.

"So I said to this guy who already knew everything but whom I was supposed to be teaching, 'Let's pretend for our first lesson that I'm the new student at the big airport with the control tower and I don't know how you do all of this, and you're going to teach me how I talk on the radio—what the proper things to say are—and you're going to correct any mistakes that I may make.' We got through it, and he later got hired as a second officer on United."

Luft was among the first women pilots hired by a major commercial airline, Continental, which at that time was a staid and conservative organization run by its founder, former aviator Bob Six.

Her appearance and mannerisms are holdovers from the efforts of early women to blend in with male flight crews. With short blonde hair, minimal makeup, and an easy way of carrying herself, Luft's appearance is that of a tomboy, in stark contrast to Joyce Kennedy's ingenue look. Although she projects the kind of asexuality that seems calculated to denote experience, inspire confidence, and downplay anything that might suggest feminine frippery, Luft's spirit and eagerness are engaging. She lives alone in a modern, well-furnished home full of piloting memorabilia. Unfortunately, her first years in commercial aviation coincided with a recession in the industry.

"I was a 727 second officer when I was hired, and I upgraded later to first officer on the same plane. Right after I upgraded, they started furloughing. So instead of going into reserve flying, I elected to go out to the Pacific and fly freight. I figured that might be the last time I'd get a chance to see that kind of flying, so I went out and did that for about six months. "Every Monday, Wednesday, and Saturday morning, a 727 would leave Honolulu westbound, the front section of the upper deck filled with freight and the cabin carrying up to 72 passengers. The crew flying the plane would be on duty for fourteen hours, flying ten hours, landing at six different islands with minimal to no navigation facilities in the worst tropical weather, and crossing four time zones and the International Dateline. Simultaneously in Guam, the other half of our 'fleet' would depart eastbound on a similar route, much of it flown at night. Because ninety-nine percent of the flying was over water, we spent a lot of our training time studying the Doppler and Omega navigation systems. Getting lost in the Western Pacific was a definite no-no, and everyone in the cockpit was supposed to be familiar with these two systems. 'DFWTD' had been inscribed on the Doppler in each bird. Translation: 'Don't Fuck with the Doppler!'"

Six months into her Pacific experience, Luft returned to flying Continental's domestic routes, although the air carrier was undergoing the difficulties that preceded its massive financial troubles. One Friday, Luft flew from New York to Houston, where she was based, leaving her hat and flight bag as usual to save the hassle of dragging them back to Los Angeles, and climbed on a westbound flight with the idea of celebrating her brother's birthday on the weekend. Instead of celebrating, the next day Luft discovered that the company she worked for had failed, unable to negotiate a way out of its cash-flow problems.

"Cindy Greenstreet was a friend of mine who was coming to the party," says Luft. "One of her friends had a private aircraft and they were flying up. When they were over Los Angeles, she tuned in approach control and heard a Continental DC-10 talking to the controller. Approach control said as they usually do, 'Okay, contact tower now, frequency such and such; we'll see you tomorrow,' and the Continental pilot replied, 'I don't think so,' with a real sad tone in his voice like something had really gone down. So Cindy piped up and asked, 'Continental Six, what's going on?' The captain responded that he'd talk to her on the company frequency. So she switched frequencies, and he told her Continental had just declared bankruptcy. Cindy landed up here and asked us if we had heard. Needless to say it was more like a wake than a birthday party because we were all out of work."

Pete Browner knows what it means to suddenly find himself on the street. Browner flew for Eastern Airlines from 1963 to January 1991, when Eastern stopped flying and ended the long and colorful history of an airline once considered to be an American aviation institution. Both Continental and Eastern came under the umbrella of Texas Air Corporation, part of the aviation empire founded by entrepreneur Frank Lorenzo.

As Lorenzo began to emerge as a force in the industry, he seemed to be carrying the banner of divide and conquer and appeared committed to developing a low-fare, cost-effective airline by combining weak or ailing carriers. Subsequent events demonstrated that this was in fact the way the airline entrepreneur made his mark in the deregulated industry. Lorenzo built his aviation empire on one small regional carrier, Texas International Airlines, which he merged with Continental in 1983 after a lengthy takeover battle. Two years after the Continental acquisition in 1985, Lorenzo—again under the umbrella of Texas Air—put in a bid for Eastern Airlines, which like Continental had been undergoing sustained financial difficulties. The industry scuttlebutt was that Lorenzo was after Eastern's computerized reservation system, which would enable him to compete with other major carriers. At Eastern, pilots charged that new management siphoned off company assets to bolster still-troubled Continental, speculation that was later verified during federal bankruptcy proceedings, when in 1989 Eastern was also forced to file for Chapter 11 protection. Pete Browner's remarks were made after the Texas Air takeover but before the Eastern bankruptcy.

"I've been flying since 1956. I paid for all my aeronautical ratings with the exception of my airline transport. When other kids were watching railroad trains and police cars, I liked to watch airplanes. I thought that looked like it ought to be a fun thing to do. And it is, and I'm lucky. I first soloed in '56 when I was sixteen, and I got my commercial and my multiengine and my instrument rating all while I was in college. I went to the University of Miami; it was the only school that would accept me with my terrible academic record."

Pete Browner moves purposefully, like someone accustomed to command and respect. He is tall, with dark brown hair and brown eyes. Immediately you sense this is a man to be reckoned with, that he knows what he's talking about and can back it up. A crumpled paisley tie hangs loose against an open collar; the sleeves of his starched Oxford-cloth shirt are rolled up to the elbows. Eyes merry, his smile conspiratorial, his lanky frame casually overflowing the chair, Browner gives the impression of someone familiar with backroom politics.

"I got hired with Eastern when I was twenty-three. I started flying Convair 440s, a twin-engine propeller-driven airplane. I flew that airplane for three years up and down the East coast and through the Allegheny Mountains, up to such lovely places as Lancaster, Redding, Wilkes Barre, Binghamton, Syracuse. The kind of thing that you'd generally expect of a 40-passenger twin-engine plane in the Eastern half of the universe." Browner grins, satisfied with his pun.

"Lorenzo is the junk dealer of the industry. I can remember shortly before the company was sold when I was doing some work with some of the union guys in the 'inner circle.' I had my finger pretty much on the pulse of things on a daily basis, and all I could think of was how Borman [former astronaut Frank Borman who ran Eastern for ten years from 1976 to its sale in 1986] had screwed this company up something terrible in the last ten years and [I thought] if we could just get rid of him and get some good level-headed, financially trained and understanding people to run this corporation, we could really be winners. And then we got sold. And the only thing that could have happened that would have been worse than keeping Borman was what happened.

"Don't get me wrong. I don't mind working for a tough guy, and I don't mind people questioning my decisions. If I have respect for them, that's fine. We all have to be accountable to somebody. I don't mind being accountable, but not to people [like Lorenzo] who use accountability as an intimidation tool. That's wrong. The traveling public deserves better than that."

Expressing the frustration of someone who feels his effort isn't acknowledged, Browner says, "When they bought Eastern the new management thought they had gotten themselves a ragtag operation. Of course we managed to survive for fifty years being a ragtag operation, right? The funny thing is that when you look back at the Borman era, probably at least the last five years he was in charge of the company, we had no management. But we're a fairly old company employee-wise, and everybody knew how to do their job. You didn't need to manage and direct and guide these people. They went to work, and they did their job and they got it done.

"In this day and age, you don't think of airlines as having any definable character because they don't. Management philosophy is that they're not going to allow individual employees to have the luxury of running their operation in the way it has always worked best. They're going to have everybody run it *their* way—or as close to that as they can get it. What happens is this all works fine when everything's going along all right, when you don't have horrendous air traffic congestion or an emergency in an airport messes things up. But as soon as you get a big snowstorm on the East Coast, and management sitting in Miami says it will choose where it wants you to take your passengers, you can't imagine the chaos that occurs. The dollar has set a new value on decision making within the industry. Because of deregulation, competitiveness has become the domineering factor."

His remarks prophetic, Browner says, "I think the company folding is a very possible option right now. . . . It's possible that it could all go. I think [Lorenzo] would go 'Chapter 7' [to liquidation]. Because it would allow him to take the assets of the corporation and move them to Continental if he wants. It would also allow him to get rid of the employees he really doesn't want to deal with. . . . I'll always be able to put some food on the table one way or the another. I'm luckier than most pilots because for most pilots their profession is flying aircraft. I fortunately have done air safety work and accident investigation work for ALPA for some seventeen of those years I've been with the airline. And I could probably seek employment in places like the FAA or NTSB or maybe even the safety foundations that would provide me enough salary so I could live."

Stan Page is about Pete Browner's age, in his late forties, but the contrast between the two men couldn't be greater. While Browner exudes energy and good spirits, Page is low-key almost to the point of seeming disinterested. While Browner might finesse a subject he considers important, enlarging it with a little humor, Page goes straight for the jugular. He is a solid, tight man, with sharp piercing eyes and a no-nonsense manner. Although trained in the military, Page has little patience with pilot myths. "I started flying when I was about seventeen years old. I got a private license, went to college, screwed around in college, didn't do too well, went into the military, went through a cadet program and became a pilot in the marine corps. We went through navy training, so I got my formal flight training in Pensacola, Florida, and Corpus Christie, Texas. I call it formal in that I knew how to steer an airplane before I went there. But I didn't really know how to fly.

"From there I went to Vietnam. I spent a tour over there—a year and two months. I flew about 240 missions, and I came back to the marine corps where I had essentially a staff job and was making up my mind whether to stay in or get out, and I finally decided to get out. I didn't want to go back to Vietnam. I went to work at Continental in June of '68.

"I became a pilot for the time off. It's a way to make a dollar, and I think I deliver a valuable skill to the nation. That's how I feel about it. That's it. And they make you prove that you can do your skill twice a year whether you want to do it or not. That's the hard part of the job, but it's also the most fun. When you walk out of there [the simulator at the annual check ride], you say, 'Son of a bitch, I can still do it.'"

Now and again there is an element in Page's manner that suggests he might not be as tough as he'd like you to think, that in fact the brittle exterior covers an interior vulnerability. Throughout the almost three-year strike ALPA called when Lorenzo took Continental into bankruptcy, for example, Page worked as a dedicated volunteer, offering assistance to other strikers. Page's attitude about the business he works for may be related to the fact that he has seen some of his dreams unravel because of events at Continental.

"We hardly do any flight planning now," Page complains. "You ask for a little more gas if you want it, if you think you're going to require it. You have to be able to troubleshoot a few systems. But if you can read the book . . . When I first went to work, you had to know everything. You had to know all of section three and section four. I mean like right now." He snaps his fingers. "Now it's, 'Get out the book; let's look it up.'

"We go through and understand the systems and all that stuff, but the smart guy is the guy that built the plane. He's what makes it work. I tell you the guys that I think were really smart were the ones who flew a long time ago. Guys like old Harry Tanehill, who was number one for a long time. He said, 'You know when we used to fly that mail, we always wanted to know where those tunnels were.' You had to be kind of smart to fly along the railroad tracks like that and fly some of those god-awful approaches that some of those guys did. I think some of those guys were awful lucky and probably pretty smart too. But the instrument flying that we're doing, it's a skill. It's a practiced skill."

Brad Prescott corroborates Page's remarks. "You're like a little puppet; it's all cut-and-dried. Everything's in the manual, which is the bible, and there's a lot of stuff decided from the ground. Jesus, you can't make any decisions."

Of Frank Lorenzo, who up until three years ago was the guiding force behind Continental, Page theorizes, "He's not interested in the day-to-day operation. He's interested in that scheme, in that maneuver. It's not like he wants to run an airline."

If you ask pilots why they fly, you are likely to get a look that is vague and confused, not so much that you are asking a dense question, but that they are at a loss to answer. It is a mystery to them why anyone should be interested. "Actually," says Bob Keystone, now retired for three years, "it's the best job in the world because when you park the airplane at the gate, you go home and you don't have a briefcase full of stuff to take home with you. You get the airplane there safely, you've done your job."

"I'm one-half of a couple supporting a family," says Lisa Johnson, "and we like a certain life-style. We like to travel. We like to have nice things. So in order for us to fulfill all of these things, we must both work."

"The whole reason you want to get into this profession is because it's a good job," says Sandra Luft. "It's got good benefits, it's got high skill levels, and people maintain those standards." She pauses, looks uneasy. "But once you start working for less and less and less, you start denigrating your own ability. And they'll be happy to keep seeing how low you can go."

In her detached way, Luft is describing changes in her profession that have occurred since deregulation, changes that cause pilots like herself who knew what flying was like before to wonder how they're now expected to behave. At Continental, for example, even after pilots agreed to wage cuts of almost fifty percent, the company was still forced to declare bankruptcy. In this light, the cynicism of Stan Page doesn't seem so far off the mark.

"I consider myself a pilot, but certainly not a professional in the same vein as a doctor," says Page. "Most pilots don't agree with me on that. I think they're wrong, and I think if they continue to think of themselves as professionals, they're going to get their ass handed to them many more times." Page's remarks suggest the generally arbitrary view pilots often have of the world, a world in which people should do the right thing and do things right.

"I don't know why the older guys are still doing it," says Page harshly. "They had it when it was great. If I had been five years older, I'd have done it differently. I wouldn't have come back to work after the strike. I would have gone out and pumped gas for seven or eight years. I would have done something else."

CHAPTER 2

Deregulation as Pilots See It

I think people take a lot of their frustrations out on pilots—why can't we leave on time, why can't we do this or that? The guy in the front office is the guy they ought to go after first. People think pilots have more control of the airplane than they do. I only have control once I get the thing going and leave the gate.

—HANK BARNES, TWA
747 captain

Ⅰt was not the kind of day they expected this to happen. Wind shear is something that usually occurs in the summer. You watch for it then; it comes along with the thunderstorms and unstable air masses and microbursts. It had been that way on the trip from Albany to Chicago last June. They had been flying at 29,000 feet. Advised that there was bad weather ahead of them, they had opted to fly around it instead of descending to a lower altitude. The captain had felt this would give them more options if things did start to go bad. The choppy jet stream had moved north with them, however, and they had run smack into the weather.

To the three men in the cockpit, when the weather hit, it felt like the plane had smashed into a brick wall, as if the nose of the massive DC-10 had hit sideways and been deflected. Within seconds the wind speed and velocity changed, causing the aircraft to thrash and wobble like a small bird on a swollen sea. It had only been twenty seconds, but in that kind of weather seconds are crucial. In that kind of turbulence, it takes no time for a loose food cart to go careening down an aisle or a piece of unstowed luggage to be pitched through the cabin or someone without a seat belt on to be bounced around. Luckily that day they had had warning. Passengers had been advised, flight attendants had stowed the leftovers from the lunch service, and carry-on bags were safely under the seats. The copilot had called for a last-minute clearance to descend to a lower altitude, and this had gotten them out of it. But still, it only takes seconds.

And on this day, just before Christmas, the seconds counted. The weather had not seemed to be extraordinary. It was the kind of very cold, very clear East Coast day that is usually predictable; it was not weather in which you'd expect wind shear. During the initial descent into JFK things seemed normal for the Boeing 747 crew—Capt. Bruce Arnt, copilot Bud McKenzie, and flight engineer Jerome Davis. At 10,000 feet, however, Arnt and McKenzie noticed the ride seemed bumpier; there was a perceptible choppiness in the air. They had talked to Kennedy ATC about approach path weather, but the tower had assured them the weather was suitable to land.

Reassured, Captain Arnt continued his descent, maintaining the reduced engine speed that would gradually slow the big plane to its prescribed 500 feet per minute, lowering it to the ground and a safe landing barely eight minutes away.

As they passed through 5,000 feet, however, both the captain and copilot McKenzie noticed an increase in wind and turbulence. Unexpectedly the bulky 747 began to lurch, tossed by a powerful crosswind. Simultaneously the plane began losing altitude, dropping uncontrollably, as if some invisible force was pulling on it. Without hesitating, the captain called for more power to counter the downward pull and provide increased maneuverability. As the engineer pushed the heavy throttles forward, the three men in the cockpit each counted silently to themselves: one . . . two . . . three . . . four. Slowly the big engines kicked in, even as the plane bounced and ebbed its way through the turbulent air. The increase in power was enough to regain control, but the turbulence still buffeted them. Five thousand feet, two thousand, one thousand. Despite the crew's struggle to manage the plane's wild maneuvering, the bouncing and jostling continued. They seemed powerless to stop the six-hundred-thousand-pound aircraft from hitting the ground. Five hundred feet—still going down and despite the increased power the captain had ordered, the plane was shaking dangerously toward a stall. Somewhere, far in the back of his mind, Captain Arnt was struggling to remember about wind shear—the downward pull, six to eight miles across, the most violent in the center. "Why the hell did this have to happen now?" he thought to himself, frustrated and irritated by the fluky weather conditions. "The tower had said the weather was off to our left. What happened?"

Copilot McKenzie could feel himself begin to sweat; his eyes were locked dead ahead watching the altimeter. The bright lines on the cockpit instruments went in and out of focus as the plane lurched from side to side. No one spoke. Behind McKenzie the flight engineer sat leaning forward, as if by stubborn force of his own will he could keep the aircraft from falling. The engineer had a vague feeling of being in a car with no brakes going downhill, trying to dodge the other cars in front of him, his own vehicle pitching and swaying from side to side while he hoped for a clear stretch or an uphill grade. He knew the only thing the captain could do now was keep the nose up, try to keep the engines from stalling, and in that way, try to fly out of it.

Three hundred feet—suddenly the plane began to even out and

the three men could see the runway break out underneath them. At two hundred feet, the wind speed and velocity abruptly changed; the crosswind diminished and became less dramatic. As the crew sighted the runway, the electric atmosphere in the dark cockpit began to dissipate. The flight engineer turned away from the windshield and back to the lights and gauges of his panel. He sat up straight in his seat and let out an involuntary sigh, unaware of whether the captain or the copilot had noticed. Almost at the last minute, the plane had begun to respond. Within seconds they were on the ground.

In silence, they taxied to the gate, shut down the engines and completed the landing checklist. "Well," said Bud McKenzie, pushing his seat back from the control yoke and unbuckling his seat belt, "the plane's on the ground, but I'm not sure I am." Neither the captain nor the flight engineer responded. As they finished, picked up their uniform jackets and hats, and prepared to leave the cockpit, McKenzie looked up and saw one of the younger flight attendants standing tentatively at the door.

"You guys glad to be on the ground?" she asked faintly, trying to hold a weak smile from slipping off her face.

"Hell, yes," said the captain tersely.

"Check," added the flight engineer. Bud McKenzie was silent and turned away to stow something in his flight bag.

"Were you scared?" the young woman pressed. When no one answered, she said timidly, "I was." Smiling again feebly, she turned and went back downstairs to collect her things.

Bud McKenzie smiles as he recalls the incident. As potentially frightening as these events are from a layman's perspective, being buffeted by natural forces is to a pilot's way of thinking all in a day's work, falling into the category of what McKenzie and most pilots consider they've been trained for. For many, especially those who flew when aviation was regulated by the federal government, it is the human-induced effects of the deregulated environment they find bothersome. They fret about aircraft maintenance, changes in working conditions, and the adequacy of government agencies to monitor an industry that for fifteen years has been struggling to sort itself out. And they worry that some of what they consider important matters of decision making are being handled by people who don't understand aviation.

The reality that has emerged with deregulation has not impressed pilot-historian Rex Chamberlain. "During the times that the

CAB regulated the airline business, there was no free entry nor free exit of routes. You were a common carrier. You not only had the privilege of flying a route, you also had the obligation. You couldn't just cancel a flight for economic reasons. Today the terms and conditions of the carriage are spelled out on the ticket, and the carrier can publish whatever he wants. Nobody ever reads it anyhow. Formerly, an airline was legally obliged to get you from A to B, even if it had to charter a bus."

Industry reports have it that as a result of deregulation, airline fares have dropped some twenty-two percent from their preregulation rates and that more people are indeed flying. In 1977, airline traffic totalled 243 million passengers; less than ten years later that had almost doubled to 472.7 million. Projections for 1995 call for 633 million people, 745 million by 1997. Gallup pollsters estimate that under deregulation 126 million adults—about seventy-two percent of the adult population—have flown sometime in their lives, compared with twenty percent twenty years ago. The fact that twelve years back, fifty-two percent of airline tickets were billed to expense accounts and today the largest group of passengers are those who fly for personal reasons and at their own expense seems to indicate that from a consumer standpoint deregulation has been a success. It is also a fact, however, that in the new deregulated world, seven airlines—American, United, Delta, USAir, Northwest, TWA, and Continental—now control the majority of domestic traffic, and of the dozens of new airlines that attempted to take advantage of the open market, only two—America West, serving the western United States, and Midway, connecting the midwestern states—appeared to be viable. America West has since filed for bankruptcy protection and Midway has stopped flying. Of the majors, American, United, and Delta are far and away the key players. Like America West, TWA and, until recently, Continental are operating under the protection of federal bankruptcy laws.

"The public has an idea that the government is going to take care of them," says former mechanic Dick Riley quietly. "But the truth is the passenger now has been put in a position of making a value judgment about the airline he flies. How is he going to do that? Is the airplane on time? How many lines did I have to stand in to get my ticket? Who was nice to me and who wasn't? But these things have no relationship to whether that airplane is safe to fly or whether the airline is competent to fly it.

"I think the passenger makes the decision on which airline gets him to where he wants to go the cheapest. The business traveler has got to go for an airline that gets him there on time and has a good past history for him. But the average Aunt Jane or Uncle Joe going to visit their relatives generally will vote with their dollars for the cheapest airline ticket they can find. The deregulation advocates say that passengers will not travel on an airline that doesn't get them there on time. They will not travel on an airline that's dirty. They will not travel on an airline that has bad food. Well, if the guy only travels maybe once a year at most, what's his point of reference? No point of reference whatsoever.

"What the public likes is the low fares. The airlines of course are in it to make money, so it's in their best interest to offer the public what it wants. The trouble is they haven't made much money because they haven't learned yet how to market their wares in a sane manner in a deregulated environment." Speaking of extremely discounted fares initiated under Texas Air's management of the "new" Continental, Riley says, "Continental's methodology is a kind of a self-destruction wish. Its management says, 'We're not getting the cash flow we need; we're going to reduce ticket prices,' and then all the airlines do the same because they're afraid of losing market share. And it feeds on itself. It's a destructive pricing environment."

Rex Chamberlain offers some historical insight on how the situation Riley describes came about. "The traditional way of running the airline business was that you looked at each city pair—let's talk about Chicago to Amsterdam—as you would a small business. You knew who your customers were. You made sales calls on them. Pricing was not as critical, but a quality product was. We're talking now about the fifties, even up to the late sixties. Then in the early seventies I'd say there began to evolve this concept, which by now is fine-tuned, of the airline seat as a perishable product. Airlines began to realize that once that seat goes empty, it's gone forever. And we began to think in terms of the thing as a pricing problem for the first time.

"Simultaneously while this was going on, huge computer reservation systems were being built at tremendous risk and expense by two carriers, United and American. This changed the game radically. Naively the TWAs and the Pan Americans and the small carriers still thought they were running a reservations system. However, armed with computerized reservations, the new breed of airline businessmen—economists and marketing people who had learned their skills in the real world of commerce—said, 'If we see a certain flight's not moving too well, we can run a clearance sale.' It began as a seasonal thing. You'd let all your agents know that the airline was having a moonlight special, 'Fifty percent off, $49.95, Wednesday night only.' This new concept appeared almost simultaneously with deregulation.

"And then a further development occurred. United and American both got the capacity not only to identify individual flights, but to identify and market *individual seats*. This enabled them not just to run a special New York to Chicago for $49.99, but to determine the number of seats they were going to sell at that price. And that could be as low as ten seats on a flight, while all the rest went for $279.95. They would put a big ad in the *New York Times,* the *Washington Post,* the *Wall Street Journal,* the *Daily News,* and people would call their travel agent." Chamberlain goes on to construct his version of a hypothetical scenario, based on the common knowledge in the travel industry that airlines restrict the number of special fares available on any given flight. "So here's a gal in her little ABC travel agency out in Des Moines, and she gets a call from someone who wants to fly on a $49.95 ticket. She fires up her Apollo [United Airlines reservations] system and says, 'Yes sir, we have four seats left.' She sells two of those four seats at $49.95. Apollo picks it up and takes the seats out of inventory. Somebody else in Buffalo calls the XYZ agency who tells him, 'Yes sir, we have only two seats left, would you like those?' and she sells them. The next guy calls up and gets told, 'I'm sorry all of the specials are sold out, but we do have seats at $279.95.'

"Now over at TWA and particularly Pan American, the marketing people pick up the Monday morning *New York Times* and they see the same ad. They have to meet the competition, so they say, 'Okay, *we'll* have a fire sale at $49.95.' The problem is that they can't price the individual seat; they have to sell the whole economy section at that special price. So all 140 seats go on the block at $49.95.

"They tell me—the people who supervise these reservations offices—that you can see this kind of thing happen. You can be sitting there, and things will be humming along, and all of a sudden, there'll be a major change, it's suddenly gotten very quiet. What's happened is the phones have stopped ringing. And they know by experience that somebody has just hit the media with a promotion. So immediately they all start running around like mad trying to find out who's running the special and what it is, and then they immediately set about matching it."

Chamberlain's eyes pick up the obvious question. Although his statistics may not be accurate, his frustration is real. "Well, it's not illegal, although it is in fact a deception. There might be ten thousand seats that day in that market, and they put ten of them on special."

Chamberlain gets up from his chair and paces the room, preparing himself for another subject. He turns, raises his right hand like a politician preparing to drive home a point and begins again. "As American and United were building their complex reservation systems, American with Sabre and United with Apollo, they went to travel agents and offered them the system, which provided greatly enhanced capability for the agencies. It also meant that the agency was married to whichever company provided the system. Since approximately 75 percent of air travel in this country is booked through travel agencies, this was an influential development in the industry." (The essence of Chamberlain's remarks is substantiated in a 1991 article in the *New York Times Magazine,* which notes that approximately 85 percent of travel in this country is booked through travel agents.)

"Although an agent can call up all available flights for a specific destination, in the Apollo system the first flights listed will be United; in Sabre they'll be American. Obviously this creates a certain bias in decision making. There was a government hearing about five years ago which determined that this practice was restraint of trade. So United and American begrudgingly agreed to provide an 'unbiased' page of available flights but in parallel to their own displays. Now if you call up and say you want the cheapest way to get from point A to point B, an agent has a judgment call to make. He or she will have to weigh the degree to which a potential passenger is committed to the cheapest fare with how business has been lately. They know what the commissions are. They know what the under-the-table commissions are. They know how their sales quotas are going.

"It's a subtle interplay of forces; the airlines control the reservations system at the same time they control the ability of the agent to function. Something like ninety percent of the major travel agents in this country are either American or United. So today if you were faced with trying to counter those two airlines, you'd have a nearly impossible task. Now, compare all of this to when the airline industry was small, in the days when airlines followed up on their sales pitch and their success was built on repeat business. Compare that with the philosophy that the airlines don't care who their customers are. They don't care if they ever come back. They don't particularly care if they're satisfied." Chamberlain stops to catch his breath. "The whole system is biased against the consumer."

The difficulty is that consumers are not consistent in their demands. "We went out the other night going to Kennedy—United and Pan Am and American—on an all-nighter," explains American flight engineer Jason Young. "I think Continental was up there too. All of us following each other. A waste? Maybe. But some people won't fly American. Some won't fly United. Some won't fly Pan Am. One carrier's got a better deal than another. Somebody's a frequent flyer on one, somebody else on another. People have their preferences." Young stops a minute and thinks through an idea. "You know, it's funny; when I lived in Chicago, my buddy Greg Scott, who works for United, would come through on a trip, and I'd go meet him at the airport. I'd be standing waiting for him to come off his flight, and there'd be people yelling at the United ticket agent, 'I'm never going to fly United again. I'm going to go American.' And I've stood at our American counters and listened to them say the same thing. You can't win. You can't make everybody happy. You try your best, but there's going to be lost bags, there's going to be late flights. You tell people you have a mechanical problem with the airplane, and they bitch. Well, what do you want us to do, fly an airplane that's not airworthy?"

"What will it look like when the airlines finally do figure out how to live with deregulation?" posits Dick Riley, who is older than Young and has seen it both ways. "The poor passenger—you're going to have three or four carriers that will control ninety percent of the traffic. And you're going to pay through the nose. Because all the el cheapo fares will evaporate as the competition diminishes. We've already passed the stage where new entrant carriers can come aboard."

Reflecting on the failure of smaller airlines that were spawned with deregulation, Riley says, "Midway and America West were both niche carriers, and there'll probably continue to be a space for niche-type carriers, a carrier that serves a market that nobody else wants. The problem with the niche carriers is they reach a certain level in growth and all of a sudden they decide they want to go play with the big boys. America West, for example, reached a point where they decided they wanted big airplanes and they bought 747s. The other way an airline can go broke is the way Air Florida did it [by sustaining a high-profile accident]. People just quit flying the airline." Riley is referring to the 1982 collision of Air Florida flight 90 with the Fourteenth Street bridge in Washington, D.C. The National Transportation Board attributed the cause of the accident to the flight crew's failure to take appropriate action relative to engine and fuselage deicing and recommended better training for both pilots and aircraft controllers. By some pilots' reckoning, however, Air Florida had no business expanding into geographical areas that would expose their pilots to conditions with which they were not familiar and about which they had not been adequately trained.

Sandra Luft who, like Dick Riley is a midcareer pilot, thinks many people today expect too much of the deregulated airlines. "You get people demanding at the new low prices what they used to get at the old high prices. At the old high prices, you could see their reason to demand it. But sometimes today you almost have to say, 'Hey I'm sorry, but you guys didn't pay enough to have the right to complain.' People have to remember that what they signed up for is really a bus ride. Those are the kinds of standards the airlines are attempting to maintain these days."

Luft's brother, Al Kellogg, works for a commuter airline in central California, building the time he needs to apply to a major carrier. He has strong opinions about the dilemma in which airlines find themselves. "The advertising community has managed to perpetuate the image of flying before deregulation," says Kellogg, "the pampering, the personal service, the excitement of air travel. What else are you going to promote? Are they going to tell you the truth? This actually makes an organization like People's Express not a bad idea because they were actually doing what they said they'd do. The Eastern shuttle was a *great* example. You knew exactly what it was going to be, a high-density ride for not long enough to make it too miserable, at the right price at the right time. But you knew you were going to get from here to there. And people accept that.

"But then you get some average flight where people think they're going to be treated like royalty. That's where the problem starts. They paid $99 for the trip across the United States, and they wonder why they're being treated like a bunch of Greyhound passengers."

One of the hallmarks of postderegulation aviation is hub-and-spoke scheduling, wherein an airline establishes its presence at an airport and funnels flights in and out of the hub like spokes radiating from the center of a wheel. Presently there are twenty-nine major hubs scattered around this country, processing more than twenty million people a year. Atlanta, once home to Delta and Eastern, had the distinction of being the largest hub operation. In Denver, Continental and United dominate Stapleton International Airport. In Dallas, American and Delta are the major carriers; in Boston, Delta and Northwest. A disillusioned Air Line Pilots Association official, speaking off the record, went so far as to suggest that hub dominance is parceled out by informal agreements among the major airlines, who limit the domination of any one hub to two carriers, thus reducing competition for trip slots, gate space, and passengers. Such allegations may be fueled by a general bias against the hub-and-spoke system. In fact, gate space at major airports is at such a premium that failing airlines forced to sell off their assets because of bankruptcy find the sale of gates to competing carriers a lucrative source of capital. For passengers, however, the hubs may not be such a great deal. The *New York Times* estimates that people who begin or end a trip at a hub can end up paying from ten to almost thirty percent more on the price of their ticket.

Rearranging routes so they will fit into the hub-and-spoke operation gave rise to another feature of the deregulation environment—the commuter airline. As the major air carriers abandoned less lucrative routes to consolidate equipment and increase efficiency, small upstart airlines appeared, offering service to passengers left out of the new system and filling in where the big carriers declined to fly. These commuter airlines, which are more specialized than even regional or niche carriers, represent both the promise and challenge of deregulation.

By one estimate, the commuter market is a $1.5 billion business, worldwide. Fifteen million Americans traveled on commuter airlines in 1987, twice as many as just eight years before, and there are over fifty different agreements that exist between small commuter airlines and major carriers. In some cases, the arrangement is simply a marketing one in which the commuter continues to operate as a separate entity but under the banner of a major carrier and takes on a name such as United Express or Continental Express. The commuter shares in some of the major company's resources, such as joint ticketing, pricing, and computerized reservations. In other cases, as in American Airlines' purchase of Wings West—a commuter airline operating in Southern California under the name of American Eagle—the major carrier may actually buy the smaller airline. In any case, standards of operation may be different.

"I think commuter airlines are one of the best training grounds for a young guy coming up," says Brad Prescott. "You're going into all busy airports; you have to deal with passenger relations." Prescott stops and thinks a moment. "Sometimes I have trouble getting on a small carrier because I know the guys flying them are likely to be inexperienced. After all, why would you be flying on one of those things if you were qualified? If you were qualified, you'd be with a major carrier." Al Kellogg agrees. "The company I once worked for engineered a marketing agreement with TWA by which they became TWA Express. Then they went through three million bucks in six months and ended up with fewer airplanes and fewer routes." Kellogg pauses and then goes on to describe an incident from his personal experience. "The weather was rainy and miserable, and they showed up with an airplane for me with the radar inoperative. I said, 'I don't go into thunderstorms without radar, sorry.' So they said, 'Okay, fine,' because no radar in a thunderstorm is a legitimate beef. The next day, however, they give me the same airplane back with the radar *removed*. Finally TWA just withdrew from the marketing agreement.

"Right now commuter flight is relatively sporty compared to riding some major carrier's 727. What the majors want is the code sharing, the common identification; they want the person to be able to go all the way through on American or Continental or whatever. My problem is that I've been in business, and I understand how hand-to-mouth this thing really is. Every so often the FAA would show up and challenge our management to prove that they were financially fit to do business, and then the company would panic and go get a loan."

Between the commuters and the larger regionals such as Aloha or Alaska airlines there was once another level of specialized carriers, smaller regional carriers like Air New England or Bonanza Airlines (later Hughes Airwest) that operated midsize aircraft but in very specific areas. Most of these are gone now, absorbed into other larger systems; Air New England, for example, was absorbed by Republic, which in turn was merged with Northwest. Even the kind of short-haul flights that typify this kind of operation did not prepare Joyce Kennedy for the demands of the hub-and-spoke flying she is now involved in as a Northwest 737 copilot.

"The hubs are saturated," says Kennedy flatly, "and it affects everything—flight times, flight delays, and when maintenance can be done on the airplane, which is a big problem. We have airplanes coming in that have write-ups [notations in the log book from previous crews], but the plane is due right out. There's so much pressure on the airlines now to get airplanes out on time, which means there's a lot of urgency to defer maintenance items. We wait until the next leg and then the next leg. I think it's just made a mess. It's certainly made it miserable to fly. I will never bid a trip that goes back and forth to Detroit all day because it's a madhouse.

"Putting everything up for grabs is what they did with deregulation. It just made a free-for-all for the airlines. We're going in a circle. It's going to end up being only a few airlines, fares are going to go up, and it's all going to backfire because they only looked at the short term of this. By increasing the competition, they've made such a madhouse out of the airports; everybody's trying to push as many flights as they can to outdo the other carriers, to try to take over a hub and monopolize an area. But in the meantime, they're screwing up everybody's bags. They're screwing up the airplanes. They're making it more and more frustrating for the travelers and the pilots. I mean the pilots are just as frustrated over this as the people are.

"We are always picking up that PA and saying, 'I'm really sorry, but . . .' I don't know what to tell people anymore. One of our pilots got called into the chief pilot the other day because he told a planeload of passengers, 'We're on time today, folks, I'm sorry.' When the chief pilot got after him, this guy said, 'I'm telling people I'm sorry every time I pick up that PA. I'm frustrated. You're telling us what to say or what not to say on the PA, but the passengers have a right to know we're frustrated, too.'" Kennedy's gentle face tightens. "The government, the companies don't realize how this thing has backfired. It goes down the ranks, and it's a snowball effect.

"I flew a three-day trip a couple of months ago. We left at eight-twenty-five in the morning from Detroit. We didn't finish until eight-thirty or nine o'clock that night. We had a long twelve-hour day with, I think, eight legs. We only got one meal during that whole twelve hours; that came out of Albany, and we didn't really have time to eat it because there were thunderstorms—we thought it would get rough and the food would be all over the cockpit.

"The captain didn't want to take the plane in the first place because it was a full airplane; we couldn't take any more fuel, and we had the thunderstorms in Albany. He wanted to delay the flight and take people off to put on more fuel. The company said, 'Absolutely not, you've got a full airplane; you've got enough gas; you can use Cleveland as your alternate.' We were legal to go. We would have just liked to have a little more fuel. As it was when we got to Albany, we had to hold. We finally did get in, but here's a situation where we wanted the fuel and someone else was telling us we didn't need it. It's like that all the time. We're constantly being told, 'We don't want to take people off. We need this gate. Let's get you out of here.'

"It was very tiring to have to go through a whole day like that Albany trip and hassle with the weather and with the problems, all the time knowing that the airline just wanted to keep us moving. . . . From Hartford to Detroit is normally an hour and twenty minutes; now they schedule it for two hours to make sure that we're on time."

Pete Browner agrees that a great deal of pilot decision making is now in the hands of nonpilots, but he sees this as a necessity since the people who fly the airplanes are caught in an increasingly complex aviation environment. "A lot of our decisions are controlled from the ground, and there are some good aspects to doing that," says Browner. "Let's say we're coming into Atlanta [once a hub to both Eastern and Delta] where there's a line of thunderstorms approaching the airport, and the thunderstorms beat us and the airport closes. If all of the Eastern flights or all of the Delta flights—especially if it's rush hour time—decided to go to Birmingham, can you imagine poor little Birmingham? They'd have airplanes parked all over the airport. So theoretically people have to make some decisions about what's best for the passengers, what's to be done with them once we get on the ground."

Having said that, Browner qualifies his remarks. "There comes a time though, when for instance fuel is getting to a critical state, that I don't care what the company wants. *I'll* decide where the airplane goes. As much as the new management philosophy at Eastern has tried to take this away from us, we still pretty much control the decision-making process during the trip. They're working very hard at removing our control over the flight, and we're fighting it pretty hard because we don't feel that it's the best way to run an airline."

Although his long-haul Pacific flying is substantially different from Pete Browner's shorter domestic trips, Rex Chamberlain's concerns are not dissimilar. "Decisions are being made at the very top level," says Chamberlain brittlely. "It doesn't matter whether you're talking about United Airlines or American Airlines or Continental Airlines or if you're talking about the Department of Transportation or the FAA. On the staff level, in the trenches where the work's being done, there are people who understand the problems and understand the perspective of the pilots and who make recommendations based on this understanding. Unfortunately, the *decisions* are being made by political animals at the very top who will very often ignore or downplay the recommendations of their own organizations. What we have happening in the FAA right now is that there are some departments, some staff recommending things like reasonable flight time or duty time limits for pilots, but that input is by and large being ignored. The agenda is a political one at the very top, where it is a number-crunching exercise, *period* with no willingness to understand these other issues."

As Joyce Kennedy has suggested, the airline practices that support the gimmick of on-time scheduling particularly gall pilots. "I feel like we're hauling cattle," says Brad Prescott. "Herd 'em on, herd 'em off. At Air Cal, the gate agent and the captain always talked before the gate agent shut the door. Hell, they just close the door now. They don't care what the captain has to say. We'll leave paying passengers at the gate in order to get an on-time departure. They have an electronic box inside the airplanes, and when you close the door and release the brakes, it automatically starts the time. So if you reopen the door, it doesn't matter, you've already started the time."

"They don't give a hoot if the plane taxis out with the wing missing," snaps Pete Browner. "They want it to move on time. Get it out on time, we'll worry about the wing later.

"There's an interesting thing that's going on at Eastern right now," says Browner, describing his speculations about Eastern's maintenance procedures under Texas Air. "What happens is they give low- to mid-level supervisory personnel monetary bonuses if they exceed the goal of on-time performance for their department in terms of the number of airplanes that actually depart. Let's say ten airplanes a night lay over in Boston for maintenance. This includes routine maintenance, additional minimum equipment list items [things that must be fixed to make the plane legal to fly] and other logbook write-ups the flight crews bring in on the aircraft. The goal for on-time departures the next morning for the first group out is set for eighty-five percent. But because there's such a load of maintenance items that came in the night before, it looks like they can only get seventy percent of the airplanes out on time.

"This makes the maintenance supervisor mad as hell because if he were to get ninety percent of the planes out on time, he would get a monetary bonus from the company for the extra five percent by which he beat his target. So what does this encourage him to do? It encourages him to go out and tell the mechanic, 'Hey—just pencil that thing off. Where it says the pressurization is erratic on this airplane, don't go into any goddamn elaborate troubleshooting. Just go out there and wash the outflow valves; get the nicotine out of them. Pencil whip that thing and sign it off and get it out.' And it happens all the time.

"Same thing happens with the departure agents at the gates. If they don't get that airplane out on time, they've got to write a report, and if they get three delays per month, then they get a disciplinary letter in their file. And if they get five disciplinary letters, they get their tail terminated. You ought to see them. Miami's the place I love to go because it's corporate culture down there. [Eastern's corporate headquarters was located in Miami at the time Browner is speaking about.] I was scheduled out of there three months ago to go to Washington, which meant we were going out over the water—150 miles offshore. Now, I've got a sharp flight attendant in the back. She comes up and she says, 'Captain, there's seventeen life vests missing'—the kind that are under the seat. How would you like to reach down and grab for that thing and not have it there? That would piss you off, wouldn't it, especially if we're going in the drink.

"So I called maintenance, and I said, 'Get out here and put the life vests on the airplane.' Maintenance is on the way with the life vests, but in the meantime the agent asks if he can load the airplane. I tell him no. He says he's got to load the airplane. 'Don't load the airplane,' I tell him. 'How the hell are the maintenance men going to crawl down between some lady's legs and try and stick a goddamn life vest in a pouch under the seat? Not only is the lady not going to like it, maybe the maintenance man isn't going to like it.'" Browner laughs heartily. "'Maybe she's an ugly lady.'

"But the guy says to me, 'If we don't get this thing out on time, we'll get a delay.' So I said to him, 'I'll tell you what, you tell your supervisor that the captain said *don't load the airplane!* And if there's a delay, put a code 39 on it,'—that's a flight crew operational decision—'charge it to Captain Browner and please put my name down because I'm trying to collect as many of these as I can. They don't bother me a bit. I don't give a shit if we're late. The plane will get into Washington on time, that's no problem. *But, goddamn it, don't inconvenience the passengers!*'"

From the perspective of her long experience in aviation, Sandra Luft, like Pete Browner, has some specific views about how deregulation has impacted aircraft maintenance. "Given the fact that deregulation allows anybody with a modicum of dollars to start up an airline, I'm not surprised by the Aloha incident or the fact that Air Cal leased those Aloha planes and then sent them back after they had a chance to look at them and saw the corrosion." Luft is referring to the 1989 Aloha Airlines incident in which a Boeing 737 lost part of its fuselage on a routine interisland flight. The pilots landed the plane safely, and only one person, a flight attendant, was lost. Investigation centered on whether the plane had been adequately maintained. The aircraft was one of three Aloha had leased to Air Cal. According to accounts in newspapers and the industry press, the California airline, alarmed at the amount of corrosion in the skins and formers of the planes, returned them to Aloha.

"Every time another postderegulation airline goes down, I think that's another reason why the Air Floridas can't make it, or People's Express," says Luft thoughtfully. "Once they get to a point where they no longer have the start-up rah-rah with the employees and have to begin paying them some money, and their airplanes come due for some real serious maintenance, suddenly they're faced with the magnitude of the problems and the costs the majors have. It looks real easy when you start out. What they've done particularly since deregulation is cut down the margin for error."

"During regulation," says Al Kellogg, who has been listening to his sister's conversation, "we had an incredible margin. The money was there so the equipment was up-to-date. People like the Bob Sixes of the world, who ran the Continentals and the Pan Ams and the TWAs, wanted the newest, shiniest stuff for their airlines, and they had a way to pay for it. The result was they built a cushion that was probably, if you look at it in a hard, cold business sense, way too big. I'm sure there's some economist somewhere who can say, 'Well, they weren't killing enough people.' That's hard and cold. But that's the way you look at things these days.

"Someplace there's an obvious line drawn, which if you cross it, you end up squeezing the airplane. What's happened in a lot of cases is that we've gone past the obvious line. We're starting to squeeze pretty hard, both people and airplanes. This business of Aloha and its 737 is a case of somebody squeezing the airplane. . . ." Kellogg looks at his sister and grins, repeating an industry joke. "My favorite story is People's Express—they sold one of their 747s because it needed a maintenance check. That's like selling your car because it's out of gas."

Which reminds Sandra Luft of another story, this one from Continental pilots' file of Texas Air blunders. "One of our 747s had an engine failure, I think in Tahiti, but managed to make it to Auckland, New Zealand. This meant that in Auckland there was now an airplane with three engines that was supposed to have four. So they called up the head of maintenance for that region, and he went to work on the problem. He finally figured out that the cheapest way to get an engine down to Auckland was to charter Flying Tigers out of Los Angeles. It would only cost them $65,000 to fly the engine from Los Angeles direct to Auckland, which is not bad because it was going to go right out of their maintenance base directly to where the plane was. So this maintenance supervisor made all the necessary arrangements, only to find out about five hours later that Continental maintenance in Houston had canceled it all.

"So he called up and asked them what was going on. They told him, 'Oh, we decided on a much cheaper way to do it. We're going to put it on a scheduled Flying Tigers flight to Sydney and then we're going to truck it to Auckland.'" She stops; Luft and her brother look at each other and both burst out laughing. "They're going to *truck* it to Auckland. They don't know where Auckland is. They think it's a suburb of Sydney. They don't know it's fifteen hundred miles across the Tasman Sea. So they send the engine over on the scheduled flight and then end up spending another $50,000 to charter an airplane, Qantas, to fly it from Sydney." Luft leans forward, slaps her knee, and grins widely.

Discussing the challenges of maintenance under deregulation, former mechanic Dick Riley offers some perspective. Speaking of the Aloha incident, Riley says, "My buddies at Boeing told me privately that the nose should have come off that airplane. They don't know why it didn't. Then they would have crashed at sea and nobody would known what happened . . . into the Hawaiian Deep, seventeen thousand feet of water. One minute they were just fine, the next minute the top of the airplane was gone." Riley pauses and offers his view of the circumstances. "If you really take a good look at what happened, you see a smaller airline that did not apparently do a proper job in maintaining its airplanes. The structural cracking that had to have taken place on that airplane must have happened over a period of years." (According to a *Los Angeles Times* article published a week after the incident, FAA inspection concluded that Aloha Airlines "did not have an adequate system to assure that its aircraft were properly maintained.")

Riley's voice is angry, but his face lacks expression. "This is a perfect example of how you can't count on the FAA to guard your safety. The real problem is that obviously Aloha didn't have an adequate maintenance program to get into those areas of the airplane where the cracking was present. The FAA says, 'Follow what the manufacturer says,' and in this case the manufacturer issued an AD [Administration Directive], or a service bulletin, and the FAA had an AD note about inspections. But there's thorough inspections, and there's cursory inspections. United has what they call a high-time sampling of our fleet, where the planes are literally taken down to the bare bones, the high-time airplanes. This program has been in progress for ten years, and our airplanes have half the cycles that Aloha planes have. But again, it takes a facility that has the ability to do it and the manpower and an engineering staff that shows the people what to do.

"Being a former mechanic and having a degree, I become the squeaky wheel. The idea is to document irregularities, to put it on paper and leave a paper trail. I don't have any authority. I go out there to the airport, and I trade on good will, conscience, and the fact that they know me. Everybody else that works on an airline has a monetary pressure or a scheduling pressure; they see safety from a completely different perspective or point of view. But there's never been a maintenance foreman killed in a crash. Or an air traffic controller killed or a company president killed. The pilots are the ones that have their necks stuck out. The old saying is that the pilots are the first to arrive at the scene of an accident.

"It's like the story of the chicken and the pig—about the difference between being involved and committed." Riley pauses for effect then continues. "Let's say you're having bacon and eggs for breakfast; well, the chicken is *involved,* but the pig is *committed.* Pilots are committed, and because of that we have a very parochial interest in safety. That's as it should be. I work with the pilots, work with the company, work with the FAA; I work with our staff engineers in Washington D.C.—we have ten or twelve professional

full-time staff engineers attached to the ALPA air safety branch.
Even though we're actually a labor union, we found out a long time
ago that nobody really has the safety interest in the job like the guy
flying the airplane. There are checks and balances in the system, and
we provide a balance against the bean counters.

"My biggest challenge is to prove that the nickel I get management to spend on safety prevented an accident. There's a mental set
with that group of people that we're never going to have another
accident. It's the only thing that I can think of that will explain their
actions. They think, 'We've had our last accident. We'll never have
another one.' And what is that opinion based on?" Riley glares and
tosses an unbent paper clip across his desk. "It's based on wishful
thinking."

"The biggest obstacle right now to the complete consummation
of the destruction of a good, reliable air transportation system is the
Air Line Pilots Association," says Rex Chamberlain, never a man to
mince words. "We've had two priorities over the years. Number one
has been to get the pilots as highly paid as we could, I'll admit that,
and number two has been to promote air safety. If we listen to Mr.
Alfred Kahn [Cornell University emeritus professor, former head of
the Civil Aeronautics Board, and an enthusiastic advocate of deregu-
lation], who speaks to us on TV, he tells us that a pilot's only
concern is to promote his own personal income. He totally disparag-
es the air safety efforts of pilots." Chamberlain's chiseled features
flame red. "In fact, pilots have made a demonstrable, legitimate
contribution to air safety, and they have been a very lonely voice in
protesting and fighting this tumultuous race toward the brink that
we're engaged in, in this country.

"The whiz kids from Cornell, the Alfred Kahns and everybody
like them, tell us that while deregulation has done wonderful things
for us, in fact the process is kind of slowed down right now and
we're having a little more problem prying the unions out than we
would like to have had. And the way to finish the job of deregulation
is cabotage [granting the right to foreign carriers to provide air
service from one point to another within the United States]. We'll
bring in the foreign carriers and turn them loose. And Alfred assures
us that then we will realize the full fruits of this wonderful new
world they've been promising us."

Chamberlain is referring to the fact that foreign airlines are
making inroads in the American aviation industry. Pilots seem to
fear most that foreign carriers will be granted the right to fly

passengers between destinations within American markets. Another aspect of the situation is that a number of foreign airlines have already made major investments in American aviation companies. For example, when Frank Lorenzo decided to bail out of Continental in 1990, after having been removed from Eastern management by a bankruptcy judge a few months earlier, he sold his $17 million stake in the airline to SAS [Scandinavian Airlines System]. Northwest Airlines has benefited from an infusion of some $40 million from Dutch KLM, and Swiss Air has invested in Delta. According to a 1991 ruling by Transportation Secretary Samuel Skinner, a foreign airline is allowed to acquire up to forty-nine percent of the equity of a U.S. carrier so long as it doesn't control more than twenty-five percent of the company's voting stock. Indeed some Washington insiders under the Reagan and Bush administrations were known to see foreign capital as a panacea for what ails the American aviation industry. Complicating the situation is increasing demands for gate space at foreign airports by American airlines looking to expand overseas. Last year's maneuvering by American carriers for London airport slots increased demands from the British government for corresponding consideration in the United States.

For pilots like Rex Chamberlain, however, the situation that has created the need for investment of foreign capital in American air carriers is a disgrace and a symptom of major failure on the part of American business generally and deregulation specifically. To him and other pilots, the preeminence of American aviation in the global industry is a matter of pride. To see these major American institutions floundering because of what he and others consider greed, bad management, and poor government leadership is deeply lamentable. Chamberlain is also frustrated by the fact that the mergers, acquisitions, and takeovers that appear to be integral to the current industrial climate have meant a loss of employment for American labor.

"That will finish the job," says Chamberlain, speaking about the expansion of foreign carriers into the U.S. market. "That will finish off ALPA. That will finish off this deterrent to the bottom line that we represent. If they do that and finish it off so that U.S. air transportation is essentially a foreign enterprise, it brings me back again to the question of what's the purpose of all of this anyway? What's the purpose?"

CHAPTER 3

How They Get Ahead and Is It Safe?

Sid Stanhon is a senior guy on the DC-10. He's nine months from retiring. He decided not to go for a 747 bid because he wouldn't be the senior guy on the 747, but he is on the DC-10. He flies to Kona and back eight times in a month and has twenty-two days off. That's an eighty-hour month right there. Our contract is based on seventy-eight hours, so he gets a couple hours of over-time.

—GREG SCOTT, United Airlines
DC-10 flight engineer

B ack in the early sixties, Capital Airlines was what today would be called a regional carrier, serving mostly East Coast cities up and down the Atlantic seaboard and as far west as Washington, D.C., and Chicago. One day back in the 1950s, a four-engine Capital Constellation was making a routine takeoff from Miami airport with a full load of passengers and a cockpit crew of four. The sleek plane, one of the darlings of the propeller age, began its takeoff roll and accelerated at proper speed past the airport tower, gained altitude, and turned on a heading that would take it east of Miami. What began as a routine flight ended abruptly, however. As the controllers in the airport tower watched, the whirl from the propeller on the plane's left outboard engine slowed and then stopped.

Even at that altitude the outline of the stilled prop blade was visible, caught in the draft of air flowing past the fuselage. The plane slowed but still flew, limping hesitantly through its turn. Just as it seemed that it might recover, the propeller on the second port engine spun to a stop. With one engine not operating, the big four-engine Constellation was still considered airworthy. A two-engine failure was serious business, however, and the men in the Miami tower hesitated as they watched the potential drama unfold. The controllers knew as well as the pilots struggling in the cockpit that the loss of the engines also meant loss of hydraulic function, which meant the crew had to control the plane manually to keep it aloft and regulate its direction.

It was quiet inside the tower as the controllers watched the crippled Constellation head for the palm trees at the edge of the airport. No one spoke, but out of habit one man picked up the phone to emergency operations and called for the crash trucks. That done, there was nothing left to do but wait for the sound of impact and the dark smoke of the fire. From experience they knew just about how long it would take. They stood silent and waited. Experience proved them wrong this time, however. Slowly over the horizon, limping forward like a bad scene from a B movie, the disabled plane appeared. "He's coming in sideways," shouted one man. "How in hell is he going to clear that pole?" wondered another watching the plane wobble toward a heavy telephone pole at the end of the runway.

Inside the cockpit, the crew wrestled with the controls; the captain strained against the wheel, struggling to keep the nose up. His feet pressed the pedals that operated the plane's rudder. "Look at that old guy bend that thing back," shouted one of the controllers. And indeed, while the men in the tower watched, the captain coaxed enough power out of the Constellation's two remaining engines to clear the pole and land the plane.

Bob Scott was flying copilot on the airplane that day and remembers what it was like. "They got the people off," he laughs, "and then we all went over to the bar and had a drink.

"In the piston days, engine fires were every pilot's fear. I remember another incident. I was flying copilot again. We were taking off from La Guardia one day, and we heard an ominous clunk. The captain looked at the engineer, who reported that everything on his panel looked normal but the tower was telling him the number four engine was trailing smoke and appeared to be on fire. I looked out the cockpit window and saw fire shooting from the engine all the way to the tail of the plane.

"Landing with an engine fire and wings full of fuel is no pilot's idea of excitement, and the captain decided to put the thing on the ground fast. He came into too high and *too* fast, however, and when he called for gear, I couldn't lock the nose gear down. He decided to try to land anyhow, and just as we were about to touch down on the runway the gear snapped into place. We went screaming toward the end of the runway trailing smoke and fire, headed full bore for the Grand Central Parkway at the far end of the airport. The tires in the landing gear blew, the engineer asked to cut power, the captain yelled back, 'Hell, yes,' and the engineer reached up and hit the kill switch. When the plane braked to a stop, the nose wheel was sitting between the threshold lights at the end of the runway. We evacuated the passengers, got another airplane, and three and a half hours later we were on our way to Pittsburgh and New Orleans. We only lost three people. The rest climbed back on the plane with us and took off."

Modern technology has increased engine performance and reliability far beyond the expectations of old-timers who knew only piston equipment. Today a DC-10 can fly with two engines out, and in fact DC-10 captains are often called upon to land the plane on one engine as part of their annual performance check. In the old days it took a lot of effort to keep the piston engines running, balancing oil pressure and engine temperature, and keeping the moving parts well lubricated. Problems were sudden and often major. Pilots who flew the mighty Constellations remember that it was not unusual to shut down an engine on almost every trip.

Although they might not admit it, many of the men who flew the piston airplanes that predated today's jet transports carried with them myths from the old days, impressions of daredevil airmail pilots like William C. "Big Bill" Hopson, who helped establish the transcontinental airmail route, and the barnstormers who crisscrossed the country giving informal flying demonstrations. Many of these early pioneers and the young men who followed them looked across the flat landscape of the Midwest and saw opportunity in the open vistas above. Bob Scott was one of them.

The son of an Ohio working-class family, Scott had an enterprising streak, and by the time he turned sixteen he had established a small freelance photography business. After high school he went to work as a traveling portrait photographer, often flying on the company airplane. Scott now says it was those experiences that awakened him to his true vocation. Watching the corporate pilot go about his business, Scott remembers thinking to himself, "This guy gets *paid* for doing something I would just love to do."

Flying is not all Scott does, however. Aside from his work as an Air Line Pilots Association spokesperson, he and his wife are both accomplished gardeners and are active in staging gardening demonstrations for charity causes. They built and decorated the house they've lived in for the last twenty years, and these days Scott likes to spend off-duty time fiddling with his personal computer and hunting down World War II aircraft to rebuild and sell. Lines of responsibility are strictly drawn in the Scott household; he is the breadwinner, while his wife, Roselynn, keeps the house and seems quietly content to listen to her husband's accounts of union activities and his pilot exploits. For his part, Scott is quick to credit his wife's role in raising the children and holding things together.

After a stint in the service, Scott pursued his aviation career in earnest. He enrolled in the Spartan School of Aeronautics in Tulsa, Oklahoma, where he received his training and the instrument rating he needed to fly commercially. Eventually he landed a job flying automobile parts, and then went to work for a ferry service operating on the DEW line, the string of radar stations across Alaska and northern Canada.

"The planes were big C-46 transports," Scott remembers. "The airports were frozen lakes; the cargo was drums of high-octane gasoline, diesel fuel, railroad ties, and other supplies to build an early-warning radar net. The captains wore copilots out at the rate of two or three a month. They handled the takeoffs and landings and then went to sleep; the copilots flew the rest of the stuff. I did that for a while, and then I said, 'Enough of this.' The captains had a $1,000-a-month guarantee and ten cents a mile, and the copilots were doing all the flying. So I worked on it and I negotiated the first contract the pilots on that airline ever worked under; it included a $500 guarantee for copilots and a nickel a mile. That meant I was making $1,150 a month, and I thought, 'Boy oh boy, this is really great.'

"What I didn't know was that before I left, Capital Airlines had notified me that they wanted me to come in for an interview. I was living with one of the captains who worked for the freight operation, and he told his wife to hide the letter because he knew if Capital offered me a job, I wouldn't go to the Arctic. He knew I'd back out and go to work for a scheduled airline in a minute. I had no college; that was one thing. The other was that I was low time. By the time I found out about the letter, it had been three months. I called Capital up anyhow, and they asked me to come down for an interview. I was on vacation so I went. I took the tests, met with the chief pilot, and he told me they could put me to work. I had been turned down by American, turned down by United. I'd been turned down so many times, I felt like a bed sheet. But now I had plenty of time—I had 1,900 hours. I started the following Monday." Scott frowns. "That three-month delay, however, cost me 120 numbers on the seniority list."

The seniority list, compiled for each of the two or three positions in a flight crew—captain, first officer (referred to colloquially as the copilot), and the second officer, who functions as the flight engineer, dominates a pilot's professional life and to a considerable extent his or her personal life-style. Scott explains, "Seniority affects everything. It affects the trips you get, the equipment you fly, the money you make, your vacation preference, and the way you're boarded on the airplane when you're traveling on your passes. *Everything* is based on seniority. Even when you go in for a check ride, they give the senior guy the option of going first, and he gets to make the choice. Nobody wants anybody ahead of him, but they respect those that are senior to them, and they don't expect more than their seniority entitles them to."

The seniority system that controls how a pilot gets ahead in the commercial aviation industry is both straightforward and arbitrary. When a pilot is hired by an airline, he or she is given a number that establishes his or her position relative to every other pilot at that airline. The move up the ladder is a function of the number of people who were hired before and those who come after. Advancement in position and salary are also a function of how many slots are open, which in turn is a function of the rate an airline develops and needs pilots. Pilots who decide to try their luck with another airline lose the seniority they may have built up and must begin again at the bottom.

Before deregulation, when the government controlled the initiation of air carrier routes, advancement in rank to captain was generally much slower than is possible today. Second officers or engineers could wait for many years to make it to copilot, and experienced aviators could go to retirement without ever having drawn captain's pay. The competition of deregulation, however, has created a demand for pilots that has resulted in a more fluid system in which upgrading can be faster. Additionally, the more common use of two-pilot airplanes, which eliminates the flight engineer from the cockpit crew, has also functioned to shorten upgrade time. Some pilots feel these developments have in some ways thwarted the old system, which limited advancement until a pilot was proved competent to operate in his or her new position.

One of the most important benefits to which seniority entitles a pilot is choice of aircraft, which determines his or her rate of compensation. Generally, the heavier and/or the more complex and thus more productive the airplane, the better the pay. Aviation historian Rex Chamberlain explains how these circumstances came to be.

"Each step as we went from the early mail planes to bringing passengers on board was an increase in productivity. The DC-3, when it came into service, was such a dramatic improvement; it was actually fairly flyable and you could put 24 people in the thing. We'd been hauling around 4 or 5 people before that. And then the four-engine airplanes, the DC-4s, the Connies, you're talking as high as 90 people in the airplane. Then they brought in jets, and now we're talking about maybe four people in the cockpit instead of six [early crews included a professional radio operator and a navigator]. We're talking about 600 miles per hour instead of 300 miles per hour. We're talking about 170 people instead of 30 people. We're talking about an airplane that can make a round trip over the Atlantic in one day.

"This is an increase in productivity of 4- or 5-fold at one time. And then we're going to do it one more time. We're going to bring in the wide-bodied 747, and we're going to cut the crew to three and we're going to go from 170 to almost 400 people, and we're going to have a belly capacity the equivalent of a 707 freighter. We can take this 747 with three guys, we can put 300 or 350 or almost 400 people in it, and we can take nearly the cargo load of a 707 freighter in the bowels of this thing, and we can send it over to Europe and back in one day. Right now today if we talk about the freight alone, if you put forty thousand pounds or fifty thousand pounds of freight down there, that alone will cover your costs and your maintenance reserves. Which means that everything you bring in upstairs is gravy.

"Now, who benefited from this? The flight attendants didn't, because we still had to have a flight attendant for every fifty people or so. But the pilots benefited, and the operator of the airline itself benefited." Chamberlain slows himself down as if to catch his breath. "So the pilots sat down at the negotiating table in the offices of management and negotiated a contract. The traditional stalling technique of management was to stonewall any idea of a raise by saying, 'Gee, we just love you guys and you're critical and we would give you the world if we could, but your productivity just is not there.' But now they couldn't use that argument.

"The next step was to develop a way to measure productivity, which resulted in formulas that measured the speed and weight of the aircraft, how many miles the airplane could traverse in an hour and what kind of weight it was carrying. And then there were other little secondary formulas introduced as various things became automated and various skills came out of the cockpit. The first person to be replaced was the radio operator. The original radio system was a thing where you had a licensed radio operator, and he had to tune up and load the antennae and then send Morse code. He knew nothing about flying an airplane. With better radio equipment—in essence, the radio telephone—this guy was eliminated, and we were able to argue that pilots were doing the radio operator's job. The next thing that happened was that they automated navigation. Navigation over the ocean was interesting to say the least.

"The captain was the base unit and everybody got a percentage off of him. The copilot would get anywhere from forty percent up to two-thirds of the captain, depending on his longevity and so on. I'm not saying that the pilots somehow morally earned this fabulous productivity; it was handed to them by the airframe manufacturers. But consequently we saw airline captains making salaries that people didn't make unless they had horrendous responsibilities, as in the big corporations."

The process by which each member of a cockpit crew implements his or her seniority in order to select the routes he or she wants to fly is called *bidding a line.* Lines of flying are established separately for each crew base (what the airlines call *domiciles*) and can vary monthly. Pilots get a copy of each month's schedule and request the program of trips they would like to fly, prioritizing them in order of preference. If a number of pilots bid the same line, which is usually the case, the pilot who is the most senior on the list of pilots qualified to fly that particular aircraft gets his or her first choice. And so it goes until all the lines of flying are accounted for. Airline economics are based on an intricately complicated system of moving flight schedules among domiciles in order to get the most efficient pairing of pilots and trips. Flight times can change with the time of year, for example, during holidays and school vacations, when more flights may be added, or by season, when schedules may vary because of Daylight Savings Time.

A central crew desk keeps track of monthly assignments and sees that all the scheduled trips are covered. Odd trips that don't fit the primary or secondary lines or come up because of pilot illness or emergency are filled by reserve pilots. These are pilots who are the most junior on the list; they must wait to be called and literally be ready to fly at a moment's notice.

Traditionally the best trips were thought to be those that combine the heaviest equipment—nowadays the McDonnell Douglas DC-10 and Boeing 747—and the least-demanding flying: decent weather, uncongested airspace, and longer- versus shorter-stage lengths with a minimum number of takeoffs and landings. In the days before the hub-and-spoke scheduling, the heaviest equipment was typically applied to nonstop flights. Under the hub-and-spoke system, however, the heavier aircraft have been put to the service of shuttling passengers between hubs, and the smaller short-haul planes, such as the MD-80 and the 737, are used to funnel people from the hubs to their destinations. A passenger heading from Los Angeles to

Atlanta on United Airlines, for example, might fly a DC-10 to Denver, which is a United hub, and a small 737 from Denver to Atlanta. If he or she returned home by way of Chicago (another United hub, which receives more north-south traffic than Denver), the plane from Atlanta to Chicago might be a 727, which is larger than the 737, and in Chicago the passenger would probably pick up another DC-10 for the second part of the trip to Los Angeles. On the other hand, flying Delta, for whom Atlanta is a hub, the passenger would probably go nonstop on a Boeing 757, a high-capacity, fuel-efficient, medium-haul airplane.

Under deregulation, however, another variable has entered the trip-configuration picture—the accumulation of international routes by domestic airlines, specifically Delta, American, and United. Following the rules of economics, the airlines have assigned their heaviest equipment with its larger passenger and freight capacity to service these new routes, and since retirement pay is based on salary the last three years of their career, older pilots feel it's in their best interests to take on these challenging long-distance routes. The old stereotype of senior pilots flying to Hawaii and back twice a month and playing golf on their days off is being replaced by gray-haired captains flying nine- and ten-day, fourteen-hour trips to Sydney and routes from the West Coast to Europe and the Far East.

Commenting on this charge in circumstances, Rex Chamberlain quips, "You'd like to have your more experienced people fly some of the tougher stuff. On the other hand, maybe if they're older, they're less able to take it physically; maybe a younger guy can handle a more punishing schedule. Your ability to hang in there does decrease along with your interest in those tough schedules, the all-nighters. Maybe the young guy's enthusiastic and excited enough to be flying this wonderful airplane. Maybe that helps him stay up for it."

Bob Scott disagrees. Scott, who late in his career has opted for United's nine-day Pacific trips, makes a case for the fact that with the increase in low-time pilots due to deregulation, it is more important than ever to have the experience of older pilots in the cockpit on the more difficult flights. He points to accidents like the crash of United flight 232 in an Iowa cornfield four years ago, where the leadership and experience of Capt. Al Haynes, a pilot two years from retirement, is generally credited with saving the lives of almost half of the people aboard. In another United flight that same year, a 747 that lost a cargo door after takeoff from Honolulu was piloted by David Cronin, a senior captain scheduled to retire in less than three months. Scott maintains that in both accidents, circumstances could have been far worse had not the men flying these airplanes known their aircraft well and had thousands of hours of experience to fall back on. Like many senior pilots, Scott believes that it takes time for an individual to develop leadership skills and be comfortable with the responsibilities of command and that this far outweighs the fact that a younger man might be in better physical shape or have quicker reflexes.

In the opinion of management pilot Craig Donlevy, one thing that helps pilots "stay up for it" is the pay. "They're all capitalists," says Donlevy genially, as he speaks about why older pilots elect to fly the longer, harder trips. Donlevy is a former line pilot who elected to take a desk job as a flight manager at a large eastern domicile, where his responsibilities cut across a wide spectrum of human resources work, from contract negotiations to family problems. In spite of this, Donlevy is generally a light-hearted individual who easily empathizes with pilot concerns while also being able to sort out the overblown from those that have merit. Among employees who have the opportunity to know him personally, Donlevy is respected for his capacity to bridge the gap between management and labor and his talent for using humor to defuse potentially volatile situations. Donlevy is also a midcareer pilot with a particular interest in staying current with the latest technological developments in the industry. He relieves any job stress by working on an old Pennsylvania farmhouse and barn he and his wife recently purchased for their retirement.

"A guy who's thirteen months away from retirement feels that although he might be willing to give up some dollars today and fly a DC-10 [instead of a 747] because the flying's easier, he can't afford to because he doesn't know what inflation might do to him in the future. Sure, some of the short-haul guys don't want to upgrade to the wide-bodies, but they feel they have to for economic reasons. It's that inner pressure that most pilots feel, that they've got to fly the biggest equipment, the thing that pays them the most. Which is kind of ridiculous in a lot of ways.

"If you really analyze people though, you'll find they also want the challenge; they want to fly the biggest thing they can, and they want to fly the international routes. It's only after a while when it becomes routine that it becomes difficult flying. Then they realize the challenge. The other thing is that all of us who have been with

United for a long time are used to two-day trips. I can remember when we first got three-day trips we all said, 'Jesus, how will we pack?' Now that the senior guys have to fly those long nine-day trips we got in the Pan Am Pacific acquisition, it's a culture shock. It's not what they signed up for.

"And we're finding there's some real culture to this long-haul flying beyond the written word—like how do you sleep in the middle of a flight for example? That's something United pilots have never had to be involved with. How do you prepare yourself for a flight? I still think one of the problems a lot of United pilots have is that they're not preparing themselves properly for the long hauls. The Pan Am guys, the guys that *did* sign up for this stuff, come in a day before. They just kind of wander around, check things out, get their manual revisions. It's a day off for them, but they're here. And the day of their flight they take a nap in the afternoon so they're ready to go. It's a big thing to them.

"Let's take a Pan Am veteran like Rex Chamberlain. Flying his trip is a big thing to him. It's important. He's very serious about it. And he treats everybody as a professional. Those people in the back—the flight attendants—are not serving the passengers; they're his right arm. They're the people that tell him what goes on in the back. So he comes early, gives them a briefing and establishes a rapport with them and treats them as professionals. Someone like Rex is used to flying trips where the percentages are that something is going to happen and where he is likely to have to solve the problem himself, whether it's a passenger problem or a mechanical problem, because there's no place to land out there over the ocean. You just can't necessarily get on the ground right away like you can if you're flying domestic."

Since seniority is everything and can make the difference whether pilots get the flying they want, especially toward the end of a long career, they sometimes adopt unusual steps to maximize the possibilities for upgrading. And although commuting can be difficult, living in one place and being based at another is common practice in the industry. Brad Prescott estimates that some forty percent of airline personnel commute, including flight attendants. "One of our guys commutes out of Tennessee to Los Angeles. He's done it for five years. It takes him all day, but he's got a farm there and he loves it. I just had a gal on a flight who lives in Aspen and has been commuting for ten years. She has to drive to Denver, commutes Denver to Dallas, and flies out of Dallas."

Commuting serves a dual purpose. It enables pilots to live in a desirable location while they fly out of a domicile that provides the most comfortable flying and/or the best opportunity for advancement. Jason Young explains, "L.A. has always been a senior base for American, so if I wanted to fly captain, I'd have to go to a more junior base, like Chicago. Boston for us is real senior. Guys are flying copilot out of Boston with a seniority number say of 2,200. They can be flying captain in Chicago at that seniority." Young says at this stage of his career, however, seniority is secondary. He likes living on the West Coast and is willing to wait a little longer to upgrade.

To maintain schedules that keep pace with their blueprint for advancement, Jim and Joyce Kennedy have commuted at various times in their careers. "Jim doesn't mind commuting," says Joyce. "He's very laid back. He'll get in the car and light up his cigar and drive up to the airport real leisurely. He never worries about missing a flight. I leave hours ahead in case there's traffic." The Kennedys are originally from the East Coast and would prefer to live there, but in order to maintain their seniority, Jim has elected to be based in Detroit, which is a hub for Northwest. At first they both commuted, but Joyce especially found the schedule too difficult to maintain.

"Jim and I swear if we ever got divorced it would be because of living the way we do,"says Kennedy, her tight voice revealing some of the anxiety she feels about the situation. "When Jim was first hired by North Central, we both commuted. And then I got pregnant with Cindi. I commuted for six months after I had her, but I was just a basket case. I found it very difficult being away from her that long and commuting. And Jim and I never saw each other. We were coming and going, trying to have one person home with the baby.

"If Jim could fly captain out of Detroit on the equipment he's currently flying, he'd probably bid it. He'd like to fly captain, but if he could fly DC-10 copilot out of Boston, I almost think he would do it and give up flying captain out of Detroit, because he likes his time with the family too. We've both been real family-oriented and would do whatever would be best for the family at this point."

Although they attempt not to express concern, it seems likely that commuting and dead-heading—flying one leg of a trip as a passenger to pick up an airplane or the reverse—would affect pilots' level of readiness and competence. "There are guys who've commuted their whole career," says John Staitsman, who commuted for a year between Pittsfield, Massachusetts, and Chicago. His experiences contributed to his decision to specialize in pilot training. "The senior ones I can understand, but there are guys who are junior. If you're making six or seven trips to the airport a month, it takes away a lot of your days off. There were some months where it took virtually all of mine away. I missed a lot of my children's growing up during that period."

Dick Riley, who for the time being flies close to home, fills in some of the details required of the commuting life-style. "Some guys try to commute out of a hotel, and that's hard, especially on reserve. You have to be available either on a beeper or on a telephone twenty-four hours a day. We have a guy at United that came over from Pan Am during the merger who was commuting from some place over in Europe—Zurich—to San Francisco. With Pan Am he only did it once a month. He would come over here and fly for two or three weeks and go home."

Hank Barnes, a senior 747 captain for TWA, moved to the West Coast in 1961, doing most of his flying out of Los Angeles. In May of 1983, however, as he edged closer to retirement he decided to transfer back to New York in order to upgrade to international routes. Barnes is a collected, self-contained man with fine features, a composed voice, and a patient manner, the kind of individual who always goes to his child's baseball games and never makes a nuisance of himself there. "I take the ten o'clock red-eye special from Los Angeles to New York," says Barnes casually. "I get to New York at six o'clock in the morning, go to a hotel, and sleep during the day for maybe five or six hours. After that, I feel pretty good. I go to dinner about four-thirty in the afternoon; then I leave for the airport at eight-thirty. By the time I get to Europe, it's only eleven o'clock or midnight West Coast time. I go to bed for three or four hours and then get up and walk around, sightsee, go shopping, and go out to dinner that evening. It seems to work pretty good for me now, although it took about six months to get used to it. I fly a lot of trips back to back, which means I get to New York and go back out the next day. I've heard that over seventy percent of our pilots commute into New York, a lot from the East Coast, from Florida.

"I don't know if the commuting bothers me; I just don't let it. My wife and I made up our minds that I was going to fly out of New York and I was going to have to commute because we weren't going to move. If I want to fly international the last few years of my career on the 747, I have to do it out of New York. Not that it isn't frustrating. On a good day at the right time it's about two hours from my home here in San Diego to the airport at Los Angeles, although it's taken me over three hours sometimes, like after I've just gotten off the polar from London. *That* drives me up the wall."

"I'm the other extreme," grins Dick Riley. "It takes me eighteen minutes to get to the field when the highway's busy. When the highway's not busy, it's about twelve minutes. I think being in an airplane as a passenger is more fatiguing than flying it. I despise dead-heading with a passion. It's boring, just totally boring. There's generally two jump seats in each airplane, and if you have a full passenger load, it's a way to get on."

Unlike most professions, in which promotion and advancement are often related to how adroitly an individual can move from one organization to another, by the time pilots reach the ranks of the majors, they are wedded to their employer for life. As United flight engineer Lisa Johnson adds, the carrier a pilot ends up with is mostly a matter of luck—basically whichever responds first. What happens to pilots after they make this important commitment is related to the airline's business philosophy, its management effectiveness, and the pilot-airline contract stipulating the terms of employment. Events since deregulation have changed the overall character of this arrangement, diluting some of the system's traditional safeguards.

For example, when Sandra Luft returned to work after almost three years of the strike pilots called against Continental to protest pay cuts and administrative changes resulting from the 1983 bankruptcy filing, she found working conditions substantially different from what she remembered. "When I first went to work for Continental, the preamble to the pilot's operations manual explained that Continental hired pilots for the rest of their working lives. The new management took that page out. My knowledge of the fact that my employer would not honor one of the fundamental practices by which our industry functions reminds me that I am not working for a benevolent organization.

"I went back to work at Continental because I like the kind of work, and I like the people. There's still a lot of camaraderie among those of us who went on strike and stayed out. We feel that we didn't walk the streets for that long to give somebody else our seniority number, which is about the only thing we got back. I have a friend who went back to work during the strike. I don't like the fact that he did that, but I try to understand. I think guys like that can't cope. They came right out of the military into the airlines and never had to look for a job, and then they are suddenly faced with the prospect of selling themselves. Bart had worked for the company for probably fifteen or sixteen years when the strike happened, and perhaps the whole thing of starting over in an industry where you're not supposed to have to do that scared him.

"After the bankruptcy, when the company started calling people back, [they started with] some of the senior people, some of the people they liked, and some of the people [who] wouldn't have an easy time getting jobs at other places."

Regarding specific abuses of the seniority system at Continental, Luft says, "When the strike was finally settled by court order, Continental management decided they would interpret the judgment according to their own rules. Their position was that as slots became available for captains, the first seventy guys to go back would be put into them but *only after* they'd spent four months as first officers. Now you've got to remember, they *had* to call the senior guys back first, so the first guys they called back were *very* senior and they'd all been captains before. But even given their seniority, they made these guys go back initially as first officers—copilots.

"But the real kicker was that the company would assign the guys that came back to a domicile instead of letting them bid what they wanted. They would send them to terrible places; they would assign some guy who lived in L.A. to a Newark DC-9 captain slot, which meant that he had to commute. That kind of thing made their life pretty miserable. They assigned guys to Guam. They also assigned guys to airplanes they'd specifically never flown before when there were slots available for the kind of airplane they had flown—*and knew*. And they purposely took people off an airplane that they knew the pilots knew how to fly and made them train on something else. Frank Lorenzo thinks piloting is a straight mechanical skill that anybody can learn."

"I work for a nonunion company now," says fellow Continental striker Stan Page, who like Luft went back to work after the strike. His remarks pertain to Continental management under Frank Lorenzo. "We always felt we had a place to go for legal advice, ALPA, and we could always get a lawyer to defend us. If a similar situation happened today, you'd better get yourself a lawyer and you'd better get a good one because the company I work for has very good ones. There used to be checks and balances in the system, namely we had a union, and there wasn't intimidation and pressure by management. What's really going on out there today is fear.

Management by fear. The whole business is kind of a manifestation of a niggardly corporate attitude; if you pay people less, you get less but at least your costs are down. People are expendable; they're replaceable. If they don't do things the way you want, you let them go. There's no sense of working together toward a common purpose.

"Part of why I guess I'm the way I am is I would like to leave something as good as what I got, and right now I don't have it as good as what somebody else gave me. In the old days, the story was it didn't make any difference where you went. Get a [seniority] number, that was the important thing. It used to be a saying, I think, that every number's worth ten thousand bucks. I would say every number now is worth a whole lot more in the real world. One number. But today at Continental, seniority doesn't mean anything.

"One of the schedulers with whom I go back a long way said to me one day, 'Stan, never forget who you are and what you did, because the company won't. The strike cost Frank $80 million.' So I'm pretty sure that beside my name there's an asterisk and probably beside every guy that struck to the end. We have an organization of the guys who struck, the GBs—Golden Balls. We have a tie pin with the old Continental insignia and an inscription, 'Brotherhood,' on the bottom of it. Management does not like that pin.

"The other day, one of the flight managers came up to me when I was just hanging around. I had my hat on kind of crooked and my coat open. He put my hat on straight and buttoned my coat, and then he saw the pin. He pulled it out and looked at it and asked me what it was. I said, 'That's how we tell the good guys from the bad guys.' He put my hat back on crooked, unbuttoned my coat, and turned around and walked away. They have to know who *we* are, because I know who *they* are.

"Does it bother us? I was bothered when we first came back, and I think everybody was. Jack Hilgrin was one of my very best friends. We had been squadron mates in Vietnam. There were twelve of us who were in Vietnam together who went to work at Continental. But Jack was the only guy out of that whole group who went to work after the strike action was called. I called him on the telephone, and I said, 'Jack, don't do it. Come up here and talk. Let's talk about this.' And he said, 'Okay, I'll meet you at the Hilton at nine o'clock in the morning.' So I was at the Hilton at nine o'clock in the morning, and at nine-thirty Jack pushed back at the gate going to Kennedy. I flew with Jack after I came back to work. I didn't say a word to him, not one. I haven't spoken to him to this day. He is the enemy."

"I think Frank Lorenzo should be hung up by his balls until they think of something mean to do to him," says Brad Prescott. "The destruction that did to families. I can tell you some horror stories of guys at Air Cal who come over from Continental. None of them crossed. Air Cal wouldn't hire anyone that crossed. I've got a friend who was my training mate; he was with Continental for nineteen years as a captain flying the Pacific routes. He ended up losing his family. He also lost a beautiful home in Laguna and was over $125,000 in debt to the IRS. He told me it was like living a nightmare." (Like Page, Prescott is referring to Continental under Lorenzo management.)

"The reason why Continental exists today is because the American public is cheap, and they don't care. I listen to people say they're taking Continental because the fare is X number of dollars. I always say to them, 'What's your life worth?' They don't even know what I'm talking about."

An additional factor resulting from the Continental strike that worries Sandra Luft and others is that they believe many pilots hired to replace those who wouldn't cross the picket line had minimal qualifications and experience. Because of the demand for pilots, however, they think these new-hires moved up through the operation much faster than they might have ordinarily, bypassing the usual quality control gate of the seniority system. Says Brad Prescott, "I ran into this guy in Portland flying captain on a DC-9 for Continental. I was shocked. He used to fly with me when I was in corporate aviation. I heard that he was so weak then they let him go as a copilot. Now he's flying as a captain on Continental. It scares the hell out of me to think that he's in the same sky as I'm in. If I had an enemy, I wouldn't send them on Continental."

"A year from new-hire to captain," says Luft. "That's awful fast, and it's awful scary. I spent a long time as a second officer, but I learned a lot by watching. There's a reason that the seniority system exists, and it's basically so that you'll learn, so that by the time you're expected to perform you've got some basis on which to make decisions. That's not to say that everybody they hired during the strike is a wet-nosed kid. I'm just thinking that it's important to observe the progression of how an airline works—having watched decisions being made—and also having the freedom to say, 'I don't know. I want some more information.'

"Also, I don't think the people who were hired during the strike, who basically got hired because they were a warm body, feel they have the sure footing to say, 'No, I won't do it.' I feel I'm on more solid ground because I have enough of a history with the airline, and I know from what I have seen that management is a little more hesitant to can people with bigger experience levels. It's the new people . . . I don't know that they fear they will lose their jobs if they make too much noise, but they have seen a lot of people come and go.

"One of the things we have always objected to," says Luft, as she continues to describe Continental under Texas Air management, "is this bad habit of training people for a new position, sending them back to the old airplane for a couple of months and *then* expecting them to go back and fly the new one. They were going to try to do that with me recently, and I talked them out of it. They wanted me to fly captain on the 737 [after she had trained on the DC-10], but I argued that I had become noncurrent on that plane. I reminded them that they would have to send me back through training and that would cost money, and then they'd have to let me go out and do three landings and *that* would cost money."

Although some pilots characterize the violations of the seniority system initiated at Continental by Texas Air Corporation as particularly vindictive, the recent trend of mergers and acquisitions throughout the airline industry has threatened the safeguards built into the system and made pilots apprehensive. The merger of one carrier by another requires some plan for combining the seniority of the combined pilot force. So far the proposed solutions have generally been viewed as inequitable. In some cases such arrangements have resulted in open hostility.

When American Airlines bought Air Cal in 1987, increasing the American pilot force to 7,400, American flight engineer Jason Young lost 332 numbers. Says Young, "In the long run, I think the Air Cal guys got the best deal around. There are a lot of pilots who aren't happy, but I don't know whether Air Cal would have survived against the big boys. They could have had a hostile takeover by Continental. They could have merged with somebody they wouldn't be happy with. In my opinion the Air Cal guys got a good deal, but you can't keep everybody happy.

"Then again Air Cal brought all their flying with them. We had a lot of flights up and down the West Coast. Now we've cut out a bunch of flights, and we've grounded a bunch of the airplanes they brought over. So *their* pilots are flying *our* airplanes without us having the advantage of their extra routes. So now I'm not as happy as I was. And *those guys* are complaining. Tough. You didn't buy us. We bought you. You're lucky to be where you are."

Brad Prescott is one of the Air Cal pilots Young is speaking about. "As soon as I get a chance, I'm bidding out of here. I'm history. I'm going someplace else. American didn't want to do a lot of cross-training, because it would cost the company too much money, so they stipulated that for the first two and a half years we were locked into flying the Western sector on Air Cal equipment and on Air Cal routes. The first chance I get, I'm bidding out of here. I'll go to East Jesus, Kansas; it doesn't matter to me—just pay me. I could go to Dallas. I've got five acres there; I'll build a house. Or Florida or New York, it doesn't matter."

United Airlines' purchase of the Pacific routes from Pan Am in 1985 brought to a head feelings about seniority that many think contributed to the pilot strike at United that year. Rex Chamberlain remembers when United's Pacific acquisition was announced. "When I left Pan Am for United, it was a negotiated deal that was worked out jointly by the union and Pan American and United. I was given full recognition of my years of service; that is, I was given date of hire [at Pan Am]."

Bob Scott, who came to United as a result of the Capital–United Airlines merger in 1961, has a different opinion of the merged United–Pan Am list. "Rex had about twenty years with Pan Am when he came over. His number now at United is about 1,200, and he's flying 747 captain. It usually takes a guy thirty-two years to fly captain on a 747. If he came over with our seniority in place, on our list, Rex could just barely hold DC-8 captain, not even DC-10 captain. There was a lot of unhappiness about that among the United group, but it was probably the fairest way to do it.

"One thing I do think, however, is that the Pan Am crews should have been brought over in their old pay scale. People like Rex Chamberlain got a $40,000 a year increase. My feeling is that the reason the company wanted it done that way was because they wanted to show the Pan Am people they were really pushing for favorable treatment and because United thought they had 410 built-in scabs for the strike they expected in April of that year."

Nor is amiable Ted Goff particularly happy with his treatment in the merger of Western Airlines with Delta. "When Delta bought Western, I took it in the shorts. All the Western pilots slotted in six, seven years behind the guy who was hired the same time at Delta.

Before deregulation Western was a great carrier. We got paid just like everybody else. But about four years past deregulation, Western started hurting, and to save the company, we started giving up a lot. In two years, we gave up, shit, a lot of our retirement money plus a cut in pay. I was making less than some United Airlines flight attendants for a while.

"When Delta bought us they thought we were just a bunch of low-rent scum because we were getting paid less instead of looking at us like we're saving this company so Delta could be a national carrier instead of some East Coast regional carrier. I lost over six years, which is over a third of my time with the airlines. When you've only been with the company fifteen years and you lose six years, that's forty percent. They really murdered a lot of people. Now it will take me six years longer to make captain. I have almost eight hundred guys ahead of me now that wouldn't have been there otherwise."

Not that Goff hasn't had his compensations. "I told somebody if that was the first time I'd ever been screwed, I'd be pissed. But it isn't. We do get paid more by Delta. I was getting around $40,000 a year during the poor times at Western. I think this year my W-2 was in the sixties. I got that back before deregulation with Western Airlines.

"The other bad situation is the Northwest–Republic thing," Goff continues, speaking about conditions that resulted from the 1986 acquisition of Republic Airlines by Northwest. "I've got some friends who were with Republic. I feel sorry for them. They have the green book and the red book. The red book is the Northwest people and the green book is the Republic side. Some of those guys lost seven or eight years seniority."

"You can't run an airline with an adversary relationship with labor," says Dick Riley, speaking about the labor-management issues that have emerged in the past decade. Supporting this statement is Riley's opinion that, ideological arguments aside, the questionable decision making that underlies some of the abuses of the seniority system has the capacity to affect important human resource issues in the aviation industry, not the least of which is the mental attitude of the flight deck crew. Management disregard for the seniority system affects not only the job security protection that pilots have traditionally relied upon but the code of ethics by which they live. And this in turn can substantially impact how an airplane gets from one place to another.

CHAPTER 4

Training and Experience

You know, you go for years and years and nothing ever happens, and then every once in a while you get a little excitement. That's what they hire you for, though, these little offbeat things; you've got to have one happen every once in a while just to keep tuned. The worst time is takeoff and landing, when you're closest to the ground. You can keep going forever up in the air with no hydraulics and all the rest of this stuff, but sooner or later, you've got to come down.

—TED GOFF, Delta Air Lines
737 copilot

O n May 2, 1988, a United Airlines 747, a four-engine aircraft, carrying 258 passengers and a crew of 19 from Los Angeles to Tokyo landed with only one of its four engines operating. According to reports, the first engine had quit thirty-nine thousand feet above the Pacific and approximately 125 miles from Tokyo's Narita airport; forty minutes later, the second engine stopped; the third engine was shut down just minutes before the pilots managed to land the airplane safely. The investigation following the incident concluded that the problem was not related to engine malfunction or failure, but that it appeared the three engines had simply run out of fuel. Because there had been adequate fuel taken on board the aircraft, initial speculation centered around the crew's ability to determine the nature of their problem and to take the necessary steps to remedy it. In this instance the factors that led to what could have been a tragic accident involved a junior crew flying an aircraft that was new to them and which had recently been put into service in the United system.

"The fact that this particular crew was assigned to that aircraft was just a total happenstance," says Dick Riley thoughtfully. "They all came from a United domestic background, and they each had reached the point in their seniorities where they could fly the 747. The captain had been a DC-10 captain; I don't know what the other two did. But the crew was brand new out of the training center, the absolute scenario that everybody fears."

What Riley is suggesting is that what happened in Tokyo that day in May resulted from a confluence of factors: (1) the seniority system that effectively allows pilots to choose the aircraft and routes they will fly; (2) pilot training under deregulation; and (3) competitive industry practices that have put new pressures on the pilot-equipment equation.

According to Dick Riley's narrative of the events related to the incident, the United 747 headed to Tokyo that day was one of a group of five aircraft initially owned by American Airlines. Their lineage thereafter is hazy, but they had at one time evidently been pressed into charter service in the Middle East flying Moslem pilgrims to Mecca. There apparently the once-proud Boeing jets had been subject to various forms of abuse, including minimal maintenance and demanding passengers. It was said, for example, that devout Moslems heading for the Holy Land took to bringing on board everything from cooking pots to livestock.

The five used airplanes became available at the time United was on the lookout for aircraft for its newly acquired Pacific routes. The airline bought the five 747s to replace six Pan Am Lockheed L-1011s that had come with the Pacific acquisition but which were incompatible with United's existing 747 fleet. As Riley sees it and Bob Scott agrees, for United management, replacing the L-1011s with rebuilt 747s eliminated the cost of maintaining a separate L-1011 parts inventory and of training United mechanics to service the Lockheed planes. Additionally, it was projected that the rebuilt 747s could be put into service relatively quickly, at a time when projected delivery on aircraft from the Boeing factory was four years. A final consideration, according to Scott, was the fact that the 747s would carry about twice as many people as the L-1011s. All in all it seemed to be an intelligent decision.

The Boeing 747 was the first of the generation of wide-bodied jets. Designed for increased passenger loads *and* freight capacity that made it commercially attractive, the 747 also represented the latest in aircraft design and technology. Pan Am was the first airline to fly the big jet, and in fact there are some industry observers who speculate the airplane might never have been developed if it had not been for the unique partnership between Boeing and Pan Am, which wanted the plane for its large network of overseas routes.

"Boeing always built the kind of ugly ducklings that hauled all the freight, and so the people who had the long-haul stuff over the water would go Boeing," explains Rex Chamberlain. "Douglas airplanes traditionally were simpler machines, and that was attractive to the airlines. The DC-8 was a simple machine; they even were still using things like bell cranks and pulleys and levers and cable runs while the Boeing 707 had electrical switches and complex components to activate the flying surfaces."

Significantly, the 747 was also the first plane to be designed around the inertial navigation system. "You turned on this box," explains Chamberlain, "and you told it where it was and you let it crank away for about twenty minutes, put it in navigation mode, and it navigated. The airplane could make circles and holding patterns and could speed up and slow down, climb and descend, it could be pushed around by the wind but this box knew where it was. It was quite a joke because up until then the pilots were supposed to understand their airplanes. Of course when this sort of electronics came along, we just threw up our hands. It was a joke. People would ask, 'Well, how does it work?' which is the old question about any airplane system. The answer is, 'It works just fine.'"

The big 747 with its fuel-hungry engines fell on hard times, however, during the oil crunch of the midseventies. Eventually smaller, more fuel-efficient planes were put into service on the transcontinental routes flown by domestic carriers such as American and United, while the wide-bodied aircraft were reassigned to ferry larger loads between the new airport hubs. Newly developing airlines such as People's Express bought or leased the large-capacity planes to implement their mass travel philosophy. In 1979, ten years after their introduction, there were 131 Boeing 747s in use, and the number gradually increased to 171 in 1988. By that time, however, Boeing was at work on an advanced model, the 747-400, a technologically more sophisticated two-pilot airplane that is now in service with a variety of both international and domestic carriers.

According to Dick Riley, United's final consideration in evaluating refurbishment of the used 747s was cost. A new Boeing 747 cost $125 million "a copy," while the thought was that the used planes could be rebuilt for the price of one factory-built new one. Additionally, the five planes were part of the Seahorse Group, Boeing's designation for the original standardized 747s bought by American, United, and Braniff, which meant that the configuration of the airplane was already up to United's standards and was similar to planes the airline already owned. Riley estimates that United invested some 70,000 worker-hours rebuilding the used aircraft, about twice what it took for the planes' original construction. Only four planes were rebuilt; one was knocked down to provide parts Boeing couldn't deliver quickly enough.

As the story goes, the airplanes' critical electrical and hydraulic systems were gone over and repaired or replaced; the fuselage of each plane was stripped, and the interior treated for corrosion; the belly skins (the thin outside layer that covers the body of an airplane) were replaced, along with the formers (the ribs that hold the plane together). When all was said and done, it took six months to refurbish the planes and prepare them for service on United's Pacific routes. During this time, the additional pilots who would be needed to fly in the Pacific system were undergoing training.

In order to be what the industry calls *qualified* on an airplane, the pilots who had bid up in anticipation of additional 747 flying had to learn the systems of the new aircraft as well as new flight patterns, seasonal weather changes, the characteristics of air traffic control in the new corridors in which they would be flying, and the configurations of airports along their routes. They had to pass a test in a simulator and complete a successful check ride. In all, the process took approximately six weeks. The cost and responsibility of retraining was to the airline's, but the initiative belonged to the pilots. The specifics of retraining usually means two weeks of ground school at the company's training facility, where the process of learning an airplane's systems includes training on cardboard cockpit replicas and classroom briefings. These are followed by multiple sessions with a pilot trainer in a simulator that mimics the systems of the real airplane and can be programmed to feign a variety of possible emergencies and incidents. The pilot is a student again. In a system that relies on individual initiative and responsibility, training is designed to insure that a pilot bidding up to new equipment is qualified to fly that aircraft according to industry standards.

Pilots who for some reason don't successfully complete training or who don't become proficient are not upgraded to the new equipment, although they may repeat the training and evaluation again at a later date. Flight manager Craig Donlevy explains the case of a 747 first officer who bid up to 737 captain and began the required training. "The guy did not make it through school," says Donlevy. "His flying abilities were okay—passable—but he couldn't put his priorities in order. Therefore he would get things all screwed up. Training programs are set up to filter out people like that. He was sent back to first officer on the 747 for eighteen months. After that he can bid up, and he will be reevaluated at that time. But he'll have to go through training again; actually he'll have to be reevaluated before he even gets into training. Is it likely that he'll be able to do it? Knowing the individual as I do, I'm not sure."

As Sandra Luft explains, once pilots are trained and checked out on a new aircraft, their skills and expectations are essentially redirected. They have spent weeks studying the plane's systems, hours practicing their role in making the equipment work. As Luft, who recently upgraded from copilot to captain, describes it, they effectively "brain-dumped" the information about the aircraft they used to fly. Their psychomotor skills become adjusted to the requirements of the new airplane, and they become emotionally directed

toward flying it. Pilots upgrading to the generation of more technologically advanced aircraft must also acquire computer programming
skills as well as become familiar with new cockpit notification and
warning systems that are part of computerized aircraft. All things
considered, as veteran Bob Keystone points out, becoming really
proficient on a new airplane takes a lot of practice.

"We all get into the airplane with the supreme confidence that
we're going to get that airplane from point A to point B with
absolute safety," says Keystone. "We've done it before. We know we
can do it again. In order to maintain top proficiency, you have to be
almost continuously flying. You can't take three months off or six
months off and expect to come back and be as good as you were
when you stopped."

In Bud McKenzie's opinion, one thing practice provides pilots
is a feel of the plane, a kind of sixth sense of how the aircraft is
going to respond to a variety of specific situations. And as far as
McKenzie is concerned, this knowledge and experience are essential
for getting out of sticky situations. "I remember one time we had a
flight instructor who was just back six months from Korea. I think he
had knocked down four MiGs and generally had a lot of experience.
We went off one morning, three of us students and him. We were
flying against targets in the desert, old tanks and trucks and things
like that. I was number two on his wing, which put me behind him
when he rolled in on this old tank at about five hundred feet. I
thought it was real close so I backed off, and the other two guys
followed me. After we landed, the instructor asked us how we
enjoyed the run on the tank. We were all quiet until finally I said,
'Well, I thought it was too low so I chickened out,' and he said, 'It's
a good thing because I almost killed myself. You guys made the right
decision.'

"You must make it your intention to always stay ahead of the
airplane," adds McKenzie. "Before you even start out, you must have
already formulated a lot of the decisions that will have to be made
downline in the course of your flight so when the time comes, you'll
know exactly what you're going to do. When you're a pilot, you don't
want to have a spring-loaded brain. You should have your alternatives
in mind and have your decision points in time set, but you must always
be ready to fine-tune them. You can always take a little more time, and
if you do, you'll have the comfort of knowing that there is a point
where you've decided to make a decision. I like to think of it this way:
takeoffs are optional, landings are mandatory."

Aviation has come a long way since the days when pilots like Bob Scott joked that their training consisted of two hours of practicing takeoffs and landings, a quick fix on the radio and the rest learned on the line. Training programs differ from airline to airline, but one common complicating factor is the increasingly automated cockpit. In 1987 when Northwest Airlines Flight 255, a DC-9, crashed on takeoff from Detroit, killing all but one of its passengers, a primary factor implicated in the NTSB report of the accident was the crew's failure to deploy the airplane's flaps correctly and the fact that the cockpit warning system didn't indicate that the plane was misconfigured. After the crash, however, the airline's vice president of technical services went on record with his opinion that increasingly sophisticated aircraft technology has made flight deck crews more and more dependent on the airplane to tell them when something is wrong.

Aviation researcher Earl Wiener, a former Air Force pilot who has made a career of studying human factors issues in aviation often in conjunction with the National Aeronautics and Space Administration (NASA), believes that because the automatic cockpit demands a different set of piloting skills, it also requires different training methods, "a reexamination," says Wiener, "of what goes on during those precious two weeks in ground school. . . . One can never be completely sure when the chips are down that the right response is going to come from that human crew." And although Wiener differentiates between the challenges that fall to aircraft designers in developing systems that are user-friendly, compared with those of airline training departments in developing pilot proficiency, he suggests that a primary challenge to modern airline management is what he describes as the downward movement of automation. By this he means that with more advanced automation occurring earlier in a pilot's career, airlines will have to revise training procedures to compensate for errors that might evolve in the course of adapting to new technology. "We need to modernize the FAA and Federal Aviation Regulations," says Wiener, "including the manner in which performance checks are conducted and the subject matter of the proficiency checks." When Wiener speaks of proficiency checks, he is referring to the manner by which a pilot is officially certified on an aircraft. Currently pilots train exclusively on simulators. The first time they encounter the actual airplane is on their line check, in which they are evaluated on a regularly scheduled flight with a check airman from the company and usually an FAA examiner. The examiner's job is to observe that the check airman's test of the pilot is sufficient to assess his or her ability to fly the aircraft.

Despite the challenges of technology, pilots say they enjoy the predictability of modern aircraft. "I've been flying for twenty-five years, and I've never had an engine failure," they'll tell you, or a hydraulic failure or anything of major consequence. Yet airplanes still fail and cause loss of life. Among pilots there is in fact some speculation that the very predictability of the new generation of airplanes can work against them by inhibiting their ability to respond to an emergency. They have a saying about flying in the automated age. They describe it as, "Countless hours of sheer boredom interspersed with moments of stark terror." Such self-deprecating humor aside, pilots are concerned that the technological reliability of modern aircraft may indeed decrease their opportunity to test their thinking and flying skills.

The simulators used by all airlines to replace real-time practice have become an accepted tool of training. Although simulator time is expensive, it costs much less than having a pilot learn on the line. It can also be said that simulators are more effective in preparing pilots to handle a variety of sticky situations because the incidents that can lead to difficulties can be programmed in such a way that develops and tests specific piloting skills. However, simulator training also has its limitations. "The simulator's the best tool we have," says Brad Prescott, "but you still don't get the same feel—the wing load, the feel of the airplane in the air, the turbulence, wind conditions. They're trying to put it in, but it's not the same. You're flying a computer, not an airplane. Every airplane will fly different, but all simulators fly alike. A lot of pilots who come out of the simulator having made a mistake feel like shit. That's because we're trained that we're not going to ever make a mistake. I don't care who you are, you can be broke. If a guy's weak in something, you should work with him until he's up to proficiency. That doesn't happen. Air Cal rented their simulators; American owns their own so if you need extra time they give you extra time."

Bud McKenzie, who has seven thousand hours on the DC-10 as a captain and copilot, talks about the simulator experience. "With the kinds of training and simulators that we have today plus the on-line training, people who are, I would say, average in qualification will be brought up to that level with a few years' experience. And like any other industry or profession, you're going to have a few people who are slightly below average who will require more training, a little more time on-line flying with more experienced captains."

Navy veteran Bill Fredericks wonders whether pilot training is focused correctly. "We can train ourselves for an emergency," says Fredericks with the vehemence that typifies all his conversation, "when an engine falls off, for example. That's what the simulator is all about. But pilots are not trained to think horizontally, and that means there are several traps we fall into. We process information very well; we process by the numbers though. If things start going awry, we may not pick it up. Sometimes we depend on the numbers too much or on routine and don't think creatively to come up with some other solution if by-the-numbers doesn't work. Sometimes our intelligence gets in the way, and we think we know it all."

As Fredericks suggests, pilots are by nature creatures of habit, most comfortable with routine. In aviation the enforcer of routine is the checklist. Although three manufactures—Boeing, McDonnell Douglas, and Airbus Industrie—provide most of the aircraft used by the major airlines, each makes a variety of models designed to suit the various flying needs of individual carriers. Manufacturers and the airlines themselves invest countless hours developing manuals that spell out the systems and procedural operations pertinent to each aircraft, and pilots make a comparable investment in time digesting this material. Because of the complexity of aircraft systems, however, the most important procedural information is contained in a checklist, literally a list of all the steps that must be accomplished at various stages of a flight. Sandra Luft explains her early experiences as a flight engineer.

"There's a before-start checklist and an after-start checklist, one for taxi, one for before takeoff and then after takeoff. Then when you get where you're going, there are in-range, approach, landing, after-landing, and parking checklists. All of these are read by the second officer [or in a two-person cockpit, by the first officer or copilot] from a laminated card and answered by the other two crew members. On the receiving aircraft checklist for a 727 flight engineer, there are forty-two memory items, from crew baggage to checking the plane's 472 circuit breakers and checking every gauge and testing every warning light on the flight engineer's panel. Once the flight engineer does his inspection, he hands the list to the copilot, who reads it back and 'challenges' the flight engineer."

"You've got a multitude of instruments in the cockpit of a 747, and each of them has to be in a certain place," explains old hand

Bob Keystone. "Before takeoff there's something like twenty-five or thirty items you have to complete on the 747 checklist. You check that everything's in its position, where it's supposed to be. It only takes about thirty or forty seconds, but it's crucial. There are so many things pilots take for granted that we've learned after years and years of flying, we don't even think about them. But you do call them out, one pilot naming the required procedure, the other indicating that it has been done. The captain calls for flaps; the copilot answers, 'Thirty degrees.' Next he calls for gear handle; the copilot answers, 'Down.' And on it goes until the checklist is completed.

"If you try to go through it too fast somebody can make a mistake and answer the normal answer but not check it. That's one human error that can take place. We all know that and we all guard against it. You're very careful to be sure that when you say something, it's done. Each one of these things becomes a part of you when you get qualified on an airplane."

In addition to routine procedures, there are also checklists for diagnosing problems and for procedures to be implemented in case of an emergency. Bob Scott explains how it works. "If we have a problem, we have a series of irregular procedures to which we refer, and if we follow the prescribed procedure successfully and if nothing else happens, we can continue to operate that way and the situation never becomes an emergency. However, if something else is discovered or if something else happens, we have to go to an emergency procedure, and we can still make a safe landing under emergency conditions. Sometimes you never get to an irregular procedure; sometimes you've got to go directly to an emergency procedure. The thing is to recognize it. Recognizing the situation is half our job. Deciding on the proper action is the other part, and the third part is executing it."

The problem is that sometimes the idiosyncrasies of an airplane can confound using the checklist and the emergency procedures the cockpit crew is mandated to follow. DC-10 flight engineer Lisa Johnson talks about such an experience. "The DC-10 is such an electric airplane. The big joke is when something happens, just sit back and wait a few minutes because it will usually correct itself. On one occasion we took off from Maui, and we couldn't get our slats up. [Slats are devices on the front of the wing that provide extra lift at slower operating speeds.] We obviously couldn't go to Los Angeles that way, and we couldn't go back into Maui. So we worked out the problem. The copilot flew, and the captain and I worked on the problem.

"I had to go back [to the passenger cabin] two or three different times to check the positions of the slats on the wings. We were on the phone to maintenance, but they couldn't help us. We could not do anything with the problem, and we were just getting ready to discuss dumping fuel and going into Honolulu and putting all the people on a different flight. Then the captain said, 'Let's just give it one more shot,' and he flipped the switch and sure enough it worked, for no reason. We had circled for probably about thirty minutes working on this."

The additional factor in all of this is that airlines are at liberty to interpret checklist procedures according to their management and flying philosophies. "In the early days, Continental used to have an interchange with Western," explains Sandra Luft. "Western would fly a 727 from Anchorage to Seattle, and then we'd fly it from Seattle to Dallas. We would get on their airplane with our own checklists and fly it on down. Of course we'd see the Western checklist still in the airplane, and we'd be amazed at some of the things they did. We used to laugh about it. They had this procedure of tossing the logbook out the window at every stop, which we thought was very funny. Our policy was that the mechanic came on board. I was amazed at how every airline flew the same plane slightly differently.

"I remember when I had my FAA oral to qualify for the 727. The guy asked me to describe the operation of the brake lockout deboost system. I described it, and he disagreed with me. I knew I was right, however, and we went to the manual. The problem was that he also gave exams for Western, and their 727s worked differently. He had just gotten it mixed up."

Complicating these circumstances is the consequences of the mergers and acquisitions now prevalent in the commercial aviation industry. Aside from causing confusion in the personnel area relative to pilot seniority lists and pay scales, these often complex transactions have also resulted in hodgepodge airplane fleets, a situation that United Airlines was attempting to avoid in rebuilding the used Boeing 747s. Pilots on both ends of such deal making may find themselves adjusting to different aircraft and to variations in operating procedures. Texas Air Corporation, for example, through its subsidiaries Continental, Eastern, People's Express, Frontier, and New York Air, at that time owned airplanes of *nine* different types, most of which were over twelve years old.

"The problem in modifying procedures on things like the checklist is the resistance of most pilots to change," says Ann Alexander, a young MD-80 first officer who was caught in the PSA-USAir merger. They've been doing something for so long; some of these guys have been doing this for twenty or twenty-five years, and the checklist has always been the same. We always felt that PSA had a real good rapport with the FAA, and we felt that we were meeting very high standards in their eyes for our checklists and our procedures. But USAir's are definitely different.

"You see, USAir's not used to the DC-9-80 [which PSA flew]; they're used to the DC-9-30. So what it appears they did when they made these new checklists was just take the '30 checklist and turn it over to an '80 checklist. And the procedures are a little different. We had guys fight for a few things on that checklist, and they eventually got them, but there's still a few things that need to be changed. And I think that with the people that we have in management now, it will eventually get there. But as of right now you just kind of remember a lot."

Alexander stops and then adds, "The other thing with the checklist is that at PSA the copilot was allowed to read the landing checklist, for example, and look at the items that he was checking. At USAir, no matter how busy the captain or the flying pilot is, the other person reads the checklist, and the flying pilot has to answer. It's very annoying at one thousand feet when you're concentrating on your landing to have someone yelling in your ear, 'Spoilers, spoilers.' Finally you just say, 'Okay, fine, you do the checklist. I will listen to you. If I don't agree with something you've said, then I'll talk to you. Say it out loud so the voice recorder's got it.'

"So what it actually has come down to is we do half and half. We do the checklist the way USAir wants us to do it; and then the last checklist before landing, where the coordination just isn't there, the nonflying pilot will read the checklist and the flying pilot will respond to the really important items like 'gear down,' for example. The other things are nonsense items that are not safety items. On a short flight, all of that stuff can back up on you, especially if the person flying is on a tough approach or something and they're really concentrating. For them to break that concentration, for them to look up and see if [something like] the 'No smoking' sign is on is ridiculous."

Brad Prescott talks about the procedural changes that occurred when American bought Air Cal's equipment. "The checklist is three times as long. They went military. Everything's redundant; you do it three or four times. Right now, I feel that American's out of control on their checklist. Like all the instruments—if there's not a flag on it saying there's something wrong, why check it? Your eyes should be outside the cockpit. Instead you're inside checking all this bullshit. When you're taxiing out, you're reading off a lot of stuff instrument-wise." He stops, realizes what he's said. "Sure all that stuff is supposed to be done before you taxi out, but that's bullshit. It should be, but it's not."

At Continental under Lorenzo management, Sandra Luft retrained on the MD-80, an airplane added during the strike that was a significant change from the DC-10 she was used to flying. "This was my first experience with Texas International training, with a two-pilot airplane which I'd never been on, and with the left seat [as a captain]. I thought coming from a DC-10, which is a Douglas product, and going to a DC-9 [the MD-80 is basically an updated version of the DC-9], which is a Douglas product, there would be some similarity. And I was real surprised when I found some complete reversals. Texas Air teaches things one way, and Continental taught things another, and they're still fairly separate. They've got different terms for the same stuff. For example, descending through eighteen thousand feet, Continental wanted you to set your altimeters at the current setting; that's the first thing on the in-range checklist as they call it. And those two words tell you exactly what you need to do. The Texas Air guys say, 'flight instruments.' Why don't they just say what you mean?" Luft's concern is that the Texas Air checklist was not specific enough. "What you mean is you want me to make sure my altimeter's set properly, and you want to cross-check the airspeed to make sure both the captain and copilot agree.

"Somebody ought to get together and talk to each other. Things are different even in terms of their basic crew concepts. I have never worked for any other airline, but I've ridden in the cockpit with a number of different airlines. One of the things that has always amazed me is even the little differences in how they start engines—the task assignments for the various crew members. But I guess it will probably always be that way." Luft sits back in her chair, a look of anxiety on her face. "The key is to get everybody who has to fly together to be trained in the same situation."

Like Luft, Joyce Kennedy also flies with a merged carrier (Republic into Northwest), and she has some apprehensions about procedural changes that have occurred as a result of combining the two companies. "When they changed our checklist, they eliminated one call for flaps. At Republic we always had two. On both the taxi checklist and the before-takeoff checklist there were flap calls. The new checklist did away with the call before takeoff. The Republic pilots fought for that; we wanted to keep it. I went in to protest. Everybody I know went in. The reason Northwest cut it out was because they felt it was redundant. They were trying to make us more efficient. Who cares if it's redundant . . . ?

"It's such a habit, putting those flaps right down when you're taxiing out, and then you look at the gauge on them before takeoff. All the pilots I've flown with *still* call it, even though it's not on the checklist. Because none of us liked not calling it. The accident in Detroit, which was immediately blamed on the pilots' failure to deploy the flaps, happened after that. If we'd had the second call on the checklist maybe it wouldn't have happened. I know the black box says there was no call for the flaps, but going through a day of work I just find it hard to imagine a situation where you'd miss putting flaps down. . . . So I find it hard to believe they didn't catch it.

"The other thing is there's been instances of the flaps retracting after having been put down. A couple of weeks ago I took an airplane that somebody brought in and on which they had noted that there was something weird going on with the flaps. The problem was they didn't stay down in the detent [the mechanism that holds them in place]. I called the mechanic out to look at it, and he found the detent was full of dirt. It was a simple thing like that. And that really brought back my thoughts to flight 255.

"People keep saying that they did not set the flaps. And I still don't believe that happened. In my mind if it did, however, I wouldn't be surprised if it had to do with the morale in the cockpit. I talked to an NTSB guy about that. He was riding around in our jump seats trying to get a handle on morale and what's going on with the pilots right now. He was on the NTSB human factors committee, and he was dealing with human factors considerations in that particular accident and among pilots generally.

"Pilots are talking about that a lot in the union. People are so angry. The job used to be so much fun. That's what everybody says. We were doing what we like to do. We were respected by the company. We were trusted. Right now if you have an accident, nobody is going to be out there to stick up for you. The company won't; the chief pilot won't. Nobody out there really wants to stick their neck out."

)n to the retraining and adaptability that may be
em in the case where one company buys another, pilots
erned about challenges faced by airline maintenance
which must keep current with merged aircraft fleets.
commercial airline maintenance was supported by
elaborate engineering departments whose responsibility was to test
new equipment, provide input to airframe and engine manufacturers,
and in the days when planes were much less technologically complex
but had more moving parts, to help operations and management
understand the capabilities and liabilities of new aircraft and the
needs of the pilots who would fly them. Rex Chamberlain remembers those days fondly.

"The philosophy of someone like Juan Trippe, who founded and
ran Pan Am, was that the United States would have a single flag
carrier to represent us the way BOAC represents the British; Air
France, France; and Lufthansa, Germany. He created an organization that had two salient features, one of which was technical
expertise. He was not interested in economics. He wanted to have
the cutting edge of technology in terms of what airplanes could do,
and he had a very elaborate technical department, heavy into
engineering and communications and that sort of thing, a department that was capable of telling the Boeing company what Pan Am
wanted regarding the capabilities of their airplanes.

"Pan Am's engineers developed airway structures; they had
expertise in airport operations. They would go down into the jungles
of South America; they'd go out into the Pacific on the islands, and
they would actually build what was necessary to support their
operation. At one point in the history of Pan American, I've been
told that they had the largest, most sophisticated nongovernment
communications network in the world.

"You don't see our European counterparts or our Asian
counterparts racing toward this precipice [of suspending their
support operations]. This is uniquely American. The structure of the
Lufthansas and the Air Canadas and the British Airways—and
Qantas and Cathy Pacific and Air France—is a well-balanced
managerial approach which addresses costs, marketing, and technical
operations in some semblance of balance. These organizations don't
kill the messengers; they're not demolishing their technical departments."

The subject is dear to Chamberlain's heart. In his opinion, "The
U.S. carriers are throwing away their engineering departments, their

maintenance expertise, their display flight-following functions, their meteorology departments, their piloting departments. And they're putting people in place who will proceed with the political agenda. All of that is very much a function of deregulation and the Wall Street orientation toward the short-term bottom line. We are *absolutely* and totally at the mercy of the short-term bottom line of the bean counters. And it wouldn't matter if there was a manager who had a different perspective. I can't fault Mr. Jones of XYZ airline. If it wasn't him it would be Mr. Smith. It's the structure that introduces these elements."

In the case of Pan Am, in addition to the elaborate support it constructed for its worldwide operations, its flight deck crews developed the expertise that made Pan Am pilots perhaps the industry's longest-running specialists at long-haul overwater flying. Take for example Pan Am's inauguration of scheduled commercial flights across the Pacific back in 1935 using Martin flying boats. The China Clippers, as the planes were called, flew at a speed of 143 miles per hour and took six days to cross the 8,200 miles from San Francisco to Manila with an actual in-flight time of fifty-nine hours and forty-eight minutes. Today the same trip takes fifteen hours in a 600-mile-per-hour jet. It was not only expertise in flying the long schedules that set the Pan American pilots apart, but also their proficiency in solving in-flight problems when they were out of reach of airline maintenance support.

"Those Pan Am people have flown out there for fifty years," says Bob Scott, who has spent the last years of his career flying the old Pan American routes. "And they've evolved a system that works. They're reliant upon themselves. They have the information they need, and they're able to get the job done. And United comes in and says, 'Aha, we bought this system from Pan Am because they're having financial difficulties. We obviously know better than they do how to run it.'

"We are very unhappy that the company has chosen not to recognize the expertise of these people, the Pan Am pilots," says Scott harshly. "Because the information that they're bringing is good. When I fly with a Pan American copilot, I'm really impressed. I watch him very carefully. I watch all my crew members very carefully. These people are professionals. They're good, and they know what they're doing."

Unfortunately the crew of the United Airlines Tokyo-bound 747 that day in May did not have this depth of experience on which to draw. All three were from the United domestic force and had not previously flown on international routes out of easy reach of company maintenance bases. Each of the crew members had met his training and check flight requirements, and technically all three of the crew members had been adequately prepared to fly the airplane for which they were responsible. However, all three were new to the aircraft and had not had time to develop the important intuition that comes from long hours of flying a particular piece of equipment in a variety of situations. In the best of all possible worlds, these particular three pilots would not have been scheduled together as a crew, and they would not have been assigned to an airplane with suspected technical problems. In the best of all possible worlds, crew schedulers would have used Pan Am pilots who knew both the routes and had special expertise in managing the airplane. But the flight scheduling system does not work that way. Crew desks are not necessarily on the lookout for this kind of thing, and there are effectively no safeguards to prohibit such a situation from occurring. Circumstances were such that this particular line of flying had fallen to these particular three pilots, either because each had bid it or—a more likely happenstance—because all three men were so junior that they were left with a schedule more senior pilots didn't want.

Apprehension about such circumstances is expressed in the saying among pilots that an individual's first flight on new equipment will be fraught with error. "You spend years and years working up to be a captain," says Rex Chamberlain, "and when you finally go out and take your first trip, it will be in the middle of the night, the weather will be the worst you've seen in eighteen years, and you'll be brand new on the airplane, a DC-9 or whatever it is. And you'll turn to your other crew members, and you'll ask if they've been flying this run long, and the guy next to you will say, 'Gee, I just transferred in. This is my first DC-9 flight.'"

Pilot-engineer Dick Riley was close to the investigation of the Tokyo incident. He has a more serious opinion. "Although those airplanes were completely gone through, they didn't do or they missed the fuel system for some reason, and they were having major fuel system problems with the airplanes." Bob Scott agrees with Riley's view and gives his assessment of the situation. "You understand that those airplanes were not ready to go into service. They're out there flying around right now. I may have to fly one Saturday. The other day the crew that flew the plane from Honolulu to Sydney after it was released from maintenance said that every eight minutes they had to rebalance the fuel. On an eleven-hour flight, every eight minutes they had to get in there and rebalance the fuel.

"The Tokyo guys couldn't trust their gauges," continues Scott talking about the problem with the rebuilt planes. "Well, I prefer to err on the safe side. If there is some discrepancy, if it looks like I've either got three thousand pounds or five thousand pounds, I'm going to shoot for the lower and say that's what I actually have and take action as a result of what I can see. I prefer to err on the conservative side." Scott's eyes narrow, and he raises his voice. "Of course nobody's going to complain about the training. They think, 'I got through the check ride, see, why should I complain about it.' That's the theory I'm afraid that many of us operate with, 'Heck, yeah, I got through it; I'm up to a minimum standards.' That's all the FAA deals with—minimum standards—and perhaps that's the right attitude as far as they're concerned. But airline safety is never built on minimum standards. We've always had a big cushion."

"Obviously," says Dick Riley, "there was something the flight crew could have done to prevent what happened. They failed to do it, and they failed to do it because they had inadequate training. They failed to do it because they had an airplane that they thought had a fuel gauge problem instead of a problem with a failed cross-feed valve. The airplane led them down the garden path. If they had known more about the situation, they wouldn't have gotten trapped that way."

Riley thinks about it a moment, and then agrees with Scott's opinion about training. "They were unprepared to deal with the problem they had because we cut corners on training—as do all other carriers. Everyone's trained to a bottom-level standard. We're fighting an attitude that we can fly the Pacific just like we fly Moline to Chicago. Unfortunately United isn't capitalizing on the experience of the Pan Am guys."

The irony of the Tokyo situation was that, unknown to the men in the cockpit who were struggling with a problem of unidentified origin and conflicting opinion on how to solve it, on board their aircraft was a crew of former Pan Am pilots on the way to Hong Kong to pick up another 747 to fly back to the West Coast. Says Dick Riley, "All of those guys from past experience on Pan Am knew exactly what to do to fix the problem. The airplane had a similar problem a day or two before with a Pan Am flight engineer, who used a procedure which United prohibits. He didn't write it up because he didn't want to be disciplined for using an unauthorized procedure. It involved using the fuel jettison system to get the fuel out of the tank.

"The first thing the Pan Am crew asked when they found out what had happened was why the United guys hadn't done that. The United engineer's jaws dropped, and the crew pulled out the United directive prohibiting them from doing what the Pan Am crew recommended. Well, that would have solved the problem."

Although partially agreeing in principle, management pilot Craig Donlevy takes issue with the specifics of Dick Riley's explanation of the events of the Tokyo trip. "What the crew did was misanalyze their problem. Had they analyzed their problem correctly, it's in the book how to fix it, and it's not against policy at all. Page 126 says that if this valve doesn't work, you do these things. What they did is they thought the valve was working. So they misanalyzed their problem. If there was a crux to the whole thing, that was it. It's hard to fix something when you don't know what the problem is. You've got to start out with the right assumptions. And without the right assumptions, you're bound to go down the wrong road. The incident will require an in-depth study, but my first blush answer is that it was the dynamics of the crew *that* day, *that* time, *that* moment. If the same crew was together at a different place and time, they may have come up with a different answer."

"The entire incident reads like a comedy," sighs Dick Riley. "It's like the Keystone Cops, if it weren't so serious."

CHAPTER 5

Pilot Error

Just like the old story of the sea being unforgiving, aviation is unforgiving, and it takes dedication and constant application and expenditures of sums of money and all kinds of human effort to make this system run as smooth as it has.

—REX CHAMBERLAIN, United Airlines
747 captain

An airplane just never falls out of the sky . . . if an airplane doesn't fly, there's always a reason.

—DICK RILEY, United Airlines
737 captain

E

ven at five o'clock in the morning, the temperature at National Airport was forecasting another hot and muggy August day in Washington, D.C., another day of frayed tempers and short fuses. Traditionally summer means vacations, and vacations mean more people traveling, some first-time travelers, many more on their once-a-year excursions. Planes are crowded, schedules overloaded, and patience lacking. Summer weather also adds to the inconvenience. The hot weather brings thunderstorms, and thunderstorms cause flight diversions, bumpy rides, and delays.

From the outside things aboard the Eastern 727 looked normal for a seven A.M. departure from Washington west to Kansas City and then on to Albuquerque and Tucson. Capt. Pete Browner arrived at the airport in the predawn to prepare for the typical kind of short-haul trip he has spent most of his career flying. At Tucson, Browner and his plane would turn and backtrack their earlier route, arriving home in Washington the same evening.

As Browner tells the story, however, he never got the chance to fly the trip. Completing his preflight check, Captain Browner observed that the distance-measuring device (DME) on the copilot's side of the cockpit was inoperative. The DME, which assesses the distance between an airplane and on-ground obstacles, is particularly important during takeoff and landing, especially at airports adjacent to natural obstacles or heavy settlement. According to Browner, a check of the 737's logbook showed the equipment had gone out of service in Miami the afternoon before and the repair had been deferred. (Given the tight scheduling of aircraft, deferring repair or replacement of nonessential equipment is common industry practice. Such maintenance items are taken care of when the aircraft is at a down time in the schedule. Additionally, not all airports are equipped as maintenance stations.)

The details of what needs to be working for an airplane to be considered legal to fly are spelled out in the minimum equipment list (MEL). The MEL is the pilots' bible. When a new model of aircraft is certified for service by the Federal Aviation Administration, a master equipment list (MMEL) is developed by the agency and a flight operations board of industry representatives. Using the FAA's recommendations, individual airlines proceed to establish their own MELs based on their maintenance philosophies, business parameters, and input from pilots and mechanics. Often these are more restrictive than the FAA's master list. The MEL is then spelled out in manuals carried on board in the flight crew's bags. Although the MEL provides an organizationwide bottom line, it is also subject to individual interpretation.

According to Browner's reading of the minimum equipment list for the plane he was scheduled to fly that day, both of two DMEs on board were required to be operative. Browner indicates that Eastern policy further specified that an airplane should not depart with an inoperative DME from a station (airport) where repairs or replacement could be made. To Browner this meant his faulty equipment had to be fixed before he left Washington. All the more so since the DME had gone inoperative the day before and had not been replaced at stops that included Miami (Eastern's headquarters and a designated maintenance base), Washington, and Boston (another Eastern maintenance base) or on the overnight back in Washington, when presumably there would have been ample time to do the necessary work.

To Pete Browner's way of thinking, the inoperative DME in his aircraft needed to be replaced. He called Eastern's Washington dispatch office, made his request, and asked for action. Instead of checking on the situation, the dispatcher told him to disregard the inoperative equipment and put his complaint on a captain's initiative (CI). That, however, was not what Pete Browner wanted to do. According to Browner's version of the story, he told the dispatcher that he disagreed with what was being suggested and that his reading of the aircraft equipment list required the DME to be fixed before the plane left Washington. "So," he said reasonably, "let's fix it."

Satisfied that he had made his point, Pete Browner went back to the routine of takeoff preparations, although in the back of his mind he suspected the action he'd taken with the dispatcher was likely to result in complications. It didn't take long to confirm his hunch. Five minutes before the trip's scheduled departure, a mechanic showed up in the cockpit carrying a computer printout that indicated Washington didn't have a replacement DME or the parts to fix the one that wasn't working.

Pete Browner now considered he had two options. He could give in, write off the incident, and be on his way, or he could raise the stakes. He chose to raise the stakes. He told the mechanic his excuse wasn't good enough. "Find a DME and put it in this airplane. I don't care if you have to steal it from TWA. I have approaches out there at all those airports with mountains, including Albuquerque, that predicate the conduct of the approach on a DME." Without responding to Browner, the mechanic turned and left the cockpit.

Pete Browner realized that he was now in the game for keeps. He pushed his seat back, folded his arms and waited for the next round. Again he didn't have long to wait. Within minutes a call summoned him to the office of Eastern's chief Washington dispatcher. To Browner's mild surprise, however, the dispatcher supported his contention that company policy required replacement of the inoperative DME. Satisfied, Browner headed back to the plane once again to wait for the mechanic with the replacement part. It was at this point that Browner says the situation began to deteriorate.

As he waited for the mechanic to arrive, Browner received a radio call summoning him to the office of Washington's chief pilot. Like many line personnel, Pete Browner considered the position of chief pilot part of management, especially after the takeover of Eastern by Texas Air, and that anyone operating in that capacity was suspect. "Bureaucracy at its best," Browner thought to himself, "but I'll play their silly game." Calculating his odds as slim to none, he once again left the cockpit and headed into the terminal toward Eastern's flight operations office. Browner maintains it was not Eastern's chief pilot whom he found himself confronting, however, but the vice president of flight operations, who just happened to be in his office that morning and had followed the developing controversy.

Browner recounts how, in the ensuing conversation, he stood his ground—the DME had to be replaced—and the vice president of flight operations retaliated by ordering him off the trip. "Go home," he told Browner, "and I'll get somebody else." Which is exactly what Pete Browner did. Forty-five minutes after scheduled departure, he put on his hat, straightened his tie, saluted his crew, and walked off the airplane, leaving a full load of passengers at the gate. Having relieved Browner of command, management now had two options—cancel the flight or find a replacement. They chose replacement.

Browner describes how, after being briefed by the original copilot and second officer, the new captain requested that Eastern's Washington dispatch provide him a copy of the FAA's master equipment list for the aircraft as his guarantee that it was legal to fly the plane despite the fact that he would be in violation of Eastern's own equipment requirements. Abruptly the game of brinksmanship came to an end. According to Browner, Eastern maintenance removed an operative DME from a backup Eastern shuttle parked next to Browner's aircraft, replacing it with a part sent down on the next flight from Eastern's maintenance base at La Guardia Airport. Pete Browner's flight left Washington three hours late, minus a good percentage of its original passengers and causing many of those remaining to miss connections on the way to their destination.

The reality of a pilot's life is that the two things he is most concerned about—his responsibilities and his compensation—are directly related. If for some reason, things don't go right, as they didn't for Pete Browner that day in August, it doesn't matter how much a pilot earns or the method by which it's computed; he is, as everyone agrees, the guy out front. Pilots have a saying that acknowledges this industry truism: "I don't worry about the people in the back because I figure if *I* get there, the people in back will be right behind me."

In this sense, the responsibilities of the modern commercial pilot are not that dissimilar from those of the aviation trailblazers who carved out reputations for themselves in the pioneering days of this century. As was the pilot alone in the cockpit of a biplane or the DC-3 captain battling his way across the country navigating by sight, today's captain is still legally responsible for what happens to his or her aircraft regardless of external factors. And however seriously pilots may take their responsibilities in the increasingly complex world of aviation, their substantial liability is expressed in two ominous words: *pilot error*. Whether something they fail to do threatens the safety of their flight or they take improper action that leads to an accident, *accountability* is the bottom line.

"Obviously, when an accident occurs there's something the pilot could have done to prevent it," says Dick Riley. "The figure I've heard is that pilot error has been implicated in something like eighty percent of recent aviation accidents. But I like to counter that by saying that no pilot ever goes out intentionally to kill himself. It's not a rational thing to do. Therefore, if he gets in a situation and for whatever reason the airplane crashes because of an action he either did or failed to do, then you've got to look beneath the surface of what appears to have happened.

"If you want to have an improvement in safety, you've got to investigate the conditions that were present which allowed this accident to take place. Just labeling an accident 'pilot error' doesn't allow you to take the steps necessary to prevent it happening again. If you dig underneath why the pilot did or failed to do something critical, if you get right down to the root of all the factors that impacted on the accident, then you can begin to take action to prevent a reoccurrence. You have to remember, the NTSB looks at *how* an accident happens, not *why*."

National Transportation Safety Board statistics indicate that in the four-year period between 1980 and 1984, for example, pilot error was implicated as a broad cause or factor in forty-two percent of accidents involving the major commercial airlines. Nonetheless, as Riley suggests, for many pilots and industry observers the issue is not that the human made the mistake, but *why*. Many pilots are concerned that the danger in using the term *pilot error* is that it is a simplistic explanation for a situation that involves an incredibly diverse set of circumstances and that a correct understanding of these circumstances is what is needed to prevent further accidents.

Robert Schornstheimer, the Aloha Airlines captain whose luck held when the top blew off his airplane, empathizes with pilots caught in similar situations. In relation to the Detroit crash of Northwest Airlines flight 255, he says reflectively, "It's easy to say a person screwed up. Well, obviously the person was doing the best he could to avoid that situation from happening."

As Schornstheimer suggests, pilot error hits hard at the men and women who fly the airplanes. It touches the heart of what pilots feel they are about—their sense of responsibility and the individual resourcefulness that is part of any aviator's self-concept. To acknowledge error is to admit defeat at the hands of various elements over which pilots are supposed to exercise some control. Error is an emotional issue for pilots, not only for those who still follow the old adage, "one man, one responsibility," but also for the men and women who accept that recent changes in the industry require a different kind of pilot vigilance. Pete Browner's opinions fall somewhere in between, but his frustrations are evident.

"Looking back at Eastern Airlines for the almost twenty-five years that I've been there," says Browner, "I can say that the airline has lent itself to a tremendous amount of positive input from the pilot force. For years and years and years, there probably wasn't a thing that we pilots wouldn't have done to try and make a flight work. At one point back in maybe '74 or '75, Eastern carried more passengers than United did. Now we're a piece of junk, and they want to make us smaller.

"Back then Eastern was probably the best airline in the world for a pilot to have a job with—*back then*. It's always been known as a pilot's airline. Because of the management philosophy, we had a tremendous amount of input into operations on a daily basis. I think that came from the kind of people that started Eastern, people like Eddie Rickenbacker. I don't mean this to sound in any way chauvinistic, but he was a man's type of guy. They all were; they were pioneers. And his philosophy lived on as a legacy long after he left the airline, even after he passed away.

"We always had strong-willed, quick-thinking people at the head of the company, and they expected the pilots to be the same way because they felt that was the kind of pilot they wanted flying their airplane. You can train and train and train and train, but you can't train for every possible situation. Eastern wanted people who would think on their feet and solve a problem when it came up, rather than asking, 'Now what did the manual say about that?' or 'How did we do that in training?' In an airplane, you don't always run into problems that can be addressed that way.

"A good case in point is the famous overwater triple engine failure on one of our L-1011s. Now there is something that has never in the history of aviation been trained for. Nobody conceived that it would ever happen. The captain was on his first trip as a captain on a 1011, and the first thing he's confronted with is a series of engine failures. He finally gets one going and lands the airplane—when everybody thought they were going to have to ditch in the water—and nobody so much as got their feet wet.

"That's what a pilot's paid to do," emphasizes Browner earnestly, "think on his feet. It used to be said if you drew a box and said the four sides of the rectangle represented all the qualities that you would want in a pilot—a good aviator, common sense, education, I don't know, pick a fourth side whatever that would be, then you'd probably find all of the United pilots would fit right in the box. And all the Eastern pilots would be on the outside of the box."

Browner feels that unlike Eastern, some other airlines have tended not to give their captains enough latitude to make decisions about how they should operate their airplanes as a function of weather or aircraft condition. "That's a big thing for pilots," says Browner. "They want to be able to make decisions about inoperative components on their aircraft because this influences whether they want to fly it or not."

"We end up being the brunt of everything," snaps Bill Fredericks with typical fervor. "Have you ever heard of management error? No. It's always pilot error. Ever hear of doctor error? How about the attorney going to jail for his client? Or the doctor dying on the table? That doesn't happen. Pilot error doesn't cost the airlines anything like lack of maintenance would or breaking a federal law would.

"The real function of our safety work as it exists today is that it provides a cushion against the things that happen in the air. Remember, you're traveling at close to the speed of sound. Most human beings are not acclimated to living or working at that speed. If you're going to hit something, you have a certain limited time between the point at which an accident begins to occur and when it actually happens—the crash. Our analysis shows that this is normally about one to two minutes. The way we look at it, picture a line, a rope of any length; hanging from that line are a series of doughnuts of any number and they're swinging around. When the rope stops swinging and all the holes line up, that's when an accident occurs."

"There's a game that's played in aviation," says Dick Riley, describing his own view. "The game is called 'Let's Kill the Crew.' And the rules of the game are that there are no rules. The aircraft manufacturers play this game, and the airlines play this game, and the air traffic control system plays the game. The weatherman plays the game and dispatch plays the game, and you even try to play the game on your fellow pilots—let's kill each other.

"For a pilot, the challenge is, number one, to know the game is being played. And number two, if you know the game is being played, then it's up to *you* to keep everybody else from killing you, including the computer that figures out your fuel load and the guy who tells you the weather's going to be fine. If you address your everyday operation from that [basis] and recognize that you are playing a game, then your challenge is to stay alive." Riley's smile is hollow.

"Things happen—like we had a cargo plane go down outside Salt Lake. In the investigation we discovered that among other things, our maintenance base cycled through a particular part six times without fixing it. They did this because the test they were using was faulty and wouldn't pick up the problem. And take the Continental Denver crash that killed the pilot and copilot." Riley is referring to the incident involving Continental flight 1713, a DC-9 that crashed in a snowstorm immediately after takeoff from Denver's Stapleton International Airport. The incident, which occurred on November 15, 1987, killed 25 of the 77 passengers aboard along with the captain and the copilot. Five years after the Air Florida accident in Washington, D.C., which occurred under similar circumstances, complications from faulty de-icing procedures were again implicated as a contributing factor in the accident.

"Preliminary findings, as they always do, pointed to pilot error," continues Riley, "the fact that the plane was not properly de-iced, and the crew was inexperienced. Okay, let's look at the pilots who were flying that plane. During the public hearings it came out that neither the captain nor the first officer had ever received training in the particular model DC-9 they were flying that night. The model that crashed is what's called a DC-9-14. It doesn't have leading edge devices, and because of that it flies differently. This fact was testified to by Douglas Aircraft." Thus far, Riley's reading of the accident agrees with the NTSB report.

"We also know that the captain had come back to work off strike. He flew as a copilot for a while and then got his captain's bid. They sent him halfway through training on the DC-9, and then he was taken out of training and sent back to fly as a flight engineer on a 727. They simply were harassing him because he was a striker. After four months as a flight engineer, he came back and finished his DC-9 upgrading.

"Added to this was the fact that this particular night the normal copilot who should have flown that sequence was displaced because the company had a copilot who had not flown for a while, for three weeks. [FAA regulations require a pilot to execute three takeoffs and landings in ninety days.] In fact, this copilot was brand new out of school." So you let him sit for three weeks, put him in an airplane he's never flown before, on a dark and stormy night with a new captain who's been beat on the head pretty badly . . ." Riley sighs heavily and doesn't complete his thought.

"Number one, you've got to ask yourself, is this particular captain going to go back for de-icing a second time because he's been out on the end of the runway twenty-seven minutes, or is that going to be another black mark on his record at Continental? He gets a brand new copilot he doesn't know anything about. Normally when you have a new copilot, the captain flies the first leg. But in this case, because the captain didn't want the copilot landing back in Denver where the weather was projected to get worse, he gave the copilot the first leg. Ordinarily in this situation, the logical thing to do would be for the captain to fly both legs, but you have to remember this copilot had been sent out *because* he hadn't flown for a while.

"What we're doing here is building a chain. The airplane is delayed on the runway for over twenty minutes. It sits there in such a manner that they're collecting ice on one wing only. If you collect ice to the extent of about number fifty or sixty grit sandpaper, you lose from thirty to thirty-five percent of the lift on your wing. In this case, it was happening on one side. You put an inexperienced copilot in the airplane and you require that he execute one of the most difficult maneuvers in a jet airplane—to take off in low-visibility conditions where the minute you pull the nose in the air, you're on instruments. And he's going to do this with one wing iced, so one side's lifting thirty-five percent less than the other side.

"So they climb into the plane, they do their preflight checklist, they go through the de-icing maneuver, sit on the runway for almost half an hour, and then finally take off. The copilot calls for gear up, the captain reaches down to get the gear handle, and suddenly he sees he's in a forty-degree bank. Right off the ground. He probably reaches over, overcontrols the airplane—because they're in an airplane that is much more sensitive than he's used to. They drag the other wing on the ground, and the airplane just rolls over on its back, and they crashed."

In reviewing the Denver accident, the NTSB noted a number of factors that Dick Riley's remarks address. First, although the captain was an experienced pilot, he had little flying time in the DC-9 and was unfamiliar with its unique flying characteristics under icing conditions. Second, the first officer had "a record of performance difficulties" before joining Continental as well as in the Continental DC-9 training program and was in fact dismissed from employment prior to Continental for his inability to pass a check ride. Furthermore he had not flown for twenty-four days prior to accident, which the NTSB noted probably contributed to skill erosion. Third, procedural difficulties in the control tower and in the Continental cockpit contributed to the accident, the probable cause of which was the captain's failure to go back for a second de-icing after the takeoff delay.

Riley summarizes his view of the accident. "What happened in Denver was a plain and simple chain of errors committed by an outfit dedicated to minimum dollar outlay. The psychological pressures put on that captain by the airline were such that he was not about to buck the system. And bucking the system is what it's all about. Having the ability to do what Bill Fredericks and I do with an airline—where if I do something as a union representative, they cannot come back at me and take personal punitive action against me. There's an insulating layer, and Continental doesn't have it. Air Florida didn't have it.

"What does the protection of a union contract do for you? I'll tell you what it does for you. United had a trip to Boise out of Denver that same night; we canceled it because of the weather. Some of the passengers from our trip went over and got on Continental and crashed."

The variables a crew of a modern jet aircraft must deal with on an average flight are myriad, and it is easy to understand pilots' contentions that management personnel "flying a desk," as Bill Fredericks puts it, may not be sensitive to the scope of the piloting job. There is a constant current of information flowing toward pilots even on a routine flight—from the headset, from other crew members, from the back of the plane—information they are constantly called on to utilize and about which they must make decisions. A layman sitting in an airplane cockpit would find it difficult to follow the constant cross communication, especially at peak periods of activity, such as takeoff and landing. At cruise things slow down somewhat, and pilots transition into the role of monitor, scanning gauges and dials for developments that appear to be out of the ordinary.

This is not to say that on every flight pilots are heavily overloaded, although it may sometimes seem that everyone in the cockpit is talking at once against a constant drone from the company frequency or air traffic control. Add a problem or two, and the noise level rises; perhaps a passenger is smoking in the rest room or a lavatory sink is stopped up or a flight attendant slips and injures an ankle or an electrical power supply fails. Or suddenly the flight deck crew finds they're heading into unexpected thunderstorms that force them to divert to an alternate airport. The smooth resolution of such circumstances requires attention to the emergency *and* to the routine flying of the airplane as dictated by checklist procedures.

"There are ways you can track whether you're approaching an accident or not," says Dick Riley. "Historically it's the number of incidents that accumulate. How many goof-ups you avoid only by the grace of God or happenstance or a little bit of luck, the close calls. There are probably four or five million separate parts on an airplane. The large systems, of course, are maintained on a regular basis. But let's say an electrical switch quits working in your leading edge slat actuator—the switch that tells you that the thing is in proper position for takeoff and landing. It's one of the things that *must* work on your airplane unless you can look out the window and see the thing, which is pretty much impossible in jets. There's no way you can do preventive maintenance on something like that.

"I'm not going to say *most,* but *much* of the stuff we have break is electrical in nature, and there's no way you can maintain an electrical item; preventative maintenance on an electrical item is meaningless. We're always going to have the random failure that nobody can predict. The general design philosophy, however, is that no one thing should be so critical that if it breaks it will cause safety-of-flight problems. To ensure that this doesn't happen, there's one or two backups to each critical item. That's why you have more than one engine. That's why you have more than one flight control and more than one hydraulic system, up to what's called 'fail active,' which means you can have two complete failures and still have a system that's workable, that's perfectly safe.

"I'm sure that the airline would like to say to pilots, 'Maintenance has determined that this airplane is acceptable; you must fly it.' They want the thing out of town. It's a black mark on their record if the airplane doesn't go on time for a maintenance reason. But because we're fortunate enough at this point in time to have a union, they can't pressure the pilots into accepting something they consider not acceptable. Even at United it happens. I'll hear about a guy refusing an airplane maybe once or twice a month. Out of the sixty thousand flights we have a month, it's an infinitesimal amount. But they will attempt to browbeat the captain. You have a scene at the gate with a fully loaded airplane going to Tokyo, and you only do that once or twice, and they get the airplane fixed. The poor people in the back are caught in the middle."

As Riley suggests, maintenance is one of those crucial variables over which pilots would like to have control but don't and where a small slip can be multiplied exponentially. Investigation of the Eastern Airlines triple-engine failure that Pete Browner spoke about, for example, determined that the incident resulted from the fact that Eastern maintenance failed to properly install O-ring oil seals in all three of the L-1011's engines.

Ted Goff offers his opinion. "Deregulation has certainly changed things and maintenance is surely one of them. I mean you just have to think of the economics of the whole thing. Everybody's trying to cut corners now, and they're going to cut everywhere in order to compete and stay in business. It's expensive to keep all those spare parts around, and it's expensive to keep these maintenance guys all over the place."

Goff's sentiments aside, it must be remembered that maintenance is not simply a matter of spare parts and sufficient labor. Take for example American Airlines flight 191, a DC-10 on takeoff from Chicago's O'Hare International Airport that crashed into an open field about five thousand feet from the end of the runway, killing all of its 271 passengers along with two people on the ground. The cited cause of the accident was the loss of the DC-10's starboard engine, which literally dropped off the wing of the airplane. In its report the NTSB cited "deficiencies in Federal Aviation Administration surveillance and reporting systems" that "failed to detect and prevent the use of improper maintenance procedures." The procedures to which the report referred involved the servicing of the DC-10's engines.

"It's a combined item," says Riley explaining his view of the cause of the accident, the substance of which is confirmed in the NTSB report. "Obviously American Airlines took that DC-10 and abused it to the point where it caused a crash, and they did this by changing an engine with a forklift. When you want to change an engine, you bring in an overhead crane and an overhead hoist. Between the hoist and the engine, you have a scale—a thing that is just exactly like a fish scale—and you put so much pull on the fish scale, which tells you how much you're pulling on the engine. You pull the weight of the engine plus a little bit, and then you disconnect the engine from the airplane.

Riley continues with his opinion of what caused the crash. "Well, American Airlines and Continental and a few others got in a position where they didn't have an overhead crane with a fish scale on it, so they began using a forklift. In that kind of a situation, you haven't the faintest idea how much pressure you're exerting on the structure, especially if you're using a forklift that will pick up fifty thousand pounds and you are only picking up a one-thousand-pound engine. They put so much stress on the structure of that airplane, they broke it. The break was a crack; it was not a total break. But the crack at some point failed, and the engine came off the airplane.

I don't see how in the world you can say that the DC-10 is not an acceptable airplane or has a bad safety record when you're changing engines with a forklift. . . ."

In its research of the accident, the NTSB interviewed a variety of American Airline personnel, including mechanics and their supervisors, who noted that using a forklift rather than a fish scale would result in a savings of two hundred worker-hours per aircraft. When consulted by American about its intent to use this procedure, McDonnell Douglas, the plane's manufacturer, indicated it "would not encourage" this. Further explaining its forklift rationale, American maintained that in addition to labor savings, this procedure reduced the number of hydraulic and fuel lines, wiring, and electrical cables that had to be discounted and reconnected and that it considered this to be a safety advantage.

"The problem with the pilot profession," says Craig Donlevy, as he sits in his airport office presiding over a constantly ringing telephone and piles of paperwork, "is there's no human who really checks up on a pilot's performance on a daily basis, whereas here in the office I know what my staff's doing all day long. I know if they're performing or not. And they know that I know. Do [pilots] need to know that? I think we *all* need to know that somebody cares and is informed about what we're doing. I want a pat from my boss; I want somebody saying, 'Hey, you did a good job.' Or if I made a mistake, I want him to say, 'Boy, you really screwed up on this.' I think for pilots it's worse when they screw up and no one says anything.

"The average pilot is a pretty ordinary person. He really doesn't have any other skills nor a lot of other interests. Why? He's so focused on a particular thing. I see that in other people with intense occupations. It's a tough world out there. There are not a lot of great jobs out there, especially for pilots. In some ways it's easier to stay with the group. Whichever way the herd happens to go, it's safe there. It's warm and comfy. When you stand out, when you start shouting, 'Hey, this is wrong,' when you get away from your peer group, then it isn't so warm and comfy. Those are tough things to do.

"I think pilots are type A personalities. They want it *now*. They want it done *right now—right* and *right now*—because they're perfectionists. They are also very self-critical. They have high standards for themselves, and they have high standards for those around them. If somebody falls short, they'll be told about it. And in reality, that's the kind of person you want running your airplanes. You don't want a guy who you ask, 'What do you think?' and he says, 'I don't know; what do *you* think?' I see somebody that really runs the airplane as having to be a type A, demanding personality. They're out there. Their life depends on it, and everybody else behind them."

Donlevy's eyes narrow. "A pilot's life depends on him. Whoa! There's not too many jobs that are like that. His skill and knowledge and whether he survives today depend on him. Do I think pilots think about that? No, I really don't. But I think it's down there underneath someplace. Because most of them will tell you, 'If *I* make it okay, then *they'll* make it.' The standard question is, 'Don't you feel really responsible for flying four hundred–plus passengers?' The answer is, 'We don't think about that. We only think about the cockpit—if the cockpit makes it . . .'

"Yeah, they tend to have large egos. They know they can do the job. But I don't want somebody who says, 'I *think* maybe I can, I don't know . . . uhhhh . . .' How would you like it if you asked a pilot, 'Do you think maybe you can take off and fly to Sydney?' and he said, 'I don't know, I'll *try*.' Your immediate response would be, 'Oh great, no thanks.' But you don't get that answer. The answer is, 'Hell yes, I can.' And if you ask him, 'Well, what if something happens?' he'll tell you, 'I'll take care of it.'

"Yeah, I think they really believe it. Certainly at the conscious level. I think at the subconscious level—especially since there are so many things they can't control—they may feel a little iffy. There's things they know they don't know, not so much the technology, but other things, like there's nothing more frustrating than coming into a foreign country and not quite being able to understand what the controller's saying—the person who's telling you where to go, where to steer the thing. One guy will look at the other and ask, 'What did he say?' You see this fearful look staring back at you, and you have to answer, 'I don't know, ask him again.'"

Donlevy shuffles some papers on his desk and considers the subject further. "Because of all of this need to be in control and to feel they can handle anything, pilots tend to act as if outside problems—that is, problems outside the cockpit—shouldn't bother them. The question for us in management is how to handle that. How do we know that something's bothering someone, and how do we assess how deep the problem might be? The difficulty with pilots is they tend to internalize everything. All along the line they're told, 'Whatever happens, you have to take care of it.' If you ask a pilot if everything's going okay, he'll say, 'No, but I can handle it.'

"You ask him what's wrong, and he'll say something like, 'I'll tell you if I can't handle it.' So you ask again, 'What's wrong?' and again he'll say, 'Nothing,' or 'I don't want to talk about it now.' And the door slams. What's happening is his wife's dying of cancer, and if he verbalizes it his eyes will well up, and he can't do that in front of you. So he's sealing it off. Pilots who do well are able to compartmentalize things like that, put them off and say, 'That's something else I have to deal with; I'll deal with it at some point in time.' But a person *can* get built up to a point where it's right on the surface, and all you have to do is scratch it. Or you see this look where the eyes are open but there's no lights on.

"The challenge for management is how to handle that. We don't have a good way to analyze the depth of people's problems. You can say to a pilot, 'How are things today, Bob?' And he'll tell you everything is fine, and we in management have no way of knowing that some major event happened in his life so that mentally or emotionally, he's not even in the same room with you. The frustration is that if you don't know what the problem is you can't fix it.

"Pilots have certain standards, and they live up to them. They don't like pats on backs, either. They really don't like to be told they're wonderful. 'Thank you for not calling in sick this last year,' boy I'd never send out anything like that. *Ever!* You know that sounds like a good thing, 'Thank you for being available for every time we needed you.' 'Well, what'd you expect?' would be the answer."

Regardless of pilots' desire for control and perfection and despite their high expectations for themselves, what American Airlines pilot Brad Prescott calls "the take-charge mode," there are indeed things out there waiting to trip them up. And on any given day if the right number of variables combine, the result can be disaster, as it was for Capt. John Maus and first officer David Dobbs on the much-discussed Northwest Flight 255.

It was a hot summer day in August 1987. The aircraft was a McDonnell Douglas DC-9-82, bound from Saginaw, Michigan, to John Wayne Airport in Orange County, California, after stops at Detroit and Phoenix. Shortly after takeoff from Detroit Metropolitan Wayne County Airport, the plane rolled to the left and then the right, struck a series of light poles and the roof of a car rental agency, and then broke apart. Everyone on board was killed with the exception of a four-year-old child. Two people on the ground also died. The NTSB concluded that the cause of the accident was the crew's failure to use the taxi checklist to "ensure that the flaps and slats were extended for takeoff." They cited as a contributing factor the "absence of electrical power" to the takeoff warning horn but said the reason for this loss of power "could not be determined."

The flight deck crew had flown together twice before in that month and had flown three legs together that day. The cockpit voice recorder indicates that as they prepared the plane for takeoff, weather en route was a concern to both pilots, who concluded that it wasn't likely they would make it to Orange County that night. The plane was full—even the two cockpit jump seats were taken—and the combined passenger-freight load added up to 144,047 pounds, close to the 149,500-pound maximum the plane could carry under those circumstances.

Based on their experience, pilots have offered a variety of explanations about how these variables added up to what happened on flight 255. Bob Scott speculates about why the cockpit warning horn didn't sound. "The Detroit crash goes right back to [saving] fuel. They probably had one engine shut down, but in order to taxi an airplane, a heavy airplane, you have to run the power out a little bit more. This blows the takeoff warning horn that says, 'Hey, you don't have the other engine started, or the flaps are not down.' Crews don't want that, so they pull the circuit breaker. Otherwise, when the guy in the tower says, 'Expedite clearing across runway,' and the crew pushes the power up, they get this 'Beep, beep, beep.' But with the circuit breaker out when they do take off, they don't have any warning if something's not right."

"Edith?" says Brad Prescott. "That's what we call the takeoff warning horn. She's a pain in the ass. Lots of guys turn her off. I hate to listen to her—always yelling about something. It's a woman's voice, but it's kind of whinny, and a lot of guys who have been around aviation get tired of that shit. They'll pull the circuit breaker so that they don't have to listen to her mouth, which you're not supposed to do. It's like disconnecting the thing in your car."

Evaluating the events that led to the crash of flight 255, Prescott speaks about factors he feels affected the crew. "I can understand how Detroit happened. I've been there. I feel sorry for the guys. I think they were trapped. They were hurrying. There was a guy sitting in the jump seat, and they were all discussing the Northwest and Republic merger. Plus they had planned to go off one runway, and the weather changed, so they had to go off on another, which was a lot shorter. They got so wrapped up with all the problems the airlines were having, plus all the problems of the weather, they never put the flaps out. The business about them having one engine shut down makes sense, waiting for the storm.

"You know what American's done to solve that? Now this is a joke, and it doesn't solve anything. Now we must say before departure of the flight, 'Ladies and gentlemen, now we've completed our cockpit checks.' That doesn't mean shit, but some brain in Fort Fumble came up with it. That's just something else you've got to say on the PA. As far as I'm concerned, the PA is not important. The important thing is that you have the goddamn flaps out. Doing it is doing it. Saying it doesn't mean shit."

"I've never heard that part about the engine," says Bud McKenzie, discussing Northwest 255 in his reflective, slow-mannered way. "But I have made an effort to find out what transpired on the ground. On the nineteenth of July, before that accident, I was in Detroit under almost exactly the same weather conditions, and I took a two-hour ground delay because of the weather. And I'm glad I did. We got on the runway for the *third* time, and we refused takeoff clearance because of thunderstorms off the edge of the airport. So prudence plays a great role in safe operation—it really does. But in that Detroit accident, the one ingredient that came across to me in the accident reports I read and everything that I could glean from people who were there listening on the radio was that they were in a hurry. And that's bad news in any situation. They were in a hurry probably because of weather.

"The fact of the Detroit accident is that the crew got a special clearance. Air Traffic Control was not accepting any traffic west of Detroit because of the line of thunderstorms, so in order to facilitate his departure what he did was he got a tower-to-tower clearance, which is an old-timer's operation from back in the prop days. He asked for and got that kind of clearance to get himself off the ground. Then when he got to the next point on his route, he'd ask for clearance from there to his next spot, and so on."

According to the transcription of the cockpit voice recorder tapes contained in the NTSB report, McKenzie is correct in his assessment of the problems faced by the crew of flight 255. The weather was bad, they did receive special clearance, and there was a last-minute change.

"There was also a little confusion on the ground in terms of how they were getting clearance to taxi, which runway they were going to use," McKenzie continues. "But those are ordinary things. The atmosphere just made me feel that as a crew they weren't taking the proper amount of time to deal with what was going on. It was a very, very sad situation to read about, realizing at the same time that it could happen to me. Because anything that happens to anybody else can happen to any of us."

As in all aviation accidents, at Detroit it was the National Transportation Safety Board that issued the definitive word on the cause and circumstances. Accidents with multiple fatalities activate a fifteen-member "go team," and in major crashes, the NTSB is assisted by experts from the companies who have a vested interest in the outcome of the investigation. Pilots are divided about the efficacy of NTSB investigations.

"I've served on many accident investigating teams not only for accidents which United had, which there weren't very many of, but other carriers also," says retiree Bob Keystone. "The teams usually consist of forty or fifty people. Of course you rub elbows with people that are experts in the fields that maybe are not yours. For example, somebody who's an expert in engines may not be an expert in aircraft structures. When you serve on enough of these teams, you learn from the other fellows. When they put a team together, they are careful to pick out experts in each field."

Bob Keystone has been retired for a number of years now, and Bob Scott, who is still flying and is closer to the action, thinks things have changed during that time. Leaning forward in his chair and clasping his hands tightly in his lap, Scott describes his feelings. "The NTSB are a bunch of political hacks. They have very little expertise. Rarely do we have anyone with any technical background on the NTSB. Now, Don Engen, he was a test pilot and a good man to have on the NTSB. I worked for him at our Detroit crash. Very objective fellow, one that I have great respect for. We also had a Coast Guard captain. Of course he knew maritime stuff, but he didn't know anything about aviation. Most of these people don't. What they do, they have their staff people go out and make the investigations, submit the evidence to them and then they pick whatever they think is appropriate and write the report. Used to be they were very interested in really digging at it.

"The Air Line Pilots Association has been instrumental in reopening a number of these cases. The Northwest Detroit crash is one of them. ALPA has taken the position that the investigation was incomplete—and we will insist that the final report not be issued till we complete our work. It costs a tremendous amount of money for us to go out and investigate. We've got a staff of engineers and pilot representatives that go out and do this. We have reopened a number and gotten the decision of the NTSB changed when we can prove it."

"I still believe in my own mind the papers might have been padded," says Northwest pilot Joyce Kennedy speaking about the events of flight 255, by which she means the load-planning papers might have showed a lower weight than what the plane actually weighed on takeoff. "I think possibly they were over gross. People were really upset over the investigation. . . . Both those pilots were excellent pilots and had excellent reputations for being super, super thorough. From what I heard about that captain, he wrote his own manual on the 757 when he got trained for that airplane, and everybody in the whole training department—all the people who were getting checked out— borrowed it and copied it. He was known for being an expert in what he was doing. It's just hard to believe that he wouldn't put the flaps down.

"Pilot error is a real easy call. Once they've got a reason to say pilot error, they really go for that. The aircraft manufacturer is going to push for that. McDonnell Douglas is really going to push the NTSB to close the case at pilot error. . . ." Kennedy suggests that airlines themselves are primed to accept a finding of pilot error. "They don't want to look as if they're to blame, whether it's training procedures or what not. [Northwest] called it pilot error before they even had the black-box recording out." (The black box, referred to dramatically in media accounts of airline accidents, is a five-by-thirteen-inch box that contains the cockpit voice recorder, a continuous loop of tape that records cockpit communication. The color of the box is actually orange. The other flight documentation device used by accident investigators is the Digital Flight Data Recorder, which monitors the previous twenty-five hours of the aircraft's operating systems.)

Kennedy continues, "My husband, Jim, was involved in the accident investigation committee. He didn't come home for, like, two weeks during that time. He was right there when things were going on, and he came back frustrated."

"What we did mostly," says Jim Kennedy, "was sit around in the room and listen to what was going on. That was about as much input as we could offer. Then the union took it a little further on behalf of the pilots. It took quite a while, but the word that I hear is that they had several experts testify that, yes, computer enhancement of this particular section of the tape, which was garbled, indicates that the word *flap* is mentioned, and that there's a noise which corresponds to the same noise of a flap handle being moved, the clicking noise. The NTSB would not take this into evidence at that point, and the report was written without it. Maybe the NTSB had a good reason for it, I don't know. There have been other instances where the flaps didn't stay down. . . . If it were to come out that there was a general problem with the flaps. . . ." Kennedy stops and thinks further. "There certainly is a lot more money and political power behind McDonnell Douglas than there is the two pilots who are now dead." Although Kennedy's remarks could be taken to suggest some impropriety on the part of McDonnell Douglas and the federal government, it is more likely that his intent is to point out the difference in resources available to the parties in the investigation, specifically that a large corporation has more resources at its disposal than the relatives of two dead pilots. In this, Kennedy is likely to be expressing his own feelings of frustration.

"Pilot error sort of wipes out a pilot's career in one sweep," says Jim Kennedy, passing on the rumor among Northwest pilots that Captain Maus's family was the object of threatening phone calls and harassment. "That particular accident was the second biggest one in the history of this country. John's [Maus's] wife, Alison, went to all the hearings. I guess the harassment is still continuing from what I've heard. All of Maus's wife's assets have been tied up—her house. I think there was a lot of pilot error involved in that particular accident, but you can't just overlook deregulation and the morale. We'd all like to think there's never any pilot error, but there is. And I firmly believe that the pressure that's in the cockpit now, the other concerns that we have about things we were never concerned with before are certainly a contributing factor. Because you're not being able to keep your mind one hundred percent on just flying a safe flight. The pressure of trying to be on time, trying to save fuel, [arguing about] do we wear long-sleeved or short-sleeved shirts. It's bullshit."

Dick Riley takes up the story of flight 255. "That was obviously the 'cause' of the crash. The guy didn't put his flaps down for takeoff, and the takeoff warning horn that was supposed to tell him that his airplane was improperly configured didn't work." Riley pauses, fiddles with his paper clips, and then goes on to explain his opinion of why the warning system didn't work. "The takeoff warning circuit was supposed to be powered from two separate power sources. One power source gave you the takeoff warning and another power source told you whether the warning was working correctly, and if it was not working correctly, it would turn on an "inop" light. What the Douglas prints say is that this thing is supposed to have two power sources off of two separate circuit breakers. The simulator manufacturer got the Douglas wiring specs and built all the simulators to have two separate power sources. But when it came time to build the aircraft, for whatever reason Douglas took both wires and hooked them up to one common circuit breaker so that the "inop" light was powered from the same circuit breaker that powered the system. The result was that you could have a single failure that knocked the whole system out. That's apparently what happened; the circuit breaker failed internally and they didn't have a takeoff warning system.

"Now, what about the issue of the flaps? Why did the captain forget to put the flaps down? What kind of baggage he was hauling along that he missed that, I don't know. And I don't think anybody's dug deep enough into the problem to say, 'We'd like to know *why* the crew missed this. . . . Here again I say, you're not going to solve the problem with 'pilot error.'"

"When we talk about these issues," says Rex Chamberlain, "we're not talking about people like the Rickenbackers and the Trippes; we're talking about people who don't remember when airplanes used to fall in the ocean. They don't remember, as Rickenbacker once said, 'When the thing left the ground, we all stood around and cheered.' They don't remember the agonies and the lost lives and the disasters. They've been given this beautiful system and these beautiful marvelous airplanes, and they have been raised with the assumption that it is your inalienable right, God-given gift, to hurl yourself into the air, to be able to fly, and that it will always be that way unless somebody screws up to make something negative happen."

"The Federal Aviation Regulations say that the pilot in command is ultimately responsible for the safe conduct of the flight," snaps Pete Browner. "And it doesn't matter what the dispatcher thinks. It doesn't matter what the maintenance department thinks. It doesn't matter what the president of the airline thinks. The pilot is the one who's responsible, and rightfully so because he's the guy who is there at the time and has to assess all the variables that are involved in preparing his trip. A lot of people who don't know the system feel it's a large responsibility, and I guess it is, but we have a lot of authority that goes with it. And I think most pilots guard that authority very carefully and use it judiciously.

"We're all different," Browner laughs. "I love a fight. There's a lot of guys who don't like fights. They say, 'Goddamn, don't bother me with that stuff. Just let me go fly my trip and go home. That's all I want to do. I've got ten years left, I've got two years left,' whatever it is. And they won't question the penciling. . . . Don't get me wrong. Those guys, the wrench turners, want to go out and they want to fix the airplanes, and they are aghast that the damn supervisors are pencil-whipping everything.

"Pilots work hard and play hard. One of my play-hard things is the ALPA work I do. I've been involved in air safety and accident investigation work for twenty-some years. I get a great amount of satisfaction out of doing it, although it's very frustrating sometimes. Why do I do it? Gee, I don't know. Maybe I think I can make the crazy system work a little better. It's hard to effect any change. You would think that with a heap of bodies and a black hole where an airplane went in, it would be easy. But the reaction of most people after one of these incidents, including the federal government, is, 'Why would we want to change anything? If we change it, we'd admit we were wrong to begin with.'"

"The flight you're on is the one that counts," says Bud McKenzie. "And as much as you think you control it all, you don't."

CHAPTER 6

The FAA and Air Traffic Control

THE FEDERAL AVIATION ASSOCIATION

The younger pilots don't understand what the real issues are about. They haven't been around long enough, and of course the military likes the young fellows because they're not afraid to try anything. They don't have the caution that is developed over a period of years of experience.

—BOB SCOTT, United Airlines
747 captain

It was one of those warm, blue California evenings, almost twilight, when the air softens and the bright afternoon sunlight fades into an evening haze. The young college freshman was alone at the small Pomona airfield where he was working as a line boy earning a dollar credit toward flying lessons for every day he pumped gas, cleaned windshields, checked engine oil, and hosed out the airplanes when students came back airsick. The airport was deserted except for two pilots in a trainer shooting touch-and-go landings.

Watching them, the young man wondered whether the two men in the plane had noticed the wind was beginning to shift.

Intent on what they were doing, apparently neither man had observed that with each landing their aircraft was touching down farther and farther toward the end of the runway. In fact, on what was to be the last go-around for the day, the aircraft ended so far down the strip that it ran off the paved surface onto the gravel at the end. Trying to slow down, both pilots bore down hard on the plane's brake pedals. The combined weight of their reaction was too much for the small aircraft, however, and the sudden force pushed the plane's nose down and caused it to flip over on its back. The line boy could hear the pop, pop, pop of the propeller as the plane bounced along the gravel. The heavy cloud of dust from the disturbed ground was almost invisible in the deepening twilight.

Quickly the young man jumped onto the airport tug and roared down to where the disabled aircraft sat awkwardly with its landing gear stuck straight up like the limbs of a long-dead animal. He jumped off the tug, crawled on his hands and knees across the fabric surface of the nearest wing, and carefully unlocked the cockpit door. Inside, the pilot and his student were hanging upside down in their seats. Like two spectators at a Wimbledon tennis match, both men turned toward the young man and nodded that they were all right. As he reached out to help them, however, both men unbuckled their seat belts and dropped immediately downward, hitting the inside of the cockpit roof. One man fell so hard he knocked himself out; the other suffered a sprained neck and cracked collarbone.

• • •

Rex Chamberlain likes to tell this story as his first experience with what the airline industry calls negative panic, a reaction to unusual circumstances that can render passengers disoriented and unable to take the most elementary measures on behalf of their own safety. Although incidents of negative panic are not unusual in aviation, the fact is that on average airline passengers have little or no previous experience for dealing with an air emergency, few if any expectations of what it might be like to be caught in a crippled aircraft, and worst of all are generally amazingly unworried about their own safety.

When most of us board an airplane, we effectively turn over control of our lives for the duration of the flight, relying on the assumption that the cockpit crew is experienced and skillful, that flight attendants are knowledgeable and well trained, that the mechanics who serviced the plane did their job, that federal safety guidelines are adequate, and that inspection and enforcement procedures are what they should be. On a good day all of the above might fall neatly into place, but, as Bill Fredericks had suggested, aviation accidents hardly ever occur on good days. The behavior of passengers involved in an incident can be one of the more unpredictable elements.

In preliminary reports of the February 1991 accident at Los Angeles International Airport, for example, in which a USAir 737 landed on top of a small commuter airplane, reporters cited an incident that occurred during evacuation of the aircraft in which a man ignored instructions from flight attendants and stepped over a fallen woman to get to the emergency door. When he reached the door, he couldn't open it, and it took a third individual to get the door unlocked and help other passengers out.

Bill Fredericks has definite opinions about passenger responsibility in airplanes. "Ninety-nine percent of people don't pay attention to the flight attendant briefing at the beginning of the flight. When you get aboard *my* airplane, you hear about it. I've been told I talk too much, but by God everybody pays attention to what I say. Bill Buckley and I have been writing each other for years now. He said something in a magazine I didn't like, and I wrote him about it, and then he wrote me back—that's the kind of guy he is.

"I rode with him once on a dead-head trip from San Francisco to Newark. He was sitting next to an open seat in first class, and a couple wanted to sit together so he very kindly moved all the way over to the right-hand side to accommodate them. But the first thing he did when he got resettled in his seat was he picked up his material and started writing; this was while the flight attendant was going through her song and dance. Sometime after that he wrote an article about how flight attendants and pilots are paid too much.

"I had him. I wrote him a letter and said, 'You know, you wrote this article complaining that pilots get paid too much and flight attendants get paid too much. I'll bet you $100 that you have no idea where that emergency handle is to get out of that airplane. You're depending on that flight attendant to pull you out of that airplane. As far as I'm concerned, I'd tell my flight attendants to forget you. If you're not paying attention, you can die. That's up to you.' He wrote me back a page and a half in which he said absolutely nothing."

"Let me tell you what it's like to evacuate an airplane in an accident," say Rex Chamberlain. "Let's go back to the late fifties. I was a young birdman in Hawaii taking my first water survival course, which was sponsored by the Coast Guard. There were four airlines involved—Aloha, Hawaiian, United, and Pan American. We started the morning off with lectures and then we went out in a cutter to the south shore of Oahu to where there was a little bit of a swell, and we all launched our company's life rafts. We put out our sea anchors and we spun around and around, and between getting seasick and ogling the girls in their bikinis, we had a great time.

"It was quite a learning experience, because it was out on the damned ocean. The wind was about eighteen knots, and the swells were about twelve feet. We don't do that anymore. Nowadays we just talk about it. We go into a hanger and we look at a life raft, and we answer a test and we sign off. However, during the lecture part of that exercise that day, the Coast Guard cutter commander spoke to us along with some air safety experts. Then a Northwest captain who had ditched a DC-7 off the Aleutian Islands stood up to tell us what it's like in real life.

"He had a fire on his airplane, and he couldn't put it out, but he did have time to fly to a sheltered location and get a Coast Guard cutter out to pick them up after he landed. And he had a little time to get the people out of the plane, but not a lot. He got the airplane onto the water perfectly with no damage, and it floated fine. When the crew got up, however, and told everybody to proceed to the exits, to their astonishment they saw an entire cabin full of passengers struggling to get out of their seats, all of them still restrained by their seat belts. They couldn't reason and they couldn't feel, and they seemed to be completely disoriented to the fact that their seat belts were holding them in their seats. Finally, the flight attendants had to go down and unfasten each one of the seat belts.

"Now, this is an airplane that's right side up, horizontal, not on fire, and bobbing gently in the ocean. But these people were not capable of the simplest act of self-preservation because they were in shock. They were not normal."

Chamberlain's words are cautionary. "When we teach emergencies today, we teach flight attendants the orders they should give. We teach them to use language that's not confusing. We tell them not to tell somebody to unfasten their seat belt because if they don't hear the *un,* they'll hear *fasten.* So we use a word like *release.* If we're an international carrier, we study Chinese and Japanese, and we study European languages, and we pick the word that is maybe more easily conveyed in different languages. But what we don't tell our crews is that these people might be in shock.

"On an airplane where there's a couple of impacts with the ground, and the lights go out, maybe the thing slides off into a drainage ditch on the side and it's at an angle, we're talking about shock. Something like that happened to the American Airlines DC-10 trying to take off in Puerto Rico a few years ago where it slid off the end of the runway and nosed into the ocean. Part of it was on land and part of it was in the water. There was a kind of fog and steam and smoke generated by the hot engine parts in the ocean water. It was like three planets. If you opened one door you saw jungle, if you opened another door you saw dry runway, the other you saw ocean. You didn't know whether you needed a life raft or whether to take a machete and cut the trees down. *These* people were in shock. It took them a long time to get everybody off that airplane. They didn't know what exits to use or whether they were on fire. They didn't know whether or not to use the slides. Now you're talking about shock and trauma and confusion. You're talking about people not functioning.

"United procedures are good," continues Chamberlain, "but they don't deal with the idea that people are going to be in shock. I don't know what you do about it except tell flight crews that passengers may not be capable of the simplest acts of self-preservation. In fact that very phrase was in Pan American's procedures, which said, 'Passengers may not be capable of taking steps for their own self-preservation.'"

Even for a person not in shock, a disabled airplane is a frightening environment. The landing gear may have collapsed, tipping the plane to the side and putting the floor at an angle. In most accidents, visibility will be affected by smoke in the cabin, which produces an eerie sense of disorientation. Walking on the tipped or collapsed surface of the cabin floor is difficult, finding your way almost impossible in the smoke. In desperation you sink to the carpet, hoping for some clean air. If you are not hurt, you crawl along following the line of white floor lights—if they're working—to what you pray is the closest exit. If you have remembered to count the seats from here to there, you will have some idea of where you are going. In what seems urgently long and precious minutes, you are the first one to reach the over-wing exit on the starboard side of the plane. The man next to the exit is unconscious, and someone helps you try to move him. Because you didn't read the seat pocket card, you end up struggling with the release mechanism to get the door open.

Flight attendants practice accident evacuation in simulators that expose them to numerous possible emergencies, including failure of the emergency system itself, such as blocked exists and jammed emergency doors and coping with blind or otherwise disabled passengers. They at least know what the inside of a wrecked plane feels like. It's nonetheless true that in this age of modern jet transport, even when we realize the hazards and prepare for them, passengers in an airline accident still need all the help they can get. Bob Scott remembers how it used to be.

"When that Constellation came to rest just short of Grand Central Parkway years ago, the thing I recall significantly is that after we got the airplane stopped, we sat there. We didn't make a big effort to get out of the airplane in a hurry, to evacuate. We should have, but I guess our training was a little deficient in those days. Nowadays, boy, you get out of that airplane right now." And one of the reasons that you do that is because of the composition of materials used in airplane interiors.

"We know you've got ninety seconds to get out or you can lose a lot of people," says Bud McKenzie, who has studied aviation safety at the University of Southern California. "When the inside of an aircraft burns, it gives off toxic gases. And if you don't get the people off and there's a fire, you're going to lose a lot of them because of inhalation of that stuff. I think some of the seat fabrics and some of the plastics are going to be replaced and probably in the newer airplanes they'll use different kinds of materials."

United flight engineer Lisa Johnson offers some words about evacuation and accidents. "I think if you get on the ground, and you get to the point where you can evacuate, your chances are real good. I have to say in defense of flight attendants that the reason they are hired is basically to get people off an airplane when there's a problem, although most people think they're hired primarily for the in-flight service. Flight attendants are very professional. I watch them when I first get on an airplane, and I'm always impressed because whatever position they're flying—and especially on the DC-10 they can work eight different positions—they go right to their station and they sit down and they adjust their seat belt so they know it's right.

"They close their eyes, and they know exactly where to reach for the PA. They know exactly where to reach for the emergency evacuation button. They know exactly how to operate that particular door, because the doors are all different—I don't understand why aircraft manufacturers don't do something more consistent about emergency exits. Each flight attendant knows exactly how he or she is going to get out, and they're just spring-loaded to shout certain things in an evacuation. Pilots go through basically the same training, but they don't pound it into us. Flight attendants practice it, whereas we don't practice it at all except once a year."

The safety gate regarding aircraft evacuation in case of an accident is certification by the FAA. To certify an airplane in the United States, a manufacturer must show that its emergency evacuation procedures are feasible and can be accomplished. It does this by demonstrating that a full load of passengers can be evacuated in ninety seconds with half the emergency exits inoperative. The problem Rex Chamberlain describes is that in undertaking this exercise, manufacturers use their own employees, who are preselected and have been prepared to get off the plane quickly. They don't necessarily represent a cross section of the traveling public, in which there may be children, individuals who are incapacitated, those who might be frightened of air travel, and people who have overindulged in alcohol during the course of a flight.

"So they put all these people in the airplane," says Chamberlain, "they dim the lights and leave only the emergency exit lights, and then they blow the whistle and start the clock running. Under those conditions you can evacuate a 747 in ninety seconds out of one side only. You can also do it without using the over-wing exits. You can use four of the ten [doors], and it still works. But nobody's in shock.

There's been no traumatic event. Remember the Tenerife accident, when the KLM plane tore the top off a Pan Am 747 in the Canary Islands? It was the worst disaster in aviation history; it killed 579 people. The first officer is a fellow that my wife and I know personally. He was a captain for Pan American, and he's now a Kennedy-based 747 captain for United. That day he was in the right seat, flying copilot. He said that for an instant when the KLM airplane came out of the fog at them with the lights on they realized what was happening.

"The captain of the Pan Am airplane shoved the throttles all the way forward and turned and tried to taxi off the runway into the mud in order to get out of the way. Ending up in the mud would have been fine compared to what happened. But it takes time to accelerate that thing. They went to full throttle and called for hard left rudder, but the airplane hadn't begun to respond when the collision took place. They had turned but a few degrees and their speed hadn't increased at all.

"My friend said he very distinctly remembers that he was looking down into the intake of one of the KLM engines, which is about eight or ten feet high. He was looking right into the intake of this thing through the fog, and he realized that the plane was going to pass right behind him. Then there was the collision, but he has no real awareness or recollection of the noise or the violence or anything like that. The next thing he remembers is the emergency evacuation, a drill that is practiced incessantly by pilots. You're supposed to set the brakes, put the speed brakes down, and put your flaps out. You shut down the engines. You turn on the emergency exit lights. You notify the tower you're evacuating. You make a public address announcement to the passengers. If you have an evacuation alarm system, you turn that on. And then you get down to the nitty-gritties. You reach up and you pull all four fire handles on the engines.

"When he reached up, however, there was nothing there. The top of the airplane had been sheared off. Now this thing, the KLM engine, had passed six inches over his head and sheared the top off, and he had no recollection of it at all. There must have been this god-awful ripping and tearing racket; you would think that he might have had some thought that maybe there was some damage up there. But he was astonished that the top of the airplane wasn't there.

"You see, that's shock. That's complete shock. I don't know the physiology of how you function in that environment. I suppose some people perform better than others. Some people go back to their rote training, and some people freeze. I guess you don't really know what type you are until you really experience it."

It was not a great coincidence that it was two Boeing 747s that collided that day in Tenerife, given that the 747 is the most frequently used overwater passenger jet now in service. Depending on its cabin configuration, it can hold as many as 500 passengers. According to newspaper accounts and industry speculation in designing the new 747-400 model, Boeing wanted to eliminate an over-wing exit on both sides of the aircraft in order to increase seating capacity. When objections were heard from flight crews, Boeing went to work and calculated that the loss of the extra wing seats in the new plane could mean as much as a million dollars a year to an airline. Rex Chamberlain thinks the payoff is too risky. He explains his assessment of the rationale for removing the two exits.

"The 747 has five exits down each side, two in front of the wing, two behind the wing, and one over the wing on each side of the airplane. By deactivating that door over the wing, they can put four or five more people on each side of the plane and carry ten more fares. But there has been a hue and cry raised against deactivation of these exits by pilots and flight attendants. . . . Eliminating those two exits means that Boeing salespeople can go to a company with a bottom line management and say, 'Here are the economics of my airplane, here is Airbus's airplane, here is Douglas's airplane. Look at how much better my airplane is.' That puts enormous pressure on the other airframe manufacturers; it puts enormous pressure on the people who are trying to drag their feet and trying to say, 'Gee, we really shouldn't walk away from a usable exit.'"

For some pilots, raising the issue of the FAA and its capability to decide issues such as those Chamberlain is speaking about is like raising a red flag in front of a bull. "The FAA's in bed with the American Transport Association, the organization that represents the airline carriers," is Dick Riley's opinion. "That's why I say its erroneous for the American public to think the FAA is going to protect them. That is the furthest from the truth of anything that I can think of."

"These FAA guys have offices in Boeing," explains Sandra Luft's brother, Al Kellogg, "and at Douglas. They're there all the time. They get taken out to a cup of coffee and somebody says, 'Look, it's going to save us a couple of hundred grand here if we do it this way.' It's inevitable. It's like the people that represent the FAA on an airline. It becomes rather chummy—even if the guy's the most objective person in the world—because the people on the airline deal with this guy all the time, the POI [principle operating inspector]. At the company I was working for, our POI came and sat through one of my ground schools. He was actually helping teach ground school. It was very helpful, but it wasn't real objective."

"Don't get me on the FAA," snaps Brad Prescott. "I swear to God, five percent are good people; ninety-five percent are *losers;* that's why they're in the FAA. That's the God's truth. I'll tell you what, it's the worst organization I've ever been around, and I was in the military. The FAA inspectors who do check rides on airplanes, every one of them has got a different idea about how to do it. I said to one of them who was giving me a hard time about something, 'Wait a minute, right here it says. . . . I can read.' But it doesn't matter, they interpret it differently. These FAA guys, they all have their little power tree to climb up, and I see that as their biggest thing. The whole thing is so political."

The Federal Aviation Administration, as the government agency designated in 1978 to replace the Civil Aeronautics Board, is charged with a variety of responsibilities, a situation that many pilots and other industry observers feel leads to a conflict of interest. The agency is responsible for setting safety standards for commercial and general aviation. It inspects the operations of airlines and of aviation manufacturers. Through the air traffic control system, it's responsible for guiding and routing flights, and it has the additional obligation of promoting economic prosperity in the aviation industry. Some observers feel the agency is hampered by its government status and that it should be independent of the federal bureaucracy and its budgets and that this would make it more capable of acting expeditiously and efficiently.

"The difficulty," suggests Sandra Luft, "is that the FAA has been given two incompatible duties—*regulate* and *encourage*—and they're not competent to do either. To ask them to do both is insanity. It's also important to separate the two. My feeling is the FAA has demonstrated its incompetence; I'm ready for a change."

"The FAA should be shit-canned and start out fresh; they really should," says Brad Prescott. "The money they waste. Here's a good one, and I mean it took a rocket scientist to figure this out. A VOR [very high frequency omni-range radio] is a radio fix by which they create something like little highways in the sky. You fly from one radio fix to another. About five years ago, some dummy crashed because he thought the VOR was at the airport. Let's say he was shooting an approach into Van Nuys airport and the VOR was called Van Nuys even though it was co-located; that means you would shoot an approach to the VOR and then you let down off of that to the airport. Let's face it, he screwed up. But the FAA said, 'Oh my God, the reason he crashed was because the airport and the VOR both had the same name.' So they changed every name of every VOR. Think of all the money that cost—when the things that are really needed at airports are things like DMEs [distance measuring equipment] on airports like Burbank. When you're flying there, you don't know how far away you are. You have to compute your distance by time. Meanwhile, Van Nuys has an ILS [instrument landing system] and a DME, and it's just a general aviation airport.

"But instead of fixing things like that, the FAA spends all this time and all this money to change the names of the VORs to a bunch of new names pilots aren't familiar with it. It has nothing to do with flying, but the FAA made a big deal of it. They had to change the charts. It was multimillion dollars worth of bullshit. But that's the FAA for you. That just shows their mentality."

Although FAA responsibilities are diverse, the agency's image is often associated with the air traffic control system. For pilots, mention of FAA jurisdiction in this area can induce strong reactions. "One thing I think about," says American Airlines flight engineer Jason Young, "is the FAA cutting costs and not hiring enough controllers. They have something like $8 billion in a trust fund, and they're saying they can't use it because they need it to balance the budget." Young is referring to the $7.6 billion Airport and Airway Trust Fund, monies collected from airport taxes and the surcharge on airline tickets and cargo and designated for improvements in the domestic aviation system. The money has never been spent, however, because government officials prefer to use it to help offset the federal deficit. At one time the revenue had been earmarked for interim air traffic control (ATC) equipment and to expand existing airport capacity. In 1990 hearings on the subject, the FAA indicated that they wanted to use eighty-five percent of the $7.6 billion surplus to finance the FAA's annual operations budget.

"They froze that money and yet we need navigational aides," says Young with unusual fervor. "Ontario airport's been looking for a DME, and the FAA wouldn't put one in. So who paid for it? American Airlines. I heard it cost them a million dollars. Ontario's a substantial airport and needed the capability. But with all that bureaucratic red tape, it takes forever for something to happen. We also opened up an operation at the Raleigh–Durham airport. They built a runway there—I don't know whose fault it was—but the runways ended up too close together to allow simultaneous approaches under instrument conditions, so the FAA wanted to test a new radar out there. Who paid for the testing of the radar? Not the FAA, not the airport, but American Airlines."

"The FAA's primary interest is not really to promote safety," says Joyce Kennedy's affable husband, Jim. "It's to keep things going, to keep things running. But you have to ask, is that really happening? Pilots are inundated with paperwork and reporting, and yet the FAA says it's still legal to take a plane into an airport at night with no vertical guidance. That's dangerous to do in a 172 [a one-engine general aviation aircraft], but we do it all the time in a 727 or a DC-9.

"That was one of the things that North Central was working on, because on that airline we would go into a lot of airports that were like black holes, where there would be nothing out there for miles. On a thick, black, overcast night, you can't see; you can't tell exactly where the trees are or if there's anything else out there. And you can't tell exactly what lights are on, either. That's one thing I will never do as a captain—go into an airport without vertical guidance in the middle of the night. It's totally fly by the seat of your pants, and that's no way to fly an airplane. What we have now is ludicrous, but it would necessitate a lot of money to put vertical guidance in a lot of these airports. Most major airports have it, but a lot of the small ones don't."

From his viewpoint as a union spokesperson, Bob Scott predictably has some very specific thoughts about the FAA. "With the FAA, you're guilty until proven innocent," says Scott. "Believe me. No way, shape, or form can you prove yourself innocent. And it can be awfully hard in an emergency situation to think of what you have to do to take care of the emergency and keep yourself legal at the same time. If you use your emergency authority, the FAA administrator may request that you explain it to the agency within twenty-four hours. They don't *have* to ask, but your company is going to ask you to report it. So you don't want to declare one when you don't have one.

"If you run low on fuel and declare an emergency, they're going to ask why it happened. And if you explain it by saying, 'Well, I didn't put enough fuel on' or 'I had a wind burst' or 'I should have diverted' or something like this, they'll hang you for that. So it's not necessarily a good idea to use your emergency authority to circumvent something that may have gone wrong or you may have done wrong because the FAA's position will be that you put yourself in the emergency situation, that you created it yourself.

"So everybody's reluctant to declare an emergency; but then you're stuck with the situation that they're liable to come back and ask why you didn't and then hang you for that. There is one way you can get around it, and that's *special handling*. You can call 'minimum fuel,' and the air traffic system will give you priority handling ahead of somebody else to get in. And you don't have to explain it. Your company may ask you to explain it, but the FAA will not question it. This is the reason I say it is so difficult to stay legal. It's almost impossible to fly a trip and not violate some rule or some regulation."

"It used to be if you had a problem with an air traffic controller or with an inspector, you could talk the situation out," says Brad Prescott. "Now they just write you up. It's like the higher-ups require them to give so many citations a year."

But the FAA does not, in the opinion of Rex Chamberlain, have its own house in order. "Mr. McArtor [T. Allan McArtor, FAA administrator at that time] had to make the decision [regarding 747 emergency exits]. Now there is some reason to believe that the previous administrator, Don Engen, was faced with more of this political reality and more of these political decisions than he cared to face. There is some reason to believe—there is rumor, folklore in the industry—that he was becoming an obstacle to Boeing and the Air Transport Association. He's gone; Mr. McArtor's come in, and there was incredible pressure on him to cave in on this exit thing."

Addressing the issue of passenger safety in May of 1988, the FAA decided to take action. Sidestepping the matter of dangerously flammable materials, the agency approved installation of airline seats that would better protect passengers from impact. The proposal was based on a five-year joint study between the FAA and the National Aeronautics and Space Administration. It will take seven years to retrofit existing aircraft. Concerning the number of required emergency exits, the FAA did not allow Boeing to reduce the number of exits on the 747-400. Although not addressing the Boeing issue specifically, it mandated that emergency exits on aircraft designed for the American market could be no more than sixty feet apart. The issue of the flammability of aircraft interiors remains unresolved.

AIR TRAFFIC CONTROL

> *The thing we don't like is that somebody*
> *else is making a decision for us. They say,*
> *"Oh, we've got thunderstorms out there;*
> *you can't go." I'm the one that's going to*
> *fly this thing. Not the controllers sitting*
> *down there on the ground that feed you*
> *only the information they think you should*
> *have, which is not necessarily the informa-*
> *tion you* must *have in order to operate your*
> *flight safely. And they're not even aviation*
> *people. They're controllers. Some of them*
> *have never been in an airplane. How they*
> *do their job, I don't know.*

> —TED GOFF, Delta Air Lines
> 737 copilot

Although acknowledging increases in air traffic since deregulation, advocates offer the opinion that advances in technology have minimized accidents and kept things safe. They cite more sophisticated radar, weather forecasting, and navigational equipment and more automated airplane backup systems. No matter how you look at it, however, a major consequence of deregulation has been an increase in the number of planes flying, and many industry experts feel that this has put considerable strain on the capabilities of an antiquated air traffic control system and outdated airports. In 1989, 430 million passengers flew in the commercial aviation system; the number is expected to grow to a billion by the year 2000. And by most accounts, the FAA is not gearing up to meet the challenge.

FAA statistics indicate that pilot reports of near midair collisions of the type that killed 82 people over Cerritos, California, in 1986 were up forty-eight percent in the first nine months of 1987. In releasing this information, the FAA was careful to qualify its data, indicating that while near-miss incidents have increased, air traffic has also expanded and the numbers of near misses versus planes flying is at an acceptable level—which probably makes sense unless you were in one of the seventeen collisions between airliners and small planes that have occurred in the last two decades. In reporting its near-miss statistics the FAA also noted that in a good percentage of the reported incidents, the relative proximity of the planes to each other reflects "no real danger."

Bud McKenzie expresses a different opinion. "When Alfred Kahn [Cornell University professor who was one of the architects of deregulation] or anyone else gives me a meaningless statistic about the fact we've got more flights operating now than we ever did and the accident rate is lower than it ever was, that doesn't mean a hill of beans. Especially if you're on an airplane that's going down, or you've lost someone in an accident. Then statistics really have no value in terms of trying to achieve what we always strive for—a zero accident rate. That's certainly what I strive for when I get into the cockpit of an airplane. We're conditioned to the impact of numbers. People are more or less—right or wrong—conditioned to the fact that we have car accidents. But there's a whole different perception when it comes to an airplane accident. It's more dramatic, and usually there are more people involved. And there's so much less control from the viewpoint of the passenger."

In 1983, a Gallup poll commissioned by *Newsweek* found that twenty-one percent of people who fly on commercial airlines are frightened some of the time, three percent are frightened most of the time, and eleven percent are *always* frightened. Respondents indicated they are the most apprehensive about the risk of midair collisions and accidents. Other researchers report that people with an intense fear of flying cite claustrophobia, fear of heights, fear of a panic attack, and a reluctance to relinquish control of their life to a pilot as the reason for their anxiety. Had they talked to pilots, they might also have worried about the state of air traffic control and the efficacy of the FAA.

"There's 101 little things that have changed since deregulation," says Ted Goff, his face slowly expanding into his classic smile. "But I'll tell you the one big thing I think is a problem, and that's the air controllers. The old guys we used to have came out of the military, and they'd been doing it forever. The guys today are just fighting to keep their heads above water; the experience is just not there. Yeah, I've heard the equipment's no good, but it seems the old guys made it work.

"Sure, there's a lot more planes, and maybe the equipment *is* outmoded, but the old guys knew; they had a *feeling*. And, Jesus, that shows up in a million ways. The way guys talk, the jams they get into and then want us to straighten out for them. Like getting us too close to other traffic and then wanting us to move on out somewhere for a little while before we start coming back in. You can tell these guys are just hanging on by their fingernails.

"I'm talking about things like when you come into the approach into Los Angeles, and way out there, five minutes before the event needs to be talked about, this guy is telling you something, just to get it out of the way so that he doesn't have to think about it later on. Like when you're heading for Santa Monica, for example, and the guy says, 'Take a heading of zero seven zero.' Well, shit, you're two VORS [checkpoints] out. You don't need to be talking about Santa Monica for another five minutes. What happens is the burden's put on us. It's not such a heavy burden, but it's just an example of how these guys are. They're not as coordinated. They can't handle as many aircraft as the old guys could. They're constantly asking you to speed up, slow down, do this, do that. A lot of times it's bordering on the limitations of the airplane, and it certainly borders on comfort to the passengers."

Beneath his usual flip manner, Goff's exasperation begins to show. "They'll tell you they want you down, and they want you to do it right now. So you've got to push the nose down, and then everybody in the back starts looking around apprehensively. I think air traffic control is probably one of our biggest problems. The Delta crash in Dallas they said was caused by wind shear—if that had been the old controllers, I don't think that would ever have happened." Goff is describing his impression of the 1985 crash of Delta L-1011, which crashed short of the runway in Dallas, killing 134. The NTSB cited the crew's decision to try to land in questionable weather as the probable cause of the accident and that a contributory cause was lack of "definitive, real-time wind shear hazard information" available to the crew. Goff speculates, "The controllers knew there were thunderstorms out there. They knew that there was a lighter aircraft in front of the heavy. The older guys would have been more sensitive to the fact that the speeds were not compatible, and they wouldn't have put them that close. These inexperienced controllers had the planes too close, and then they asked Delta to slow down to speeds that made them susceptible to wind shear. Maybe the captain shouldn't have slowed down. Maybe he should have gone around or something. You always have that option. You can always say, 'I can't do that' or 'I don't want to do it.'

"*I* think personally, that if it had been the old controllers, that would never have happened. There would have been more space between the planes. Those guys were more attuned; their whole life they've been directing aircraft."

As Goff implies, many of the controllers who eventually found themselves in commercial aviation got their training and experience as military controllers. Currently, civilians who take up the occupation train for thirteen weeks at an Oklahoma City facility after which they undergo three years of on-the-job probation. Salaries begin at twenty thousand dollars but rise steadily with the number of years on the job and with lucrative overtime. The present air controller work force is mostly men in their midthirties; only four percent are women.

Although the common image of an air traffic controller is someone in a headset scanning the skies from an airport tower, there are actually three groups of workers engaged in the business of keeping air traffic moving. Controllers in airport towers clear runways and guide planes within five miles of an airport. In the terminal radar control office, often located in the basement of an airport tower, another group controls planes within thirty to forty miles of the airport. The job of this approach control contingent, whose only view of the aircraft is on a radarscope, is to manage traffic approaching the airport by separating it at various elevations and distances. Much farther away is the regional air traffic control center, which assigns cruising altitudes and may be in contact with pilots hundreds of miles from the airport at which they are scheduled to land. The system is reversed on takeoff, as pilots are handed off from the tower through a series of stations en route to their destination.

In 1981 Pres. Ronald Reagan fired over eleven thousand air traffic controllers who had walked off the job in an effort to focus attention on working conditions and safety issues. Reagan's action was based on his contention that the strike was illegal, as well as the expectation that a $12 billion computerized system approved in 1981 called the National Airspace System Plan would make the jobs of many of the lost controllers obsolete. The target date for implementation of this system was 1992, but observers suggest that because of FAA foot-dragging, it will be another decade before controllers get equipment relief, despite the fact that in many cases ATC equipment actually dates back to the fifties and sixties. Controllers joke that the

U.S. air traffic control system may be the largest user of vacuum tubes remaining in the country. The additional problem is a labor shortage. According to Raymond Spickler, executive vice president of the National Air Traffic Controllers Association, to meet demands on the system, one thousand new controllers will be needed each year from 1990 through 1995. The current FAA hiring rate is less than half that number.

"They had some real growing pains after the strike," says Pete Browner. "They had some young controllers who were good kids. They were working their hearts out and were trying to do the job, but they didn't have the experience to cover that scope and scan it and provide the secondary information to the airliners the way the old guys used to do. They were working to capacity just to get the thing done on a routine basis. Now they're getting a little more experience, and they're up to speed."

Not all pilots are so generous. USAir's Ann Alexander describes a routine day at Los Angeles International Airport (LAX), the third largest airport in the United States in number of planes handled daily. Among pilots it has also been voted the most dangerous, although the airport public relations office dismisses the view as unsubstantiated. During peak time at LAX, a plane lands every fifty-six seconds. "Coming in today," says Alexander tightly, "it was just ridiculous. It was an IFR [instrument flight rules] day so they had to have a certain separation between airplanes, plus the fact that we were behind a 'heavy,' which means that we have to have at least five miles separation for wake turbulence. Twenty miles out they told us to maintain 180 knots, which we did. All of a sudden this really excited voice came on and said, 'Slow to your minimum speed, now.' Well, it takes a few miles to slow that airplane down; otherwise the passengers would be through the windshield. So we started to slow, and we switched over to the tower frequency.

"The tower said, 'If you can't see the guy ahead of you, maintain two thousand feet; don't continue your descent.' The guy ahead of us was *five* miles ahead of us, and it was foggy and hazy so you could just barely see the runway. I couldn't pick out an airplane out there, which meant we had to maintain two thousand feet even though we were getting closer and closer to the runway. Finally we saw the guy on the ground. When we told the tower we had him, they said, 'Fine, clear to visual,' but by this time the runway was almost right under us. So we decided to try it, and if we didn't make it, do a go-around.

"That was poor, poor controlling on their part. They should have kept us at least six miles apart, and they should have seen way back there that we were going faster than the guy up here in front of us. If they needed us to slow down, it should have been way back there. There should have been none of this 'Maintain two thousand feet.' I realize there might have been extenuating circumstances, but we couldn't see anything." Alexander stops, offers a what-the-hell grin, and then adds, "We made it just fine, but it was a steeper approach than normal."

"You hear from the air traffic controllers that they're just swamped, and I've seen a lot of errors on calls," says Joyce Kennedy. "Jim flies long-haul stuff over to San Francisco, but on the DC-9, I fly little short hops, which means I have more contact with controllers. Jim's up in a high airspace for a longer period of time, but down where I am, I have a hard time, for example, even getting on the frequency. You call in and give them your number, and it takes a long time sometimes. I don't know how many times I've made a call and couldn't get through."

Despite the difference in their flying experiences, her husband agrees. "Two people call at once and neither one can get heard. Sometimes we want to divert for weather. We can't get through to anybody, and we're sitting there right in front of a thunderstorm. What they need to do is have more frequencies and more manpower. I definitely see a problem in that area."

Brad Prescott, who usually takes the position of the outsider, has mixed feelings about the subject of aircraft controllers. "I feel sorry for the controllers; they're under the gun. Now they have this SNITCH system in which they're allowed, I think, three miles and one thousand feet horizontal between airplanes. If planes get closer than that, the electronic surveillance system goes off, and then the poor controller's written up. Who *cares?* All this does is make them more worried about getting told on by this new system than about doing their job."

"My father and I disagree on the way to remedy the ATC situation," says Bob Scott's son, Greg, who flies as a DC-10 engineer. "He thinks that the fired air traffic controllers should stay fired, but I believe that one way to solve the problem is to bring those people back. Legally they had no right to strike, that's true. They were a government agency, and the folks in air traffic control right now say that if they did come back, the old guys wouldn't know the job anymore because it's changed so much. My personal opinion is they knew what the job was before, and they're going to be able to adapt because they know the system. They know how things are supposed to go."

Gene Scott's chum Jason Young disagrees. "Yeah, I can see there's certain controllers they could rehire—the noninstigators. But I think they'll still have problems. How can you take a guy who's been out of work and who was a striker and bring him back into that? They should've taken care of this stuff right after it happened years ago. They say training takes a long time, but they're not even training as many as they can. It's a typical political bureaucracy thing that's going to take forever to go through. It's classic. The FAA blames the airlines. The airlines blame the FAA."

The National Transportation Safety Board has characterized the current air traffic system in this country as running "flat out." Despite the increase of air traffic from deregulation, the United States has not built a new airport since Dallas–Fort Worth was opened in 1973, although Denver is scheduled to open a new international airport in the mid-1990s. Smaller airports serving general aviation are slowly being closed down, victims of land development and disuse, which puts more pressure on smaller planes to use the larger commercial airports. Additionally, the number of domestic flights reportedly rose twenty-five percent in the four-year period between 1985 and 1989 alone, and the aviation infrastructure has not changed considerably since deregulation. The FAA's answer to increased traffic at peak times is to slow down the system to make traffic more compatible with ATC capacity, which results in substantial delays at hubs and other major airports.

"I don't believe there are too many planes flying," says Greg Scott. "I do believe in updating or increasing the ability of pilots to see and avoid other airplanes. It's not exactly see-and-avoid, but *have knowledge* of aircraft around you, so you can avoid them. Mr. McArtor seems to think that you can look out your cockpit window and spot anything. It can be very hard; in fact, on the days when it's clearest, it can be the hardest to find an airplane. And that's not the only problem. There are all kinds of people up there with all kinds of reflexes and ability and different levels of experience and preparedness.

"Last night I was flying at Van Nuys Airport. We were flying in a rectangular-type pattern, shooting takeoffs and landings. There was a guy behind us who was told to follow us, and there was also another airplane down below us heading right for the runway. The instructions for us and the other plane behind us were to turn left and left again to get to the runway. Well, the other plane didn't see us and went after the other guy, who was closer to the runway, even though he had been told that he was number three following a Cessna, which was us. He followed the other airplane instead because he couldn't see us. That's just a small instance of what can happen up there. In a commercial airliner, particularly, it makes it difficult to rely on see-and-avoid. We're going faster, things happen faster, and we also have to keep our heads inside the cockpit, keeping track of things that need to be done there."

What pilots commonly refer to as *see-and-avoid,* as casual as it may sound, is actually a procedure dictated by the FAA as protection against midair collisions. In the absence of mandatory position-establishing equipment on general aviation aircraft, all pilots in both general and commercial aviation must rely on their own ability to visually locate conflicting traffic in their airspace and then take the necessary steps to avoid an accident. Pete Browner explains.

"*See-and-avoid* is a law, one of the federal regulations—ninety-one point something or another. What it basically says is that each pilot shall operate his aircraft so as to *see and avoid* other aircraft. It's an old law that comes from the days of the sea; it has to do with right-of-way rules. When you have head-on objects on a collision course, like ships or airplanes, both pilots turn to the right to avoid each other. In aviation the regulation stipulates that if you're converging, the aircraft coming in from the right has the right-of-way, and the other aircraft will alter its course to pass behind it. This is of course provided you can see it. That's the problem."

Browner pauses, the muscles around his mouth tighten. "I'd love to see and avoid other airplanes. I'd like to see and avoid all the other airplanes that are potential midair collisions. But sometimes, because of physical limitations, as good as a pilot's eyesight is supposed to be, he just plain can't see the traffic in time to avoid it. Or see it at all. Below ten thousand feet and outside the airport traffic area anywhere between 200 and 250 knots is the average aircraft speed. To convert that to feet per second, you multiply by 1.68, so you're traveling somewhere between 350 and 400 feet per second, which means you're galloping up the land. When you're on approach to land, you are actually reducing your speed from about 220 knots to about 120 knots.

"Now what happens in reality in the see-and-avoid environment if you don't have anything else to help you, like radar control indicating unidentified traffic here or there, which gives you a point to look at. You're just randomly scanning the horizon to try and pick up objects. Obviously that's not very efficient. It's probably going to take you twelve to thirteen seconds to see something, recognize what it is, make a decision about what you want to do to correct the flight path of your airplane, put the input into the aircraft, and have it react.

"I know it sounds absolutely ridiculous that it takes that long, but that's the physical limitations of the human being and the machine. Don't think that it takes thirteen seconds to do every maneuver in an airplane, but it takes about that much time in this kind of a problem situation. There was a study that was done by some people up at MIT [Massachusetts Institute of Technology] on collision threats. They planned it very carefully. They had the airplanes separated by a known vertical separation, not much, like fifty or one hundred feet, and they would have a guy fly along. The intruder aircraft would aim at him, and they would determine how far away the pilot could see the intruder, first with random scanning and then with the intruder being pointed out to him by a radar controller.

"They found that when the controller gave the pilot an indication of where to look, he could pick up the traffic considerably farther away than he could with a random scan. Even if the controller simply said, 'Unidentified traffic at ten o'clock, three miles.' Bingo, that gave him a focus point, thirty degrees left of center, and the pilot would scan out there and could pick the traffic up.

"There have been some recommendations developed relative to scanning techniques when you're in this see-and-avoid environment, but nobody that I know of, no airline for instance, as part of their training program teaches a scan technique. I don't think in fact that there's a good one around. AOPA [Aircraft Owners and Pilots Association] developed one a number of years ago which is okay if you're flying very slow-moving airplanes. They recommend that you go 90 degrees on either side of you from the point where you're looking dead ahead and that you should take that distance in 10-degree segments and scan with a dwell time of a second on each 10-degree angle.

"My opinion is that you should refine that to 60 degrees to narrow the time in which you're away from the start position. But even then it's a 120-degree sweep. A second for every 10 degrees is twelve seconds from left to right and when you come back the other way it's another twelve seconds, which means you've used up twenty-four seconds. We just said it's going to take thirteen seconds to see, recognize, and avoid an airplane that may be a threat to you. My God, I could have had a midair collision while I was looking to the right. Or I could have one when I come back looking to the left if the intruder comes in from the right. So how do you scan? I don't know, I wish I knew. Somebody teach me quick—I don't want to hit anybody.

"What we're really talking about here is, how well does a little airplane stand out up there? Well, the fact is he doesn't stand out very well because he's small. You've got to get close to him to see him. Very seldom do little airplanes or other airplanes for that matter hit 747s. That's a big chunk of iron moving through the sky, and you can see it a long way off. A small plane may get close, but they don't hit them."

The FAA defines a near midair collision as an incident in which two planes come within five hundred feet of each other below twenty-nine thousand feet or when a pilot must take evasive action. Although to a layman such an occurrence might seem like a momentous event, pilots don't necessarily think so. "There was some hell being raised," says Pete Browner, "because we didn't think the government, necessarily the FAA, was processing all the near midair collisions. So one of the things we did at ALPA was to encourage pilots to file near midair collision reports. Pilots don't like paperwork, so if they see something going across the windscreen, they might say, 'Jesus, that was close. I wonder if we ought to report it?' And the answer is likely to be, 'Ah hell, no. It doesn't make and difference anyway. Nobody does anything.' So they don't report it. But with ALPA encouraging them to do so, right away the number of reports went up."

However, keeping track of near misses as a strategy for understanding how planes collide in midair has not substantially improved the system. On December 3, 1987, Mexicana flight 906 from Mexico City came within ten feet of Westair flight 3558 (flying as United Express) in the sky over San Diego. The Mexicana pilot maintained that he was thirty feet from the Westair plane, while Westair's chairman of the board claimed the two planes were no closer than one thousand feet. The Mexicana plane carried 138 passengers and a crew of 13; Westair had 13 passengers aboard and a crew of 2.

In November of the same year a United Airlines 767 taking off from Long Beach airport narrowly missed a single-engine Cessna.

United flight 76, with 108 passengers and crew had to dive to avoid the small plane. In December, 1987, United Flight 14 on its way from Los Angeles to Newark with 289 people aboard was speeding toward takeoff from Los Angeles International Airport at 175 miles per hour when it narrowly missed a taxiing Delta 737 by 200 feet. The NTSB called it a runway incursion; the FAA labeled it *pilot deviation*. And in another Southern California incident, an Alaska Airlines 727 narrowly missed a light airplane at seven thousand feet over the inland city of Pomona. The smaller plane had not checked in with flight controllers.

The limitations of commercial pilots and their aircraft, however, are only one aspect of midair collisions. The other involves the general aviation pilot flying on visual rules, especially in controlled air space. "The problem in the L.A. basin is that when the visibility's good, and everybody runs to go fly, the winds are very bad," says United flight engineer Lisa Johnson. "People don't realize the potential for wind shear. And then when the winds die down, the visibility is usually bad, and you can't see who's out there. Also, for the most part, the Sunday flying pilots really don't remain proficient. I've had all sorts of offers to fly people around, to the mountains and Catalina and San Diego, and I just won't do it. I could, but I figure it's not worth it for me. There's so much to keep up on flying in the L.A. basin, I think only a professional pilot who is flight instructing or flying charter or flies every day can really remain proficient. I just stopped my recreational flying."

Probably the worst midair collision in recent memory took place in the crowded Southern California skies Johnson describes. Pete Browner carefully followed the investigation. The 1986 Cerritos accident involved a collision between an Aeronaves de Mexico DC-9, flight 498, and a Piper PA-28. Fifty-eight passengers and 3 crew members of the DC-9 were killed. The pilot of the small plane, his wife, and his daughter also lost their lives, along with 15 people on the ground. Says Browner, "Cerritos is *the* midair collision that probably shouldn't have happened, because it happened in controlled air space. The ultimate thing that accident proved is that the see-and-avoid concept of traffic separation isn't worth the powder it would take to blow it off the face of the earth. We're killing a lot of people because of it.

"Of the small planes out there flying around, most of the pilots are fairly wealthy people. Let's face it, to be able to fly a light airplane these days, you've got to have some money. Most of these people are also well educated. They're not dumb. Even given that, the general aviation traffic density is high enough out there in the L.A. TCA [terminal control area reserved for commercial aviation] that the probability of them running together or hitting an airliner is greater there than probably anywhere else in the country. Maybe anywhere else in the world. And that basically is the problem that confronted the Aeromexico pilot that day.

"You can go the other way and say, well, if the guy flying the little PA 28 had never gotten up into the six thousand to seven thousand foot shelf of the terminal control area out there, the accident wouldn't have happened. Sure, absolutely—I agree. But have you ever tried to identify the TCA for Los Angeles? You ought to see that airspace as it's depicted to the controller on a radarscope. You ought to see what he's dealing with and then take a look at a terminal control area chart. You would have to be a navigator in the Strategic Air Command to figure out how to stay clear of that damn thing. And here's a guy flying a little airplane who is a meticulous individual by definition. He even had a brand-new TCA chart in his lap, trying in the only way he could possibly do to stay away from it. He had talked about the specific trip he was taking that morning with a distant relative who is a pilot in the Los Angeles area. They talked about how to stay clear of the terminal control area. So what concerns me is why the accident happened.

"You take a fellow like that pilot, who had every intention in the world of staying clear of the TCA, who understood the ramifications of getting into it. How could he possibly have allowed this to happen? That's what concerns me. Because you know he didn't go climb in that airplane in the morning with his wife and his daughter with the idea of running into that Aeromexico airliner. That was not his intent.

"What happened, I think, and this is pure speculation on my part—I have no evidence to prove it—involves the freeways in that area. There's the Artesia freeway that runs east and west down there, somewhere south of L.A. and down toward Cerritos, and there are about three or four parallel freeways that are southbound and hit the Artesia freeway perpendicularly. I looked at the TCA chart, trying to figure what I would do if I were an inexperienced light airplane pilot, how I would convince myself that I could follow my progress along the ground and determine where I was relative to those various sections of that TCA. And I think one of my strategies would be to orient myself by the freeways, so that as I went along the Artesia freeway heading out toward Seal Beach, I would eventually get east of that six-thousand- to seven-thousand-foot-layer of restricted airspace and then go ahead and climb.

"Had I left the airport with a turnout to the right, I'd have flown somewhere along or a little bit south of the Artesia freeway, and as I went across each of those freeways, the perpendicular ones to the Artesia, I would have looked at those and said, 'Okay, I'm *here* on the map, I'm *here* on the map, now I'm *here* on the map, now I'm *here* on the map, and now I can climb to about nine thousand feet to go on out to Big Bear, which is what he'd have to do to clear the mountains.'

"But supposing he miscounts by one, suppose his attention gets diverted. Maybe he and his wife are looking at the Queen Mary sitting down there or the hangar where the Spruce Goose is at Long Beach. Or his daughter asks him a question—we don't know what went on in the cockpit of the airplane—but he looks back and he miscounts by one freeway. And he says, 'Okay, now I can climb.' Up he goes, and wham! Simple. I don't know that that's the answer to it, but I mean, why else? He wouldn't inadvertently go up there and climb into the TCA. The receipt for the TCA chart was found in the back of his car at the airport; he'd just bought it the day he left."

In fact, the NTSB report of the Cerritos accident indicated that the pilot may have been doing just what Pete Browner has suggested, navigating by freeway. The Piper PA-38 pilot had recently moved to Los Angeles and had only a little over five hours flight experience in the area. He was known to prefer navigating by landmarks, and the NTSB suggested that his inadvertent intrusion in the Los Angeles TCA was a result of his misidentifying one or more of the freeways that he was using to find his way. In reviewing midair collision data as background for its report, the NTSB also noted that the FAA began to delineate airport terminal control areas in the 1970s in an effort to minimize the incidence of midair collisions. By the time of the report, twenty-three such areas had been designated around the country. The NTSB noted that during the year 1984, TCA hub airports handled about eighteen percent of all reported domestic aircraft operations, which amounted to about sixty-four percent of passengers flying on U.S. domestic routes.

Responding to the suggestion that the Aeronaves de Mexico pilots should have been able to see the small plane for several minutes before the accident, Browner says, "Ridiculous. What the NTSB report will show you, if you look at the cockpit visibility study, is a series of dots which demonstrate as time goes by where that small airplane would have been on the Aeromexico windscreen. That's kind of misleading in that it makes one think that maybe for five minutes or six minutes that airplane was visible to the crew of that DC-9, which is not true.

"A crew of an airliner descending into the L.A. area and trying to pick up a little airplane like the PA-28 they ultimately collided with out there would have a very difficult time seeing him with the ground as a background, especially a residential area. It's like a camouflaged area down there, because the PA-28 was light-colored and the houses are light-colored, and it was a very clear day. Also, the two airplanes would have been perpendicular, and they were probably looking at a 30-degree angle at the profile of the fuselage of the small aircraft. They were probably not going to be able to see him very clearly until they were just about at him or just a little less than a mile separated them.

"And, of course, that's if they were looking right at him at the time and that they could pick him up and recognize what he was. After that they would have had to make an immediate turn to try and change the flight path of their aircraft.

"What did the NTSB end up saying about Cerritos? It seems to me that they identified the primary cause of the incident as the light airplane pilot's inadvertent transgression into the terminal control area. For the first time in as long as I can remember, they didn't blame the pilots for not complying with see-and-avoid. They recognized in that report the inadequacies of the see-and-avoid concept. Jesus, what a milestone. It's about time somebody with a little prestige, other than pilots, recognized that this is not the way you should separate airliners and light airplanes in an airport traffic area. Because if we keep this up, we're going to have some more dead people laying around. It's inexcusable. We've been fooling with it long enough now. Let's get rid of it; let's do it right. Of course McArtor jumped on it and said we're going to put T-CAS [threat alert and collision avoidance system] in the airplanes, but he did it in a way that instead of going for the Hope Diamond, we're going to get a cubic zirconium."

Browner is referring to the original regulation proposed under former FAA administrator McArtor, which called for all planes operating within forty miles of 254 domestic airports and flying higher than six thousand feet to be required to carry Mode C transponders to identify their position. However, the outcry from general aviation regarding the expense for small aircraft owners was such that the agency was forced to modify its proposal to 138 airports nationwide. Transponders are now also required on all planes flying above ten thousand feet and in a thirty-mile radius of this country's twenty-seven busiest airports. Additionally, the legislation required that, by 1990, all planes operating in Airport Radar Service Areas surrounding 109 medium-size airports must carry Mode C transponders.

"If you think about it," argues Browner, "back in the early days before we had radar, *all* flights operated on the see-and-avoid concept. And we had midair collisions, didn't we? Like the one over the Grand Canyon [in 1956 a TWA Super Constellation and a United DC-7 collided, killing 128 people, at that time the worst accident in domestic aviation] and the one over Brooklyn–Staten Island [in 1960 a United DC-8 collided with a TWA Super Constellation while both planes were being tracked by radar; everyone aboard both planes died]. So we said, 'My God, we've got to put radar in.' That was the be-all and end-all, because that old radar antenna is going to go around, and the controller is going to see all these airplanes, and he'll point them all out, and we'll never have another collision.

"Well, that didn't work either, did it? We still had midair collisions. Then they said, 'Well, my God, what we'll do, we'll put altitude reporting on the transponders on the airplanes so that we not only know where they are azimuthwise, we'll know how high they are. And we'll keep them separate.' But we 'still have midair collisions, don't we? So maybe what we need to do is put the collision avoidance information and responsibility back in the cockpit where it belongs, with the pilot. And give him the tools to work with to perform the job adequately, something other than his eyes. The controller has a lot of other responsibilities. Really, his *only* responsibility is separating known instrument-flight-rule targets. Reporting and separating VFR—visual-flight-rule—targets comes down on a priority scale much lower, and in some cases he doesn't even have to do it, depending on the air space.

"I think the public assumes that because radar and air traffic controllers are in place, traffic is being controlled." Browner stops and heaves a heavy sigh. "That's not true," he says solemnly. "That's not true at all."

CHAPTER 7

Technology and Air Safety

The paradox of automation is that it works very well when it's not needed; it doesn't work very well when it's needed. It reduces workload when the workload is low, and increases workload when the workload is high.

—EARL WIENER, retired pilot and
NASA human factors consultant

To celebrate the introduction of 747 service to the South Pacific in the early 1970s, Pan American World Airways staged a festive inaugural flight from Honolulu to Australia for travel agents, news media, and related public relations people. The plane scheduled for the celebratory trip was a new Boeing 747, just released from the Seattle factory, flight-tested and accepted by Pan Am. Among the VIPs on board the Australia-bound 747 that day were two representatives from the Boeing factory riding shotgun in the cockpit.

Although Pan Am's chief pilot and other invited guests were not scheduled to join the flight until Honolulu, the trip was to have originated from Los Angeles International Airport with a full load of passengers. And although the real celebrating wasn't planned to begin for another five hours, there was an air of expectancy aboard the big plane as the cockpit crew prepared to depart the gate and begin taxiing toward the runway. The atmosphere of anticipation faded quickly, however, as the pilots discovered they had lost pressure in one of the plane's four hydraulic systems. To fly the trip as planned was now impossible, and the crew radioed the control tower that they were aborting takeoff and returning to the gate.

Rex Chamberlain, then a Pan Am pilot, tells the story as it circulated within the Pan Am pilot group. A cursory inspection of the airplane's exterior revealed a spill of hydraulic fluid beneath the 747's huge tail section. The Boeing engineers joined Pan Am's ground crew in taking a more complete look at the aircraft, and when they had completed their assessment, the incredulous investigators were forced to conclude that not one, but all four of the plane's hydraulic systems had failed, an occurrence described by Boeing engineers as a statistical impossibility. Since the hydraulic lines are the mechanism with which pilots control the aircraft's flying surfaces, failure of all four systems rendered the plane virtually unflyable.

Boeing had designed the 747 so that each one of the plane's four rudders was attached to two of the plane's four hydraulic systems; each system had a supply and return line through which the hydraulic fluid flowed. The high-pressure supply line was designed to withstand a pressure of three thousand pounds per square inch, but the return line could sustain a working pressure of only one-third that amount. The problem on Pan Am's brand-new airplane was that the supply and return lines had been reversed on *all* four hydraulic systems. The result was that lines designed for a thousand-pound pressure were carrying fluid at three times that amount. The overloaded return lines had, in effect, sprung a leak and caused the entire system to fail.

According to Chamberlain's insider account, the subsequent investigation revealed that the error in attaching the hydraulic systems had been made at the Boeing factory on the 747 assembly line. Human error had defeated the theoretical calculations of the engineers who had factored in what were thought to be all contingencies, from age deterioration to component reliability. What they hadn't considered, however, was the effect of human error on their supposedly fail-safe system.

Human error of another kind was involved eight years ago when another 747, this one operated by Japan Air Lines (JAL) on a domestic Japanese flight, crashed into the side of a mountain, killing almost all of the 500 people aboard. Investigation revealed the cause of the crash to be failure of all four hydraulic systems. This time the failure was traced to an improperly executed repair to the aft pressure bulkhead. The resulting explosive decompression produced mechanical damage to the airplane's structure that took out all four of the hydraulic systems.

Dick Riley describes the horror of trying to fly under such circumstances. "You're fighting for your life. It was probably thirty minutes from the time the bulkhead blew and they hit the mountain. We know that an airplane can fly without a tail from the incident when a B-52 came back from doing research on mountain waves, hit a wave, and lost the whole vertical stabilizer and rudder off the airplane. They made it, but they had a mechanical backup on their flight controls."

Even before the South Pacific fiasco, and long before the JAL disaster, Pan Am had another near-fatal incident when one of its 747s plowed through the approach piers on takeoff at San Francisco International Airport. The damage to the plane's fuselage knocked out three of the four hydraulic systems, and an angle iron came precariously close to taking out the fourth. Incredibly, in designing the placement of the hydraulic lines, the engineers had not considered the possibility of external damage to the fuselage. Subsequently,

Boeing changed the routing of the hydraulics so the lines are not positioned so closely.

Nor does the 747 have a monopoly on this kind of failure. The cause of the crash of United flight 232 at Sioux City, Iowa, on July 19, 1989, was the loss of all three of the DC-10's hydraulic systems, which were destroyed when the number two engine blew apart. The resulting damage to the hydraulics meant that the crew lost control of the plane's flying surfaces, steering, and brakes. In an article in *Airline Pilot,* the magazine of the Air Line Pilots Association, Capt. Alfred Haynes described the drama as he and his copilot, engineer, and a United flight instructor riding in the cockpit attempted to land the disabled aircraft. Haynes referred to what happened to them that day as a "once in a billion" occurrence.

Aside from carrying more passengers than any other airplane, at the time of its introduction, the Boeing 747 represented a whole new dimension in aircraft flight control. During the early days of aviation, when planes were smaller—and therefore lighter—and their engines less powerful, pilots controlled their aircraft by exerting direct physical pressure to foot pedals and steering mechanisms. Their physical efforts were then transferred by cables to the plane's various flying surfaces. As airplanes became larger and more complex, however, the effort required for control eventually outstripped the physical ability of the crew in the cockpit. It was at this point that aviation entered the age of hydraulics, systems of pneumatic lines filled with fluids that amplify the pilot's natural muscle power, somewhat in the same manner as the powered controls in an automobile make it possible to drive a car with less effort. To protect against the loss of hydraulics and its far-reaching consequences, aircraft designers traditionally depended on the principle of manual reversion; that is, if all else failed, pilots could control the airplane through their own physical effort.

The weight of a 747 is such, however, that manual reversion is not a viable backup option, and Boeing engineers decided instead to base their new design on the principle of redundancy (systems duplication). As Dick Riley tells it, justifying its decision to eliminate manual reversion, Boeing announced that its new design philosophy would produce an airplane capable of flying with what in engineering terms is called ten-to-the-minus-ninth reliability. In providing the plane with four duplicate hydraulic systems, Boeing cited research data indicating that a simultaneous four-hydraulic-system failure on any given flight was a virtual impossibility within half a million years of flight time.

"So now we know," says Riley coldly, "that half a million years is really only sixteen, because it took just sixteen years for an event to occur that was unforeseen by the people who crunched the numbers. Each of the individual situations has been addressed, but the basic problem still remains—if all four hydraulic systems fail for whatever reason, that airplane is uncontrollable. The strange thing is that in 1969, when we accepted our airplane, I wrote up this particular happenstance, and it was signed off by all the engineering types. So my standard answer now is ten-to-the-minus-ninth reliability takes sixteen years."

The sometimes rocky marriage of human intelligence and technological gadgetry is one of the hallmarks of the twentieth century. The promise that has elevated technology to almost divine status in the Western world is the capacity to free humans from mundane tasks, releasing them for more complex work. This in turn makes the individual a more efficient and cost-effective resource. There is no doubt that technological advances in aviation have been accelerated by developments in defense and space, making it possible to fly airplanes more cost-effectively, safely, and reliably. In the increasingly complicated world of modern aviation, the automation of flight systems, the means to control them, and new methods of cockpit display and reporting mechanisms were probably inevitable. Modern airplanes are far too technologically complex, air safety regulations far too involved, and the airways far too busy to expect that two or three people in an airplane cockpit can function effectively without some form of hefty automated assistance.

The application of technology to aviation systems has not been without repercussions, however. Of primary concern is what human factors experts call the human-machine interface—how the human utilizes the technology. Secondarily there is apprehension, especially among pilots, about the extent to which technological modification should be applied in the industry. One case in point is the two-pilot, two-engine wide-bodied aircraft.

Among its other innovations, the original Boeing 747 benefited from a series of developments in electronics that decreased the physical workload of cockpit crews. Another leap, made possible in part by microprocessors and digitalization, combined with advances in avionic design and improvements in the jet engine, resulted in even more technologically sophisticated, long-range transports. Previously this kind of aircraft had been powered by multiple engines: the Boeing 747 has four and the Lockheed L-1011 and McDonnell Douglas DC-10 have three. The era of the 747-400, however, also introduced the 767, a wide-bodied jet powered by only two engines, and the 757, an aircraft of similar design developed for short hauls that is now being used by some airlines on nonstop transcontinental flights and being considered for overwater Pacific flights. Within the industry there has been concern about the utilization of these new two-engine planes on long-range overwater routes.

"The 747 spills as much fuel just taxiing around Kennedy Airport as the new planes burn all the way across the ocean," says Rex Chamberlain. "I've burned six or seven thousand pounds of fuel just taxiing a 747 out to Kennedy for departure. The modern twin-engine transport will fly 150 people across the ocean on a lot less fuel than a big airplane will. The airplanes we're talking about are the Boeing 767 extended range and the Airbus Industrie A300 and A310. The key element here is not a smaller airplane, but the number of engines.

"What we're concerned about is a double-engine failure. We're talking about an airplane losing all power. In the worst-case scenario, it would be at night over the North Atlantic, gliding down without power to pancake into the ocean, into what could be fifty-foot waves and water so cold that if you were down there in a Coast Guard cutter, as each wave broke over the rigging, it would form ice."

With surprising vehemence, Bud McKenzie concurs. "Two engines over water is to me absolutely anathema. There was some talk of using a 767 for the presidential party and someone said, 'We can't put the president on a two-engine airplane over water.' And yet we can put hundreds of people on a two-engine airplane over water. The logic is nonexistent as far as I'm concerned. An airplane full of people with one engine operating, it just doesn't make sense to me. The morals of it are just unacceptable. Because you don't have anything left in terms of insurance or redundancy, which is what modern aviation's been built on.

"And how much experience do people have in terms of ditching in the water anymore? The people who have experience ditching in the water you can probably count on one hand. They told us when we came back with our fighters from Europe that if we went in the water over the North Atlantic we had about a minute."

On the other hand, Brad Prescott, who is a few years younger than McKenzie and Chamberlain and has spent a great many hours flying two-engine corporate jets, doesn't seem that concerned. "Two-engine airplanes don't bother me. I've flown two-engines around the world and it never bothered me. If you had an old piston-driven airplane, I'd like six engines—piss on four—I'd want six, because I know how bad they were. Jet engines? I've been in aviation since 1969, and I've never shut an engine down because of a failure. I've shut an engine down because of a false warning like a fire warning or hydraulic leak. In twenty-two years and ten thousand hours, that's pretty good."

Regarding the crew complement on the 747-400, where the use of sophisticated electronics has made it possible to eliminate the flight engineer, Bob Scott has some opinions. Scott is currently flying the original 747, the product of the collaboration between Boeing and Pan Am. "Boeing says, 'Ah, it's just a two-man airplane, no problem. It's as safe as a 737. You do it all the time in a 737.' But this airplane carries 400 to 500, maybe even 600 people. It has four engines, not two. It's 231 feet and four inches long. The wings are going to stick out farther than anything we've ever flown before. They're going to have to modify the taxiway at Los Angeles so there's enough wing clearance. And this airplane is going to be flown by two people.

"Now two people can probably handle it most of the time. Provided nothing goes wrong. Just as soon as something goes wrong, those two people are going to have their hands full. Yeah, it's a less complicated plane to fly; it's simplified tremendously. But it's doggone *different*. Fortunately United Airlines is going to run the pilots through a full-blown school, thirty days, and we'll get all the simulator time we need. Because the operating concept is completely different.

"In writing the SOPs [standard operating procedures] for the new 747, we have decided that when we get ready to push the airplane back and start the engines, we won't move until every control is positioned properly so that when we get out to the end of the runway, we can take off. Right now, we have two or three items that we have to accomplish as we go into position for takeoff—turning on the landing lights, a couple of other minor things. My opinion is that we should not move that airplane with only two people on it until everything is in position, which means there are going to be some delays. But it's better to delay than to find out that you haven't done something important.

"It is our belief—the committee that's putting together the

SOPs—we believe that the pilot and the copilot must flight-plan together. . . . With the new plane, the captain must do the cockpit setup that the engineer formerly did, along with all the things he's got to do himself: check the flight plan, insert it into the flight management system, check all the way points, make sure that's done. . . . The copilot is going to have to go through the cockpit, look at all the consumables, anything that might have been used en route that should be replenished, and find the logbook; that's always a chore—you never know where it is—and make sure that maintenance is working on all the open items. I don't see how they can possibly launch one of those things on an originating trip in less than an hour and ten minutes. With three people, we do it in one hour. But in a two-man operation you're going to have to hurry or you're going to be late."

TWA captain Hank Barnes, who flies the original 747 from the East Coast to Europe, compares his experiences in a three-person crew with those of two-person 767 crews who fly the same route. "I know that the guys on those planes complain quite a bit coming out of Europe. During the evening when you leave the East Coast of the United States, air traffic control sets up tracks out there. Going out, going to Europe, you've got quite a bit of time before you have to get into the track. You get a clearance from New York to your destination and then the controllers in Gander [Newfoundland] give you a clearance over the track, whichever track you want.

"Say you want 'X-ray' because that's the best one for winds and everything. They may say, 'We can't give you X-ray at thirty-seven thousand.' So you're on 'uniform' or 'romeo' track. That's been no big deal, changing like that, but coming eastbound out of London, you've got to get into your track right away. When you leave Shannon [Ireland], you're on track. And a lot of these two-man crew people get very busy at that point, because sometimes ATC can't handle all the traffic. Especially in the summertime, they can't take a 767 at a certain altitude on a particular track, so they'll change it. So now you've got two guys flying this airplane, *managing* it, so to speak, and one guy's got to get his head down in the cockpit, to find out now what track air traffic control is talking about it. Over on the west side of the Atlantic, you've got plenty of time to figure it out. Out of Europe, those guys have got their hands full.

"It may sound like I'm a union man about this issue, but I think they're going to need a third man. It doesn't necessarily have to be a pilot. Because that's a dead-end job for a pilot, but it needs somebody to do the paperwork, to do the communications. If the guy wants to take a rest, he can keep the other guy awake on those long hauls. I'm kind of thankful I'm not in that seniority bracket where I have to deal with this. But it's being done that way, and until somebody puts one in the ocean, they're going to keep on doing it. The union made a mistake a few years ago when they agreed to the findings of the President's commission and took the flight engineer off the airplanes. United had an extra man on the 737 when it first came out because that's what the union wanted for traffic watch. I admit I like a third set of eyes in there, especially over here in the United States." Barnes is referring to the President's Task Force on Crew Complement, a review commission established by Pres. Ronald Reagan to investigate eliminating the flight engineer from airplane cockpits. The issue was brought to a head in part by the introduction of the MD-80. The commission upheld the ruling by the Federal Aviation Administration on the two-person MD-80 crew and concluded that in the future all aircraft, including wide-bodies, could be certified for two pilots.

"To me, a third set of eyes is very important," Barnes continues, "especially around terminal control areas. I had a near-miss about twenty years ago when we were coming in from the East on an all-nighter. L.A. center had cleared us to ten thousand. Then they came back and told us to level off at twelve thousand. We were just approaching twelve thousand, so we leveled off and asked why. All of a sudden this jet fighter came past us from behind; I mean, I could I could see his helmet and the numbers on his tail.

"They keep telling me about all this automation," says Barnes, "but what happens when the automation doesn't work? That autopilot can always fail. In the back of my mind is always the thought that anything made by man, a mechanical thing, can always fail somewhere along the line. How much backup do you build in the airplane? The best computer they've got going is right here, in the head."

"The case for the third man in the crew, and I don't mean the relief pilot, is a very real one," says Bob Scott, as he continues his discussion of the two-person cockpit. "And it's a very legitimate one. How do you think employees would act and operate if they know the boss would never appear . . . in the workplace? The captain is in command of the airplane, from the nose to the tip of the tail and everything in between. However, in a two-man crew—and on anything under eight hours you're going to have a two-man crew—how comfortable do you feel with just one pilot up front? What you're effectively doing is putting a barrier right there at the cockpit door. On my own before a flight, I go in early, even right now with a three-man crew, so I can get in there, get the flight planning done, go up and brief the flight attendants, tell them who I am, and if they have problems they've got help up in front they can count on. A lot of them feel that they can't count on the crew up front. That's because a lot of pilots say, 'The cabin's your problem; I don't want any part of it.' That bothers me. If a guy accepts the pay and the title and if he doesn't do the job, it's dishonest. It's also not the safest way to operate when a pilot figures he's in command of the cockpit only."

"We're going to treat it as a whole separate airplane," says flight manager Craig Donlevy, speaking about the 747-400. "As a matter of fact, the FAA inspector went out today on a 767 because he's going to be on the 747-400. He wanted to get refamiliarized with the 767. We're going to wind up with four people in the cockpit. One captain and three copilots on the long haul. Literally you'll have fifty percent rest time. With four people and two seats, half the time can be in rest. So on the long hauls, it will be pretty nice."

Donlevy's description is similar to what the FAA eventually decided: two full crews, one a senior captain and copilot, and their backup, a junior relief crew. As Donlevy suggests, this enables all four pilots to get some rest—approximately three to five hours on the thirteen- to fifteen-hour trip. This contrasts with the requirements for the 747 both Bob Scott and Hank Barnes fly, which uses the traditional three-man crew with one international relief pilot and allows significantly less rest time per trip. Additionally, the crew quarters on the new 747 are designed to enable longer rest periods, whereas the older plane has only one pull-down bunk.

Although the two-person, two-engine aircraft may raise eyebrows among pilots and some aviation experts, it is far and away the automation of aircraft systems, new methods of flight control, and innovative warning and alert systems that have occasioned the most discussion. Among pilots, the views differ as to whether automation has lived up to its promise. For Craig Donlevy, whose management job means he must be current on such issues, the Boeing 767 represents a whole new generation of flying. "The airplane's incredible," says Donlevy. "I flew it down to a Category 3, which is a seven-hundred-foot RVR [runway visual range] landing, on a *slick* runway, and the way I felt safest was to turn on the autopilot, let it autoland, and let the autobrakes brake. When I went to manual brakes, I really had my hands full. Had that equipment not been available, I couldn't legally have landed. And from a practical standpoint, I couldn't have done it either. I would have had to go someplace else. So what this means is that on days like today when it's foggy, a pilot can complete his mission. Those kinds of systems put some real reliability into an airline's operation. If the manufacturers ever generate the capability of zero-zero landings, there literally won't be any more foggy days. Think about it; we won't have to deal with things like we had to today, diverting a flight to another city and then trying to get the people from there to where they wanted to go."

For some pilots, however, upcoming developments may not be as exciting as Donlevy describes. Retiree Bob Keystone, who flew the original 747 in his last years as a commercial pilot, suggests the conservative view. "People say to you, 'Well, the whole thing's easy; you've got all those computers.' Baloney. The computers do what you tell them to do, but as far as flying the airplane, they don't have any brains. They don't do the thinking. The pilots do that. Normally I would fly the airplane, or my copilot would, from takeoff to cruise altitude, and then, when we were landing, about 200 miles out we'd take it off autopilot and take it the rest of the way. There are several reasons for that. First, the changes that go on all the time in vectors and traffic avoidance and things like that are easier to do by hand than they are to make the autopilot do it. Also, the autopilot doesn't need any practice, and I do. If I want to continue to be a precise pilot and a very capable pilot, I have to fly. I can't just sit there and let the autopilot do all the work."

The experts have a word for Keystone's apprehensions; they call it *peripheralization,* a reaction that occurs whenever automatic equipment is introduced into any organizational system, whether it be banking, medicine, or aviation. As humans feel themselves moving away from the center of the "action," toward the periphery, this can translate into feelings of loss of power and position, individual anxiety about the ability to apply the new technology successfully, and fears about how the system might be affected by human error. For many older pilots, this can also contribute to feelings of being devalued.

"I know all of us pilots are overpaid and underworked," says Pete Browner. "But I can think of a couple of dark and stormy nights that I would have been delighted to have the critics along in the airplane. I will say this of pilots—the environment in which we operate hopefully is very routine; however, every once in a while it can be very hectic. I think it's gotten worse during deregulation. . . . If you give me a bushel basket of bananas and a gorilla, I can teach him how to fly an airliner in three or four days. I probably won't even need all the bananas in the bushel. But when things start to go wrong, is that gorilla then going to be able to reason the thing out? Will the guy who developed the electronic checklist have thought of all the variables that go into the decision-making process and how the pilot problem-solves?"

Younger pilots, who have grown up with computers, seem less anxious about the challenges of automation and its affect on their piloting role. American Airlines flight engineer Jason Young speaks about the modern airplane. "You can't know everything about these complicated planes, and the airlines don't expect you to. What good is it to know a junction box has failed if you can't fix it? Maybe you can figure that it might lead to some other problem, but your manuals have the information you need to know as far as the manufacturer and the FAA are concerned. And everything on an airplane is backed up. Your brakes, for example, are a separate hydraulic system and even if that goes, there's accumulators in the brake systems to give you brakes. And if those fail, you have air bottles that'll get the brakes working."

Fellow American Airlines pilot Max Neeland is not only comfortable with current automated systems but anticipates the next generation of computerized equipment, *flying by wire*, a system wherein the signals from the cockpit currently being carried through hydraulic lines and cables are transmitted electronically. "Flying by wire is the wave of the future," predicts Neeland enthusiastically. "I don't see anything wrong with it. In fact I'm sure it's more reliable than we have now. Right now in a DC-10, all of the flight controls are manipulated hydraulically. Think what it takes to plumb that kind of a system with a hydraulic pressure under three thousand pounds per square inch. I would rather trust wires carrying an electrical signal than all those fittings that could leak or lines that could rupture.

"When you move the control stick in the Airbus [the first planes to be controlled by wire], it sends a signal to a computer that decides which of the flight control surfaces on the airplane should move and how much. So in some ways it's making the airplane simpler, and it's saving weight. You're not plumbing the airplane over long distances with heavy cables to move the valves."

Ann Alexander, who flies the MD-80, a McDonnell Douglas redesign of the DC-9 that gives airlines with medium- to short-haul trips the sophisticated flight management systems and navigational capabilities of the wide-bodied jets, admires her airplane but remarks that its complexity has affected ease of function and requires more mental concentration. "You have to be thinking a lot more. It's a difficult airplane to land, for example. You can hand-fly it, but you have to make constant corrections. You can't just trim it up and fly it without any hands like you can other airplanes. When I first started flying this plane, my ego went right under the table. . . . This particular airplane has the autoland capability; it can land by itself, which is fun to watch. You want to *do* something; you actually almost have to sit on your hands. It comes in constantly correcting, and when it finally gets to fifty feet—that's the magic number—the power comes back, and the nose comes up, and it just kind of drops in. It takes it all the way down the runway, right down the center line. I watched it and I said, 'I can't believe this machine just did that.' "

But while the younger pilots may feel little or no apprehension about increasingly automated planes, many of the older hands like Rex Chamberlain fear the new systems contain risks. "When pilots talk about the modern cockpit they have two concerns," says Chamberlain. "One is, as the aircraft manufacturers automate airplanes, the pilots have effectively been removed from the control loop. We don't displace controls anymore and push throttles and rudders in order to fly the plane. Now the automated equipment does that. The other loop is the information loop, which flows from the flight instruments and tells us how fast the plane's going, how high we are, whether we're accelerating or decelerating, what the true course is and so on, including things like the oil temperature.

"Pilots have not really objected to being increasingly removed from the control loop. They don't say, for instance, 'I don't like autopilots; I want to fly the airplane.' What they are objecting to is being removed from the information loop. The difficulty is that the engineers are questioning the pilot's need to know this kind of information. . . . It's like playing a video game, and what the engineers are headed toward is a system that says in effect, 'Mr. Pilot, you tell the computer what today's problem is, and it will take care of it.' For example, let's say today's problem is to move the airplane from Los Angeles to Tokyo. The difficulty is that the pilot—any kind of a pilot in the traditional sense, especially one with a pre-automation background—is going to be a little uncomfortable with all these blandishments. He's going to want to look at this thing and say, 'Well, if you're so smart, Mr. Computer, tell me how you're going to go about this problem; where are we going to fly first?' And the computer's going to say, 'We're going to fly over Oakland first.' Then the pilot's going to say, 'What course and about how many miles?' Now the pilot already feels better because he's gotten a reasonable answer, and he's going to say, 'I think it can do it.'"

"It's a whole different way of learning about flying," says midcareer pilot Stan Page with his usual brusqueness. "It's programming the computer versus flying. On the one hand it's more fun, but on the other, you've got all this magic stuff and you want to learn how to make it work. That's the challenge of it—making it work right. And if you finally get it down to where you fly a perfect trip, then you can probably say, 'Okay, I've had enough of that shit.' How long does it take to get it down to a perfect trip? Probably six months. Because there's so many different ways you can learn to think like the computer thinks. You have to learn the computer's solution to the problem.

"I had to sit and draw it out, how the computer thought about it, because the computer thought differently than I did. First of all, I didn't understand that the computer is designed to save gas. That's one of its basic parameters. If you understand that, then you can understand the logic of the computer. For instance, in a descent it wants to take you up to a point, saw off all the power, make a descent, and land. That's the computer's ultimate solution. But air traffic control doesn't work like that. So the question is, if you're twenty miles from where the computer wants you to start down, how do you do that without spending a lot of gas? So part of the problem is understanding how that scenario works, and the other part is understanding what the CRT [cathode ray tube] is telling you about how the computer views the problem. You've got to understand what's on the screen; you have to understand the profile, and you have to understand that in three dimensions in your head. Then you marry this together, and you and the computer will get along just fine.

"I can see where this system, with the FMC [flight management computer] and the autopilot and the mode control panel and all of that automation that's in there someday is going to be data-linked to a centralized computer. So that after you take off and get the gear up and all that shit, you're going to give it to the computer. You're not going to have to talk to anybody because that computer is going to take you from A to B, and it's going to serpentine you through all the traffic. It's going to be done for you. That's what it's coming to."

Based on his human factors work, Bill Fredericks expresses another pilot anxiety: concern that dependence on complex cockpit instrumentation can produce a false sense of security and an erosion of traditional piloting skills. "Take our DC-8 freighter crash in Salt Lake City, for example. They had an electrical bus go out that affected power to one engine. In that airplane, the radio is normally put on the number two bus, but in this particular airplane, somebody put it on number one [which meant the crew lost ground communication]. A whole series of things happened right behind the power outage."

Fredericks presents his version of the incident. "First, the controller made a very small error; he didn't give a specific radio course on the VOR, and things started to deteriorate rapidly as the pilots tried to figure out where they were. They became so involved in trying to pinpoint their position relative to the mountains they knew were somewhere around them that nobody was flying the airplane. And when you get into a situation like that, your mind comes *off* the flying *into* the cockpit." Fredericks pauses to speculate on the cause of the accident. "And I'll lay you dollars to doughnuts this was what this guy was doing. He was watching the flight trajectory out of the corner of his eye, paying more attention to that than what was going on outside the airplane. By the time they got around to figuring out what was going on, the accident was over. They slammed into the mountain, and nothing was wrong with that airplane that they couldn't have landed with."

"There's always an underlying fear," says Craig Donlevy, "'if all this stuff fails, can I fly it? I've got to keep up that skill.' And if you think about it, all this is just information, and the ideal technique is that you should use it as it's called for. That way every flight isn't the same. On a VFR day you fly the plane manually, and you keep up all the skills. On an IFR day, when you really have to get down, you use the technology.

"There's never been more information at your fingertips. A good for-instance is on the 767 when you go to start the engine, the starting temperature limit of each engine automatically comes up; after the engine's started, it disappears. You can't do that with mechanical instruments. Anything you want, anything you can think of that you can do on a TV screen, these new systems can do. You get timely information that isn't cluttered. It's terrific."

But line pilots have been known to take a different view of the promise of automation. "Remember," warns Dick Riley, expressing a personal opinion, "the Boeing philosophy is, 'Don't tell the pilots anything.' Boeing thinks God lives in Seattle and works for the Boeing Aircraft Company. Don't get me wrong, the Boeing company is a national treasure—it really is. But the more of the airline business they have, the harder they are to live with.

"In the new instruments there are no trends in functions presented to the pilot. When something exceeds a certain given value, then it's identified and shows up on your computer screen as a problem. You won't be able to tell a generator temperature is starting to go out of limits until it goes out of limits. The Boeing engineers figure if they don't tell you, then it doesn't take time and work for you to monitor this. The Boeing people don't want to tell the pilot anything. Their rationale, if you dig deeply enough, is that pilots crash their airplanes. They had a paper written four or five years ago on the autoland function. There's eighteen pages in this technical paper, and if you distill down what they've said, you'll find they contend they have never had an airplane crash when the plane's been flown full autoland. Their conclusion therefore is that all landings should be flown fully automatically, and the pilots should never touch their airplane. Now what they don't tell you is how many times the pilot has to turn his autoland system off because it would have landed him off the runway. That never shows up in the data." In his discussion of the Boeing report, Riley is expressing his concerns about the future role of pilots in regard to automated cockpit systems.

"What they'd like to do and they haven't figured out how to do yet—or the state of technology's not there—is build an airplane where the whole thing will be all done automatically by computer and the pilot will monitor it. The problem is that historically people have proven to be horrible monitors."

"The whole thing has evolved into a philosophical debate about what information we give the pilot," says Rex Chamberlain. "The question is, can a system be humming away down there in the bowels of an airplane providing no information to anybody, just doing its thing, and if it stops doing it, no one would know unless it affects the dynamics of the airplane in flight?

"What we have," continues Chamberlain in a high, intense voice, "is a major divergence between the pilots as a profession and the engineers and aircraft designers as a profession. The pilots are saying they want to know what's happening systemwise, and the engineers are saying, 'We have done mathematical analysis, statistical analysis, and probability studies, and the reliability of this system is one failure in ten billion flight hours.' *This* system. There are other systems, and of course the more of these things that become critical, the more potential there is for developing a chain reaction among them.

"The idea is if you can construct the scenarios, you can design the equipment to take over. Whether you can construct all possible scenarios may be a question, and what we've seen to date is that these systems are kind of limited in their imagination. They tend to be rigid in their thinking. In other words, the emergency has to unfold according to a perfect scenario or the computer doesn't recognize it. Let me give you an example. Here's an airplane with two engines over the Atlantic in the middle of the night. We run out of oil on the number two engine, so we shut it down. Now we're flying along on one engine, and the fire warning goes off. Normal response to a fire warning is to shut the engine down and press a button that sends a fire-extinguishing agent down there, except that in this case, the pilot's going to say to himself, 'No way, I've only got one engine. I'm not going to shut it down. Let's spend some more time; let's validate this problem. Do we really have a fire? Let's let it demonstrate its presence in other ways. Let's make a visual inspection. Let's look for other indications. Maybe I'll have to operate with the fire for a while. But I'm not going to shut that engine down because I'm going to be in fifty-foot waves if I do.'

"Obviously you could design your system so your computer reasons to shut the engine down for a fire warning except if it's the only engine operating. But even that's an arbitrary situation. What if the fire warning is flickering? What if it's intermittent? What if it isn't just a fire warning? What if it isn't a black-and-white problem? What if it's gray? What if the little fire warning light's flickering dimly and then it goes out? And nothing happens for three minutes, and it flickers dimly a little bit and goes out again? Do we have a fire warning or don't we? See, a computer's not going to like that. A computer is going to say yes or no. A pilot's going to say, 'Interesting puzzle.'

"He's going to draw back on his experience; he's going to

communicate with the technical center of the airline. He's going to have the maintenance department look at the history of this particular engine through satellite communications, and maybe they're going to say, 'Oh yeah, we've been having this problem with this engine.' There are all kinds of resources the pilot can utilize to make a better decision. But the question is, are we really going to be able to create enough of the real world?"

Being out of the information loop, as Rex Chamberlain calls it, concerns pilots in a number of ways, in particular by creating anxieties about being relegated to monitoring rather than controlling the systems of their aircraft, as well as worries about skill erosion and uneasiness that their performance is being second-guessed by computers. While acknowledging these difficulties, human factors researcher Earl Wiener feels there are ways in which automated systems can be designed and implemented that would make them more effective and user-friendly.

"I don't see any reluctance on the part of the manufacturers to try to advance new technology," says Dr. Wiener. "In fact, some people think they've been advancing too much, which brings me to one of Wiener's laws: *Invention is the mother of necessity.* That means that once something is invented, you *have* to have it, and you've *got* to use it. The best example is the Xerox. Once Xerox was invented, then we had to have copies of everything. I still get letters every so often with Xeroxes of other letters attached to them. I didn't need the original letter, let alone all the Xeroxes."

A former air force pilot, Wiener is now professor of management science at the University of Miami. Tall, thin, and somewhat pale, he looks more like a closed-room engineering type than a pilot. Like Craig Donlevy, however, he has an exceptional ability to empathize with flight crews about human resource problems. His recent research in fact indicates that commercial pilots may not be as anti-automation as Chamberlain suggests, although this doesn't diminish his apprehension about how automated systems are being utilized.

"Bring the crew in as partners in this thing," says Wiener. "Don't treat them like dummies. I don't think you can play peeka-boo with pilots and say, 'We've got some stuff down there in the computer, but you can't have it. When you land, the wrench benders can get on the airplane and take a look at it, but we're not going to tell you.' In the 757 there's information hidden from the pilot that's available only to maintenance; it's switch-selectable outside the airplane in the wheel well. Boeing says it's maintenance-type information. Well, the pilots want it. There's one thing I think you can't do to pilots, and that is tell them there's information they can't have. Boeing feels that this is maintenance-type information, and they don't want the pilots to have it because they'll start getting into do-it-yourself solutions and whatnot.

"Of course, the pilot can't do any maintenance; he's not saying that. What he is saying is, 'I need to make a decision on this. It's information that could be useful to me in making a decision.' And I think that's the approach the designers have to take: Take a look at the pilot's concern. *Is* there information down there that he could use? But even if the answer's no, there's going to be resentment that somebody like a maintenance man can get on that airplane and get information the pilot can't get in flight."

Nor is information the only critical issue. "We believe that the high-tech aircraft calls for different piloting skills," says Wiener. "It's a different style of flying; it makes different demands on the human. There are more alternative selections, various ways to do things. This type of flying calls for more strategic planning and less manual work, more of what psychologists call *cognitive ability*."

Rex Chamberlain agrees. "The airplanes are very complex, and every time they add another black box, the pilots have more to do, not less. Instead of the radio operator worrying about communications and the navigator worrying about navigation and the flight engineer worrying about the systems, the pilot has to worry about all of them, plus air traffic, communications, the radio, and what's going on in the cabin. None of these things have disappeared as functional requirements, but they are falling on fewer and fewer shoulders, and instead of being the squad leader and having your squad out behind you, we're now down to two fellows. Most of the time this human-automation works fine, but to assure your adequate functioning in this situation, you have to take the initiative to keep yourself in the loop.

"We hear a lot about complacency and about boredom as the cockpits become automated, and there are [fewer] physical chores to do. The pilot is evolving more and more into the function of a monitor. Is the autopilot following the course? Is the navigational equipment providing reasonable navigational information? How are the systems performing? How's the fuel burn-off going? Even though the task is one of monitoring, there's a lot going on."

"People should be in the loop and let the computer monitor," asserts Dick Riley flatly.

Bud McKenzie agrees. "The paradox of automation is that you have to be paying more attention to what really is going on in the black boxes—are they doing the right thing? Did you program them properly? You have the time to react, but you don't want to *react*, you want to *act*. In other words, if you're planning to leave from San Francisco to let's say two hundred miles out in the Pacific heading for Honolulu, and you miss the entry point into the airway which leads across the ocean—as Hawaiian Airlines once did—you probably missed it for a reason. You didn't program the computer properly or you didn't hook up the computer to the autopilot or you've fallen into one of a number of various other little traps that can lead you down the primrose path. These things have happened, and the airplane's just going to kept tootling along as long as it has fuel. A word I like is *vigilance,* and that really applies today. In fact, it even applies more so in the paradox situation where you have highly automatic equipment. The more automated we become, the more there's the natural human tendency to sit back and relax.

"Things like misprogramming an INS or missing an airway happen because of human error. You get distracted somehow; some people in aviation safety call it *complacency.* That's kind of an iffy term, I think, because it doesn't adequately describe what's going on. I think most of the time it's a combination of factors—how the person is feeling at the time, for example. Some people bring their problems to work, which can distract them through the whole course of the flight. But the word *vigilance* for me just covers it all. It keeps you focused on what it is you want to pay attention to in terms of the primary factors.

"We all have faith in technology, but there have been many incidents and accidents that verify the notion that you should never fall in love with an airplane. Professional pilots or private pilots who have flown for a long time are prone to say, 'I love that airplane' or 'This is the greatest plane I've ever flown.' That may be, but tomorrow it might fail you. That's a real possibility. If something does come up, you've got to look at it very objectively. It's easy to say, 'I love this airplane; I'd like to save it.' But that's not what the name of the game is. The name of the game is get everybody on the ground safely, or if you're on your own and have a parachute and it's time to leave, leave."

Bob Scott describes an accident illustrating McKenzie's ideas. "It was a charter—a football team on a DC-9 going into Charleston,

West Virginia. When we started to analyze the tapes, we heard that two minutes before touchdown the pilots were commenting on a sign on an automobile agency over to their right. One of them was saying, 'Yeah, I just bought a new whatever it was.' They were chatting about their sports cars while they were a minute and thirty seconds from the end of the runway. So they weren't thinking about the approach, were they? They crashed short of the runway and killed everybody. They had an instrument landing system, and there was no excuse for it.

"Complacency is something everybody has to guard against. You do the same thing time after time, and it always works out perfect. So you think, 'Well, it's going to work out perfectly this time.' In fact you don't even think about it. But you'd better. You might make a mistake otherwise. Sometimes things happen very quickly in a short space of time. The flight attendant will call from the back; you'll get a radio call from down in ATC, and maybe something's going on in the cockpit at the same time too. You just have to be able to constantly devote your attention to what the primary things are at the moment."

The work of Earl Wiener and his associates suggests there are ways to design automated systems to minimize the potential for complacency and to retain pilots as active participants, to bring them in on the action, so to speak, when there is still time for them to be effective. "I've written a lot about this," says Wiener, "and I think it would not be too difficult to have warning and alerting systems that are predictive like the one of Airbus. Other warning and alerting systems, even elaborate ones like Boeing's EICAS [electronic integrated crew alerting system], are still limited to alerting the pilot to the problem *after* it's become a problem. How fast can somebody react? The answer is by the time they react, even if they react fast, it may be critical. Why find out when you're over the Atlantic that you've got a slowly disintegrating system? Why not find it out early in the game?

"Forecasted or predictive alerting systems would completely revolutionize the alerting systems of today because they would continually recompute and forecast future parameters. If something could be forecast to be out of limits, the system would then warn the crew that in so many minutes or so many hours such and such is going to happen, and don't you want to do something about it *now?*

"Let me give you an example. The 757 starts off with I think eighteen quarts of oil, and there's a set point at five quarts. If you hit five quarts, you get a message about it. Now the question I raise is, why not forecast? The system knows the oil consumption; why wait till you get down to five quarts—and you're halfway across the Atlantic—to give the fellow the warning? Maybe he knows it; he's already thought about it. Maybe he knows what to do about it, but tell him.

"I interviewed an Eastern captain who told me he had developed his own little procedure for when he flies coast to coast. Every hour he would call up the EICAS page on his CRT screen. Normally it's blank unless there's an alert, but you can call it up anytime and look at it. In the old days they used to get up out of the cockpit and go back and walk through the cabin and look at the wings. Nobody looks at the wings anymore because there's nothing to see. So the hour came to do this, and he called up the EICAS, and lo and behold, one of the engines was low on oil. What could he do? Well, he did an intelligent thing; he continued to watch it. At that time he still had plenty of oil, but it was clear after watching it for a while that he was never going to get to San Francisco. So he had to make a decision where to go. If he had a potentially disabling problem, why continue out on over the West, which is sparse in airports. He talked to the company about it, and they determined they could land at an airport that has maintenance facilities and facilities for passengers, so they could possibly get passengers onto other planes. Had he not done that he probably would have gotten two-thirds of the way across the country, and when he got to five quarts the alarm would have gone off. And at that point, five quarts wouldn't have been enough to get him to his destination, and who knows where he would have had to land. It wasn't a critical emergency, but he might have ended up in some remote airport where there were no passenger facilities, and the chances are he wouldn't have ended up at an Eastern Airlines maintenance base.

"So that's what we're saying about warning and alerting systems. Don't wait till you've reached the critical point. The interesting thing is that there are techniques for doing that right now; we computer forecast all the time. All you need is a few lines of computer code for each parameter you want to forecast."

In his research Wiener has found that one way pilots attempt to escape the dullness of prolonged monitoring and to minimize skill erosion is to spend some portion of their time hand-flying the airplane. In a study of pilots training on the MD-80, Wiener discovered, for example, that individual pilots developed personalized programs for what they call hand-flying. One pilot's plan might be to hand-fly one leg of each trip, another's to hand-fly up to ten thousand feet. Another pilot might fly one raw data approach on every trip. Wiener took to calling these the pilot's personal FARs [federal air regulations].

"Each person set his own rules and then followed them as religiously as if they were actual FARs," says Wiener, commenting on what he found in his study. "I think that's fine, but I also think as we get to know more about this, we can't leave it up to each person's imagination as to whether to fly a flight-director approach once each trip. I think that's going to have to become part of the training regime." Wiener pauses and smiles sheepishly. "Every time I hear someone say, 'I turned it off and flew it raw data,' I smile to myself because in the airplanes that I flew, that's all we had—raw data. I didn't know it was raw data, though. I thought it was hard stuff. Now in my later years, I find out that I was flying around with nothing but raw data. And I'll tell you, if anybody ever took any of it away, you felt that the world was coming to an end."

Although the issues of monitoring and skill erosion are important human factors considerations, there are other complications related to the human's adjustment to highly automated systems. One of these is the contention that automation can affect the magnitude of cockpit error, circumstances alluded to by Bud McKenzie in his discussion of the need to be diligent when interacting with automated equipment. Says Wiener, "One of the things that we have found in our observations and accident and incident reports and interviews with flight crews is that automation is an error-amplifier. Errors may be less frequent, but they tend to be larger. Digital systems in flight increase the possibility of large blunders while tuning out those little 2- and 3- and 5-degree errors we were used to making in the past." Illustrating his point, Wiener refers to what he calls the precise twelve-hour error—setting the digital alarm clock correctly to the right minutes and seconds but for the wrong part of day—evening rather than morning.

"We are going to need more crew coordination and better intra-crew discipline. Modern machines are forcing that because there seems to be in the automated cockpit a breakdown of the traditional who does what." In a 1989 National Aeronautics and Space Administration study, for example, Wiener and his researchers found that the configuration of the automated cockpit, which includes personal key pads for each pilot, makes it difficult for one pilot to see what another is doing; most important, the captain may not be able to oversee the work of the first officer. The study also concluded that automation tends to blur the traditional distinctions of who's flying the airplane, that is, which pilot has control at any given time and which is providing backup—a central principle of cockpit procedures. In addition, the fact that the copilot may be younger and more adept at computer programming skills may cause the captain to turn over his programming responsibilities in a tight situation or the copilot to rush to help inappropriately. Wiener notes that this blurring of crew responsibilities is not nearly as likely to happen in a more conventional cockpit. The study concludes that airlines utilizing high-technology equipment will do well to take a look at their crew coordination and cockpit resource management programs, both in task assessment and standardization. This is particularly important since the need for pilots has brought younger and less-experienced young men and women into the cockpits of major carriers, and these more junior pilots, who by virtue of their relative inexperience may have less-developed piloting skills, are likely to be flying more sophisticated airplanes.

"I call this the era of clumsy automation," says Wiener. "We have remarkable capabilities, but the pilot interface is clumsy. It requires too much of the pilot; it requires too much head-down time, which everybody's concerned about—too much time with the pilots looking in the cockpit when they should be looking outside, at least one of them should be looking outside, especially going into an area like Los Angeles. But a place like Los Angeles also becomes a programming-intensive area. At times you end up with both pilots sitting there programming when at least one should be looking out the window, especially with two-person crews and especially going into a terminal area. That's why automation doesn't work very well where it's needed the most. Manufacturers go bananas when they hear me say that, but it's true. Automation works very well at cruise; it works very well at the high points of flying and the early parts of descent. But when the pressure gets on, people tend to turn it off. Pilots call it 'taking it off.'

"Flight guidance systems and sometimes the autopilot—the things that were put in there to help them—turn out to be a workload generator rather than a workload reducer. They turn it off because they feel that their workload is increasing, and they can go back to a more primitive form of flying and do it better. That's the paradox.

"Are the manufacturers listening? They're listening and getting mad. The manufacturers tend to be defensive, and yet they're professional people; they want to turn out a better product. They don't want accidents. . . . Yes, two people can handle an airplane, two people in a well-coordinated, well-trained crew supported by more pilot-centered automation than we have today. *Pilot-centered* means a design philosophy similar to what we started with—the idea that the equipment should be there to help the pilot, to serve him, not that the pilot should be at its mercy."

Perhaps the ultimate in computerized airplanes now flying is the Airbus line of aircraft, two-engine planes manufactured in Europe by a consortium of companies from Britain, France, what was West Germany, and Spain. An essential design element of the equipment is that the plane's computers are programmed to inhibit incidents of pilot error by limiting the plane's response to what it considers dangerous or ill-conceived commands. Although there was a spurt of pilot protest when the planes were being considered for use by foreign carriers, nevertheless Airbus aircraft have now been certified by foreign carriers and by the FAA for use in U.S. domestic service. As of yet, however, American aircraft manufacturers have not jumped wholeheartedly into "fly-by-wire." In their designs for the 757, 767, and 747-400, Boeing engineers included computerized controls for the engines, but hydraulics still control wing and tail surfaces. McDonnell Douglas's MD-11, which has replaced the DC-10, is fully computerized but with mechanical backup systems for the wing and tail surfaces.

"What about this fly-by-wire stuff?" smiles Dick Riley, settling into the subject. "The last time I talked to Boeing about it, they indicated they're not putting it in their new airplanes simply because they don't feel it's mature enough yet. There are too many problems with having all of your eggs in one basket in a fly-by-wire control system. Airbus is doing it because they can save about two thousand pounds in airplane weight, which is what the cables and the pulleys would require. Two thousand pounds in a three-hundred-thousand-pound airplane. But that's two thousand pounds that's going to have to be hauled around for the entire life of that airframe, which is twenty-five years.

"In the Airbus plane, the controlling device is in the cockpit, and the actuator is on the flying surface. They put a computer in the middle, and the computer filters the pilot's input. What that says to me is that the pilot's not smart enough to know he can stall his airplane or he can overstress his airplane, and the computer then is supposed to be smart enough not to let him destroy it. What it means ultimately is that the pilot really has no control. He's not flying the airplane, he's flying the computer. The computer has the ultimate decision about whether or not what the pilot tells it to do is reasonable and whether or not it should allow him to do it.

"We've already had a situation with Airbus, that accident in France." Riley is referring to the 1988 crash of an Airbus A-320 delivered to Air France two days before the accident. The plane was under the control of a seasoned pilot who was also the airline's expert on the new aircraft. The plane was carrying a full load of passengers, some of whom had won a seat on the flight in a local promotional contest, and was making a low pass over the airport as part of an air show when the accident occurred. Investigation centered on speculation that the pilot was flying too low and had waited too long to boost power.

"That airplane just flew right into the trees," says Riley. "No pilot in his right mind, I don't care what he's doing, would fail to bring the nose up and flare when he's flying into trees. Did the computer override the pilot on this thing? It looks to me like they didn't get any response from their engines when they pushed the throttles forward; couple that with a computer that's not going to allow the pilot to stall the airplane; it won't allow the angle of attack to exceed a certain fixed value. They probably got slow, the guy pulled back on the stick, the computer said, 'No, you can't go any more than you already are.' Why the engines didn't respond is beyond me. . . . Obviously he didn't get thrust when he wanted to."

Are pilots going to put up with these computers monitoring their performance? "We don't have any choice," says Riley. "The airplane manufacturers are going to build the airplane, and the airlines are going to buy it. And it's going to be federally certified as safe, and the airline will say, 'Here it is, guys, fly it.' Is it safe? I guess we're a bunch of skeptics. Not all pilots—I am. I'm a skeptic. It's going to have to prove itself to me."

"The engineers are saying that they don't envision the pilotless airplane," says Rex Chamberlain as he completes his arguments. "They say what they envision is eventually an automated flight in which there will be a pilot sitting there with a sign in front of him that will say, 'In case of emergency, break glass.' And he will break the glass, undo the safety wire and lift out this old flying stick, a side-arm control stick that is never used except in emergency. And he will able fly this thing wonderfully with all these finely honed pilot skills he no longer possesses because he doesn't do this any more. But without the airline pilots and their safety organization and so on, there would be nobody speaking up and saying, 'Let's go a little more slowly with this stuff.'"

Is technology in the cockpit a solvable problem? Earl Wiener ponders the question a moment. "It's an improvable problem. Not solvable, but improvable. I've been accused by the people at Boeing as being anti-automation, anti-technology, and all of that. Well, far from it; I'm just saying that I think we need a less clumsy, more pilot-centered, more intelligent automation. And if this is a phase we have to go through in an evolutionary scale, okay. But I think we ought to be looking ahead rather than pretending the emperor has clothes on when he doesn't."

CHAPTER 8

Home and Life-style

*The airlines have adopted policies in more
recent years in which they don't consider
pilots people. They're just part of the
machinery. But they are people, and when
you use them without concern for normal
rest periods and normal lives, they get stale
on the job.*

—BOB KEYSTONE, retired United Airlines
747 captain

The blare of the alarm fractured the silence of the unlit room. Somewhere a dog barked, and the sound rolled across the early morning, its harshness muffled by the fog and the bulky trees that hung over the low house. Under the heavy quilt, a man moved. His thin hand reached out to quiet the noisy clock. Almost motionlessly, he laid back on the pillow and fought to remember. Slowly out of the dimness it came. Five o'clock.

As he lay in the silence, she moved beside him, disturbed by the clock and his movements to stifle it. Her soft form shifted slightly, and as she turned to reach for him, he fought the impulse to return her embrace and sink back into sleep. Instead his hands sought the strong lines of her face; his lips brushed against her mouth. "Is it time?" she murmured.

"Yes," he answered as he held her close and stroked the fine strands of her pale hair. "Yes, it's time." He could hear her sigh, feel the slight movement away from him. And then in one swift movement, she was gone. Out of bed almost as if she had already erected a shield against the hurt. He lay back against the sheet and heard her walk into the kitchen, heard the big Samoyed dog rouse himself from his spot next to the window and tumble along after her. He lay thinking, unable to move, still feeling the warmth of her in the bed. Somewhere outside a dog barked again. The sound of home—a dog barking in the full, round air of the country.

He knew she was struggling against it, against the anger, against his controlled nonchalance, against this shrill interruption in the new relationship they were trying to build. He also knew she wouldn't mention it. Nor would he. Because there was nothing either of them could do.

He climbed out of bed, crossing quickly into the bathroom. There he moved by rote—soaking his beard for a shave, stepping into the hot water of the shower. By the time he finished and was dressed, she had coffee ready. She had changed into jeans and a shirt and was standing by the kitchen window. She offered breakfast, but he accepted only the mug of strong coffee, tasting its bitterness and looking out through the window at the lightening sky. A rooster crowed, and they both turned toward the clock.

"It's time," he said, putting down his half-finished coffee.

"I know," she answered, still holding her own mug against the wool of her shirt. She thought a moment and her face brightened. "Why don't you leave some things here? Then you could go right to the airport."

He winced, turned away, answered absently. "It's all right. It doesn't take that long to stop at my place."

"Have a good trip," she replied, chastened by his response. Moving toward him, she kissed him lightly on the eyes. "Be safe," she whispered. "Be safe."

Drawing back from her, he saw that she meant what she said. But he also knew that for her he was already gone. For her, he had left the night before, even before they had climbed into bed and tried to talk. She had already prepared for it. And she had done it better than he. It would come to him later—after he had gone back to his apartment and changed into his uniform and loaded his flight bag and suitcase into the car.

After he had checked in at flight operations, met his crew, reviewed the flight plan, worked his way through the briefing. Only after he had climbed into his seat in the cockpit and attended to the thousands of details that would distract him before the flight. After they had taken off and had been handed off to the first departure controller, only then would it hurt. But by then he would be in the groove; routine would overtake the longing, and then he would be on his way. He would really be gone, gone for four days. He knew he was stretching the limits of this new relationship with his erratic schedule and being absent for long periods of time. There would be no stopping by for dinner or a walk on the beach with the big white dog. That night he would be in Chicago. The next night it would be Philadelphia and the next, Boston. Working, meeting the challenges of the job he loved. "It's in my blood," he told her when they first met.

· · ·

"**I** went through a lot of relationships because of this job," says Brad Prescott as he attempts to explain the challenge of living "normally" in the face of his piloting life-style. Prescott was married when he decided on a career as a commercial pilot, the father of three children. Today he is divorced and his children are grown. He remains a bachelor, however, and it is a choice dictated somewhat by the demands of his work. "There's no doubt in my mind a couple of the gals couldn't handle my life-style. When I was flying charter I was gone sometimes thirty-five days at a time. Mostly my relationships were with working girls, but they really weren't career-minded. They wanted a relationship where the man was home a lot, where he was around to do things. That doesn't work, not with a pilot.

"Now that I look at it, that was the whole problem with the one girl I thought a hell of a lot of once—I was gone too much. And she was the type of person that needed somebody around. You develop a second sense after a while. Some women just can't handle it. They need that security blanket. If both of you have a career, I think that can help. I saw my relationship with the last gal I lived with go down the tubes because she didn't have a career, and we didn't have any quality time together. When I'd come home, we'd spend a lot of time together, but it wasn't quality time. I'd rather see somebody a little less and have that be quality time rather than just *being* there. And I have to admit I enjoy my free time. I went through a two-year period that was really rough. At forty I felt like an orphan; I felt like my life was upside down going backwards. I had lost my wife and my family, and I was really down on relationships because I felt I put a hundred and fifty percent in the first one, maybe too much. I know I'm not the family-oriented person I was when I was young.

"I raised three kids, and I was close to them. I was lucky to be able to raise them before I really started being away from home much. I went to PTA; I was the mom of the neighborhood. They can say that flying improves a marriage; they can say that bullshit, but it's not true. I think flying is very hard on families. Not only because you're gone a lot, but when you come home you're not always ready to unwind into a family life. Plus your wife has to take up a lot more of the slack. And I think wives resent that a little bit. They think you've been out partying all the time you're gone on a trip. I'll tell you what, I bet there's not five percent of commercial pilots who have been married only one time. Most of them have been married three times or more."

Asked if flying affects his social life, Jason Young answers, "What social life?" Young is ten years younger than Prescott, and also a bachelor. "I had a girlfriend who couldn't understand that and then I didn't have her anymore. But it also can work the other way. Take someone like Greg Scott; he wife doesn't work. He might be gone for maybe two or three days at a time, but he's home maybe fifteen days out of the month. That means they can go places with the kids if they want to, or fly somewhere together on their passes. Most people can't do that."

By the standards of the nine-to-five world, pilots live an unusual life. Not only does their job take them away from home a good deal, often there is little regularity in their schedule. Families have to adapt to the inconsistencies of a pilot's comings and goings, which can mean periods of functioning without the man—or woman—of the house, only to have that person home full-time for days on end, attempting to integrate in a home life that in many ways has developed without them. Some pilots feel that the adjustment has become more difficult in recent years, when schedules have become more demanding and can mean longer trips that result in spending more home time catching up for the next trip.

"It's a slightly random way of life," says Stan Page. "It's not structured. The only time you're really structured is when you have to go to work."

From the vantage of his twenty-eight thousand hours, retired pilot Bob Keystone offers commentary on the reality of the piloting occupation. "The layovers are the worst part," says Keystone. "We always said we want them to use us. And when they don't use us, leave us alone. Leave us at home. They expect us to be able to go to bed and go immediately to sleep and get eight hours. You can't do that. . . . We're people, and the fact is that we're likely to be up all night one night and maybe have a day off and then fly all day the next day. There's no rhythm. As a matter of fact, I suffer today from that. I don't sleep well at night because my night circadian rhythm was never allowed to continue on in a routine fashion. I never know when I'm supposed to be asleep and when I'm supposed to be awake."

"He's up at one o'clock in the morning," says Keystone's wife, "but he can't go to sleep until four or five. And he wants to go to sleep at seven at night. His clock is completely off."

In general, commercial pilots are amazingly nonchalant about the schedules demanded by their flying and the life-style that results. Most claim to be unconcerned about the effects of fatigue, and the industry in general appears to be uninterested in the issue and about the consequences on pilot performance. Federal regulations specify the number of hours a pilot can fly in a given time period on domestic runs, but duty times for international flying are not precisely defined. For these, pilots depend on the protection of their union contract. In addition, airlines offer no training in coping with the demands of long-haul flying or flying on the wrong side of the clock or adjusting to disorienting schedules. Pressed, pilots may offer complaints about the impersonality of computer scheduling or about losing the flight managers with whom they were able to develop relationships and negotiate trip changes. For the most part, however, pilots speak as if the schedules they fly have little or no effect on how they do their job. As one psychologist suggests, however, people who adjust to unusual routines over long periods of time often become numb to their effects. Added to this is the pilot sense of duty and belief in the necessity of getting the job done regardless of circumstances.

Although the sleep/scheduling equation is particularly acute on long-haul international trips, domestic schedules can also take their toll. Greg Scott explains, "One of the trips on the DC-10 I don't like, and a lot of guys don't like, is when we fly an all-nighter from L.A. to Newark. We get into Newark about six in the morning, Newark time, which is three A.M. our time. We sleep for about four hours and try to get up during the day, because the next day we have a six-forty-five A.M. pickup. This means we've got to get up at five-forty-five, which is two-forty-five in the morning L.A. time. How do you sleep for that?

"In the airplane, at first you're usually pretty good, but about halfway through the trip you begin to fade. You're looking at gauges that don't move; you just try to stay awake and keep yourself going. I'll change the frequency when we're supposed to. I'll push the buttons for the other guys when it's supposed to be done. You get tired, and there's no way around it."

"We'll have one guy occasionally nodding for a few minutes," says Scott's friend, Jason Young, "and actually in the long run it's the safest thing. At thirty-five thousand feet you've got lots of separation from everybody. You don't have all the private pilots out there flying low around you. If he's going to rest, as far as I'm concerned, let the guy rest up at cruise for half an hour or forty-five minutes so that when he gets down to low altitude and we're back to getting going again, he's on top of it.

"People criticize us for being up there bullshitting. Well, okay, let's think about it. If you're not going to talk, what are you going to do? You can't read a newspaper, you can't read a magazine or a book—what are you going to do? Are you just going to sit there for fourteen hours? Let's see how awake you are after *that*. You've *got* to talk. The hard part is when you've got a captain that you have nothing in common with or who doesn't want to talk. I flew with one guy who insisted on keeping the cockpit dark at night. Talk about nothing to do. For four or five hours, you look at the clock. You think to yourself, 'There's another minute.' That's hell when you're trying to stay awake.

"I think it's more fatiguing to fly at night because your body naturally sees it's dark. It's time to be asleep. Sure, you can feel the effects anytime you fly all night, and anybody, any human being who's tired, knows your reflexes and thinking slow down. There are certain times that you really hit the peak low, especially when you're not on a consistent night schedule.

"The people who plan our trips for the month are thinking about the best crew utilization, and they come out with these trips—we call them 'ominous trip pairings.' You'll get a trip where you leave L.A. at twelve-twenty in the morning or at one-oh-seven, something like that. You go to Dallas, get in at six, sit there till eight-thirty and then come back to L.A. My opinion is if you're going to have somebody fly from one in the morning till six, they should get off at Dallas and go to sleep. There's no reason why they should sit for two and a half hours and have to fly back. Even this trip that I'm going to do tonight—we go to Chicago, then on to Newark. There's no reason we should have to go on past Chicago. We could fly all night and get in there at six in the morning, which would be the equivalent of four in the morning West Coast time. That's not bad, but then we should go to sleep.

"Another thing they do, and again I don't understand it, they've got crews that are based in New York or Chicago or Dallas. Why don't they fly the seven A.M. departures and let us fly the ten A.M. departures? The logic of it is money. The longer you're gone, the more they have to pay you. You're paid, at least we are, so much per every hour we're gone. I guess all of this is just an example of how the ground people don't think about what pilots have to go through. *They* don't have to stay up all night. They don't realize our reflexes and our thinking processes slow down. Plus this system has been working for so many years, and there hasn't been a problem. But that doesn't mean there would not be or could not be."

"If I take a four-day trip, by the time I get home on the fourth day, I've just have the crap beat out of me," says Ted Goff, who still flies the typical short-haul trip Western Airlines pilots specialize in, both before and after the merger with Delta. "I can never sleep in a hotel as well as I can at home, especially when we're switching time zones. You fly from L.A. to Chicago and go to sleep, and when you get up in the morning, it might be three o'clock here. And then the next day you're in Anchorage, and that's a time zone change the other way. So you come home after three or four days, and you're really tired. That's the big one that I notice healthwise. The only other thing I guess you worry about is catching syphilis or something . . ." Goff pauses, smiles, and then gets serious again.

"The other day we were ending up a four-day trip, leaving Dallas on what we call a standard instrument departure. We got halfway through it, and they changed it a little bit. I misunderstood what the guy meant. It wasn't anything big, just a misunderstanding. But that's why you've got two guys up there—to check on each other. You have to do it fast, though. You don't want to dink around flying 600 miles per hour discussing what the guy said.

"Sitting around waiting to fly is bad. We go to Salt Lake, and we wait around for three hours for our next trip out. What do you do for three hours? What you *do* is waste time. Of course if it was really bad, and if we were really smart, we'd bring some books and study something, wouldn't we? Does anybody ever do shit like that? Hell, no. We talk to each other. We cruise the lobby, look at the people. Eat, get fat. I usually end up in the cafeteria drinking decaf and reading the paper or a book. Or I write my kids a note a lot of times. Our union contract with Western said that if we were stuck for anything past four hours, they had to get us a hotel room. The idea was to penalize them so they wouldn't sit us around like that. With Delta there's none of that. They can sit us around; there's really no limit."

From his corporate flying days, Brad Prescott remembers the effects of fatigue. "You'd leave here about five o'clock at night, and you'd get over to Europe, for example, about ten o'clock in the morning. Okay, now you've got a problem. You're tired, but if you go to sleep, you're going to wake up at ten-thirty, eleven o'clock at night, their time." He pauses, drums his hands along the top of the table. "So you force yourself to stay up, but usually then you're so goddamn tired that you don't sleep good when you do go to bed. Over the long term I think it's detrimental. Then there's dehydration. You're up there for hours, at seven thousand, eight thousand feet above sea level; it's very dry air, extremely dry. Most people don't realize how fatiguing it is to sit up there hour after hour. I get so bored. You just hope you can stay healthy.

"They really know very little about jet lag, so what I do is I do what I feel like. If I feel like eating breakfast, I eat breakfast. I used to fly with this guy who amazed me. We'd go back East, and we'd be getting up at two-thirty in the morning to come to the West Coast for a seven o'clock flight, which is four A.M. our time, and he would have to have a full-course breakfast. He'd say, 'Oh, I can't start out the day without my breakfast.' And I'd say, 'Wait a minute. This isn't day. Your body doesn't know that. We just came from California yesterday—you haven't gotten acclimated to this time zone yet. Don't tell me that shit.'" Prescott stops and then says thoughtfully, "I don't know if I'm durable, but I very seldom get sick, and one reason I think is because I *don't* change my eating habits. I don't try to play mental tricks on my body. I don't try to change it."

Medical research suggests that people coping with the effects of jet lag can force themselves to accomplish routine tasks such as shopping or sightseeing or being part of a meeting, but they cannot *will* their bodies back to a normal sleep or eating schedule because it takes time and the return to established routine for the human body to resynchronize itself and restore its normal twenty-four-hour, circadian rhythm. Pilots talk about catching up. They become expert at taking naps; they buy sleep machines and use the snow pattern on hotel TVs. They wear sleep shades and sleep with blackout curtains so they can rest during the day. But does it help?

Bill Fredericks thinks these techniques are helpful but they're not enough. Acknowledged as an authority on the effects of fatigue and sleep deprivation, Fredericks has participated in a variety of international symposiums. In addition, he teaches a course in aviation and human factors, and he has lectured extensively. Anxious to address his subject, he goes directly to the point. "The way the FAA gets around the issue is by contending that fatigue is a subjective kind of thing. Well, in some ways it is. But that doesn't mean it isn't there. It's a concomitant of all the things that happen to you during the day—whether you've got stress as a result of family problems, whether you eat properly, whether you're feeling the effects of dehydration. In an airplane the air is about eleven percent humidity; desperation and perspiration, that's about it. When you start drawing fluids out of your body, your blood volume diminishes, and you don't get the blood to your brain. The food we eat on these airplanes is awful—the crew meals. All of these things play a role in fatigue.

"Unfortunately, however, both the NTSB and the FAA say that fatigue can't be measured. That's true, but sleep loss and sleep deprivation *is* measurable. And what's more, it's costing crews. We did an analysis of the Western [Airlines] accident in Mexico City, where the guys slammed into equipment on the runway and everybody was killed—and ALPA refused to put it in their final report because it addressed the issue of sleep deprivation. ALPA's position is to stay away from it because it's the only tool we have to negotiate with. The last flight-time/duty-time regulations were negotiated in 1981–82; they came out in 1984–85, and they are so far away from reality that it's sad. There wasn't a physiologist among the bunch that developed the regulations."

Fredericks considers sleep deprivation a contributing factor in the 1978 midair collision between a PSA [Pacific Southwest Airlines] 727 and a Cessna 172 over Lindbergh Field in San Diego. When the NTSB refused to consider the mass of information Fredericks had assembled in support of fatigue and its effect on the accident, he created a paper trail, writing directly to NTSB board members and to members of Congress. The accident that focused so much of Fredericks's energy killed 128 passengers, the entire PSA crew of 9, and 9 people on the ground and shocked the aviation world. Fredericks's opinion of the accident is fairly simple. "Although it was not cited by the NTSB, it is possible that sleep loss due to poor scheduling and short-term nutrition deprivation may have exacerbated an already confusing situation that existed that day. Both planes were flying on visual flight rules, basically using the see-and-avoid concept. The controller gave them some faulty information, which he corrected, but then things got worse from there."

Working with PSA, Fredericks reenacted the duty-time–rest schedule of the flight deck crew aboard flight 182. On Friday, September 22, the crew reported for work in San Diego at three-thirty P.M., flew their scheduled flight, and checked out the next day, Saturday, after twelve-fifteen A.M. at Oakland. That same Saturday they checked in at Oakland at six-forty-five in the evening and arrived home in San Diego at nine-forty the same night. The next day, Sunday, they checked in at four-ten in the afternoon and checked out at ten-fifty-three that night in Sacramento. On Monday they reported to the Sacramento flight office at six A.M. The accident occurred at two minutes after nine on their approach into San Diego.

Fredericks's assessment of the crew's layover and off-duty times adds up as follows: from Friday to Saturday, they had six hours and thirty minutes of off-duty time; Saturday to Sunday, the time was expanded considerably, to thirty hours and thirty minutes. Between Sunday and Monday, however, they had seven hours and seven minutes of time off in which to prepare for their Monday schedule. Translating these hours to available sleep time, Fredericks calculates that from Friday to Saturday the crew had five hours of possible sleep time, and Sunday to Monday, five hours and thirty-seven minutes, which he suggests was insufficient for maintaining alertness. Citing a stack of sources he has accumulated on the subject, Fredericks maintains that the effect of one single night's sleep restriction (when a person gets only five hours of sleep instead of the usual eight) is sleepiness the next day, a condition that can manifest itself in feelings of exhaustion, lethargy, depression, drowsiness, and reduced ability to cope with interpersonal relationships. Fredericks feels that transcripts of cockpit communications on that day in 1978 bolster his contention that the PSA crew was suffering from that condition. At one point, a flight attendant is heard to ask the captain, "Tired, *are* you?" To which the pilot answered, "I'm draggin'. It was a short night."

Thinking over the dynamics of the San Diego accident, Fredericks identifies another possible factor. The coffee shop at the layover hotel was closed when the crew arrived, and members appear to have had their last meal at six o'clock on Sunday evening, fifteen hours before the accident. The conclusion Fredericks draws from his evidence is that the fatigued members of the cockpit crew, trying to follow the San Diego controller's information about traffic in their area, misidentified that traffic. The crew did not identify the small plane about which the controller warned them until seven seconds before the two planes collided. In fact, a subsequent ALPA report raised the point that there were three light planes and a 737 in the area when air traffic control was communicating with PSA flight 182—a Gruman T-Cat and not one but two Cessnas, a 172 and a 150. The contention of the ALPA report is that in identifying the Cessna 150, which was on a different track from the Cessna 172, the PSA pilots thought they had identified the plane with which they eventually collided. In fact they never did see that airplane until it was too late. Fredericks feels the fatigued PSA pilots were unable to pick up discrepancies between what they were told to look for by the air traffic controller and what they actually saw.

There are differences between mild fatigue, from which most people suffer from time to time, and what the experts call chronic fatigue. Mild fatigue is usually the result of inadequate rest, excessive physical activity, extreme cognitive effort or mental concentration, or some combination of these factors. If the situation that causes the fatigue is not relieved by a period of sleep or recreation, and it's prolonged from day to day, the condition can deteriorate into chronic fatigue, which can be difficult for a person to recognize. According to at least one expert in the field, individuals in this situation may be particularly oblivious to poor performance or any performance deficiency they exhibit under these circumstances.

Symptoms of this condition include reduced reaction time, decreased motor skills; channelization, which refers to decreased ability to see the big picture; impairment of judgment and decision making; short-term memory loss; reduced alertness, possibly manifested in pilots as "sloppy" flying or a tendency to be easily distracted; expanded tolerance of error; degradation of visual perception; loss of initiative; and increased irritability and intolerance, along with feelings of depression.

"A problem comes at you in an airplane differently than in training school or in a textbook simulation," says Rex Chamberlain, as he describes the correlation between fatigue and what can happen in the cockpit. "You're not sure what's happening at first. We make checklists, and we do these drills to get ready for these things, but when they really happen in the airplane, they never come at you clean. The first thing that happens is inquisition. 'Does anybody know what's happening? Something's not right—what is it?' We have a single indication of a problem. And the first thing we do is we try to validate that indication. What it amounts to is that we have a little piece of a puzzle. We'll spend a fair amount of time analyzing what at this point may be a deteriorating situation. Unfortunately this type of thinking degenerates dramatically with fatigue.

"The next thing that goes is tolerance, your ability to communicate and work with the other people in the cockpit or in the back of the plane to do your best to correct the situation. You get short, you get caustic, you get unresponsive, you get defensive. Another thing is tolerance of error. The guy who's deeply fatigued will sit there; the speed won't be quite right or the trim won't be quite right. There'll be displacement from the glide path or the localizing path such that he would normally take immediate corrective action to put the airplane 'back in the groove,' as we call it. When he's tired, he'll sit there and tolerate the situation.

"What the FAA and what the airlines are saying is that we have been unable to demonstrate that fatigue has been a factor in any accidents. To combat the argument that it might be, the airlines have taken crews that are fatigued and put them in the simulator and then had them shoot approaches or shut down an engine and other standard maneuvers that demonstrate competency and proficiency. And they do it. They do it successfully, even though they're deeply fatigued. And the airlines therefore equate that performance with an adequate level of safety. The real experts, however, the people at NASA, for example, who have recognized, scientific competence in this field, will talk to you about specific things like short-term and long-term memory skills, abstract reasoning power, tolerance of error, and so on. In a deeply fatigued state, there *are* certain types of skills that hold up, skills associated with crossing the needles, putting the airplane on instrument approach, and setting it down on the runway—in short, executing standard procedures, the things that the airlines test for in the simulator. What goes downhill in fatigue is the ability to reason through a new situation."

Chamberlain is concerned that United Airlines flight management personnel don't understand long distance international flying and the potential for developing fatigue-related problems. "When I tell a flight scheduler that he's creating a safety problem with some of the schedules because they're very unrealistic from the physiological point of view, he says, 'I'm not a pilot; there's no way I can judge safety issues.'"

"I would say that long distance flying is one of the biggest problems that aviation has got," says Craig Donlevy. "It really is. We need faster airplanes. That will come eventually, and everybody will laugh. We used to fly long flights to Hawaii, real long flights to Hawaii because we were flying DC-6s. Someday we'll say, 'Remember when we used to fly 747s to Sydney? How did we every stay up in the air for fifteen hours and keep our sanity?' Because it will be done in four or five hours. Guys like the Pan Am people have been doing it forever. Their bodies have a built-in tendency to be able to do that, and eventually I'm sure we could do it, too."

"But if you look at those guys, they look old," says Bud McKenzie, speaking of the Pan Am pilots now flying for United and the United pilots flying the old Pan Am routes. They age fast on those trips. You see the pilots and the flight attendants both, they look old, their skin is dry. They're pale."

Corrobating McKenzie's observations is the fact that as far back as 1937, a physician by the name of R. E. Whitehead began describing symptoms of what he called *aeroneurosis* among Pan Am pilots, a condition he diagnosed as the result of the concentrated flying of the newly introduced Clipper service in the Pacific. Pilots were then flying a Pacific duty period of 135 hours in two-week stretches, which at that time was the equivalent of nearly two months of domestic flying. The pilots would fly from the West Coast to Honolulu, nearly a twenty-hour flight, after which, instead of resting for the twenty-four-hour period common in domestic flying, they pushed on the next day. The pilots themselves complained, wanting in-flight rest facilities for the Pacific crews. Pan Am responded that not only was the idea too expensive, but it also breached the tradition of single command at sea, the model on which commercial aviation is based.

"Sure," says Craig Donlevy, "there's a lot of undesirable flying. But you have to assess the question of whether it's just undesirable or whether it's really unsafe. And to do that basically you have to go out and fly it yourself. One thing we're finding in the Pacific is that you can't just fly one trip and make a determination, because the effects are cumulative. And determining whether a trip is really unsafe is such a subjective thing. The experts are trying to quantify it, people like NASA-Ames, and ALPA, and even the company, but there is no resolution at this point.

"A good example is a 747 reserve pilot. He gets up at eight o'clock in the morning. He stands reserve all day long. And at five o'clock in the evening the crew desk calls and says, 'We've got the ten-ten P.M. departure to Sydney.' He's been up since eight. It's logical to assume that he's probably not thrilled by the assignment. Some of this is covered by contractual arrangements, and what we're always trying to do is match the physiological realities with the schedule. But you have to rely on the person to say straight out, 'I am available' or 'I'm not available.'

"And the challenge of that situation is that he's got to answer the question of why he isn't available when the next guy behind him on the list is. But at that instant in time the crew desk doesn't ask those questions; the guy makes his determination and then he stands accountable for what he does. Then I have to follow up on it. Logically I understand what the guy's saying, but the agreement is in the contract. This is what both sides agreed to. He's supposed to make himself available somehow, someway. I don't care if he takes two-hour naps during the day, or whatever.

"One of the problems with reserve is that before in United's culture, you could fly anything because it wasn't very long, and it was no big deal. Now that we've gotten into the longer trips, we've got a whole new set of problems. This is a real tough time because both sides have agreed to the contract stipulations, and I'm supposed to administer it. I don't necessarily agree with it. I see some times to break it. But I've got to ask those basic question of why a guy wasn't available. He can say, 'Well, I was tired,' and I can say, 'Yeah, I understand, but still . . .'

"I don't really worry about the fourteen-hour trips as much because we've got the fourth person, the relief pilot, and everyone can go get some quality sleep. What's tougher is when you send a three-man crew out on an eleven-hour flight, which is legal. They have to be on duty during the entire flight. They can't get any rest."

Bob Scott discusses his fourteen-hour Los Angeles to Sydney trip, currently the longest stage length commercially flown and known among United pilots as the "Sydney Strangler." After the Los Angeles to Sydney leg, Scott flies additional trips in the area and arrives back home approximately nine days later. "According to our contract, nobody is supposed to fly internationally over twelve and a half hours. Legally we could do it without the extra pilot, but the contract says put the extra pilot on. That's something we fought for because we get guys worn out and under a lot of pressure from changing time zones time after time after time. One fellow walked into the flight office off that trip, and the gal in the office told me she thought she was going to have to get up and help him sit down. He'd just landed out there with three hundred people on board, but he staggered into the doggone office. He was just exhausted.

"What generally happens on a flight like that is that each of us will take a one-hour break, starting immediately after takeoff. The engineer will take the first one, and usually whoever is going to make the landing will take the third rest period. We make a schedule out of it. By that time the people should have been finished with their dinner, and I'll go down and check the cabin and talk to the flight attendants to see how things are going. And then I get back in the seat, and I'm there until maybe the third rest period. The engineer will take his three hours in the sack, then the copilot, then me. That's about the only way you can do it. But even then, by the time you land, you're pretty well bushed.

"I have great respect for the Pan Am guys and what they've learned to do over the years, not that it doesn't take its toll. Rex Chamberlain puts it very well. It's his opinion that people who are in this operation and have been in it for some time are running on pure adrenaline and that one of these days when they get down to a critical situation—-a low instrument approach, maybe—that shot of adrenaline is not going to come. And it's at the end of the flight that you have to do your finest work. Hopefully there's going to be somebody there to take up the slack."

Aside from the question of whether pilots get adequate rest, there is also the more subtle issue of the effect of scheduling on their life-style. Do flight schedules allow enough regularity and stability, for example, to prepare pilots to return to the job and its responsibilities? As Craig Donlevy has suggested, there's no central watchdog organization that keeps tabs on pilots, how they work, or how they live. Pilots rely on their own individual sense of preparedness. Where and how they live is totally up to them. Bachelors Brad Prescott and Ted Goff both own homes, while Max Neeland, just newly married, lives on a boat in California close to his San Francisco domicile and commutes to his wife in the Virgin Islands, where she lives with her children. Instead of commuting to his job, Neeland, in effect, commutes to his marriage. Bud McKenzie, on the other hand, favors a routine that is more conventional. "I've flown with a former Pan Am guy who lives outside San Francisco and flies out of Los Angeles to Hawaii a lot. I guess that's what he wants to do, although I don't understand it. Why be married? He and his wife never see each other. The Pan Am guys are also some of the ones we see a lot in our employee assistance program because of problems with fatigue and with alcohol. I don't know how they live like that."

Industry estimates suggest that between forty and sixty percent of pilots who work for domestic carriers commute, but so far no one—the FAA, the NTSB, or the airlines—has investigated whether commuting, especially before a trip, affects a pilot's readiness. Pilot arguments to the contrary, common sense suggests that the extra time spent traveling must have some effect. "The airline pilots, in my judgment, have got some decisions to make on how they want to attack the scheduling problem," says Stan Page. "They've got something to contribute. If you're going to be flying international out of New York, you don't want to be living in Honolulu. That's *your* problem, but you're putting your problem onto somebody else, namely, the public. Or flying out of New York, you try to do that from the West Coast, and you're already beat before you start flying. If you want to fly out of New York, live there. And if the public wants to be safe about that issue, then they've got something to give too. If you're going to talk safety, you've got to talk about that issue."

Northwest pilots Jim and Joyce Kennedy struggled to make commuting work for them as a two-pilot family and finally settled on living in Boston and spending summers on the eastern tip of Long Island, where Joyce was born. On a hot August day Jim Kennedy arrives home after having just driven his battered pickup three hours through heavy summer traffic from La Guardia Airport. Before that he had flown from Detroit to New York, dead-heading in the cockpit of a packed 737. Before that he flew copilot on a Northwest Airlines DC-9 from Detroit to San Francisco. The day before he had been in bed with the flu. On this hot and humid day, he wears an old plaid cotton shirt hanging outside a pair of nondescript brown slacks and beat-up loafers.

"Daddy, daddy," his five-year-old daughter shouts, as she dances in pink leotards toward his truck. "Daddy, daddy, let's go swimming." Ten minutes later Jim Kennedy has changed into his bathing suit and is standing ankle deep in an inflatable plastic swimming pool, bailing out pine needles with a metal kitchen colander. After a few moments of semifutile effort, he looks up and says sheepishly, "Well, I guess we're going to have consider changing the water." He grins, not unlike any suburban father spending a summer Saturday with his family, anticipating the barbecue that will come later and perhaps a bedtime story beneath a big pine tree.

For Jim and Joyce Kennedy, however, such moments are far from commonplace, far from as casual as they seem. Among a number of two-career piloting families, they have had to work hard to carve out the time for their personal life. Although the Kennedys' life-style has been complicated by the fact that they both fly, Joyce, especially, went to great lengths to fly the schedules that allow her time with her family and finally decided that it would be best to take some time off until her youngest child is older. "I used to fly either two-day trips or I'd leave at four and come back at four the next day," says Kennedy. "Once in a while I'd fly a nice three-day trip, where I'd leave late the first day and come back early the third day. But most likely I'd fly what we call illegal overnights. I'd leave Detroit at eight-thirty or nine-thirty at night and fly to Albany or Providence or somewhere like that and get in at eleven that night. Then I'd leave at seven the next morning, which means I'm leaving the hotel about five-thirty or six-thirty to fly back to Detroit; and I'd be done at eight-thirty in the morning. I'd do that three nights in a row, and I'd be off four days. It was very tiring because I was only getting four or five hours of sleep, but what I did is I caught up doing naps.

"They call it an illegal overnight because we're on duty all night. Normally when you go on a two-day trip, for example, when you check into the hotel you're off-duty and you get a ten-hour rest or whatever and then you go on-duty the next day because you have to have at least a ten-hour break. You're getting paid while you're on-duty the first day, and you're getting paid while you're on-duty the second day. On an illegal overnight, however, you don't get that ten-hour rest. You're considered to be on-duty all night long, so you're getting paid all night long [duty pay, which is a smaller percentage of flight pay].

"All the flight attendants on those trips are mothers; it's just like our own little airline at night. But I'd be home every day. I'd be there to take my kids to preschool. I could pick them up. I could make all the daily functions. Luckily at that time I had a girl living with me; I could take naps, and she could take the kids out. Jim doesn't like it when I fly those overnights because he says I get too tired—and it's true. I get very bored because you don't go anywhere and you don't do a lot of flying. But it works out nice being a parent with that kind of schedule."

Like Kennedy, Lisa Johnson is married. She has a small daughter. Johnson doesn't have to cope with commuting, however, and says she finds no special challenge in combining marriage and a flying career. Holding her little girl on one hip, stirring her oatmeal and talking on the phone at the same time, she appraises her future plans. "I'm going to stay on the DC-10 for a while; I could be flying 727 copilot with my seniority. I could be a very senior copilot in Chicago, Denver, or San Francisco. But I won't commute, not with a child. And I've seen too many divorces with people who have commuted. I could commute and fly the 737 and be very senior and have all Los Angeles layovers, and it sounds good, but then I would never have that private time that I really cherish.

"When I'm on a trip, I love to go to a hotel room and order room service and just watch TV or read a book or do my needle-point, just do *exactly* what I want to do—make my phone calls, catch up. When I get home I don't even think about the job. I don't talk airplanes. In fact there are still people that have known us for years who come up to me and say, 'I just found out you're a pilot; all these years, I thought you were a flight attendant.' I definitely think flying helps a marriage. It gives us time away. We have the time to breathe apart, and then whatever the incident was doesn't seem as big as it originally was." She pauses a moment, straightens her uniform tie, and then laughs, "There are definitely times when I have three days off or if I'm on vacation or something and I think, 'Oh my God, when am I going back to work? I need a trip.'

"My husband was almost forty when we got married, so he was

pretty much a confirmed bachelor, and I've never liked anyone who tried to tie me down to a point where I felt that I was uncomfortable or I was not still free. And I don't mean free to go out with other people; I mean free to pursue my career. It's a little hard at times being away from my little girl; she's almost three. She woke up the other day and saw the uniform, and she said, 'Mommy's going to the airport.' And I said 'Yes.' And she said, 'Why?' I said, 'Because Mommy's going to work today, and I'll see you tomorrow right after lunch.' She said, 'Oh, okay,' and she was fine. So she knows; when the uniform goes on. . . . It's a way of life."

Although Johnson and Kennedy make light of it, women who fly face considerable challenges in managing the different facets of their lives. Most men seem to find flying an enjoyable life-style, especially those whose wives don't work outside the home. "It's not hard to raise a family and be a pilot," says Bob Scott. "In fact, I've probably spent more time with my kids than anybody else in the neighborhood. My neighbors used to think I was a bum, because I never seemed to work. I was always out there doing my landscaping, putting in the irrigation system. The woman I dated and then married lived in what they called a 'stew zoo' just off Midway Airport in Chicago. It was a virtual haven for a bunch of single guys. The stews at that time were all adventuresome, shall I say. You'd usually end up flying with them for a month, and you'd get pretty well acquainted. I had five years on the airline, and it liked to kill me. I was a couple months shy of being thirty when I finally got married, and when I finally made the decision, it was a good one. My wife makes the home so pleasant that I'm happy to turn around and come home as soon as I get in. I *want* to come home to her.

"I took good care of my kids. I think maybe my wife thinks I was a little hard on them, especially the first one, but now maybe she realizes I wasn't. I look at my boy as not just my son, but my very good friend. And I think he thinks of me in the same way. And that makes me feel good. We have a good rapport, we always have. From the beginning, I knew Greg was very mechanically inclined. He'd come to me with a broken toy, and I'd say, 'Okay, let's take it apart and see if we can fix it.' We find the time to talk frequently. It's the type of rapport that I always hoped to have with my kids."

"I think flying helps a marriage," says Ted Goff. "It lets you get out and let's you have a little peace and quiet and be alone and just kind of rejuvenate yourself. I think rather than being a home-wrecker, flying gives the family a little time to be by themselves. Not everybody likes that, of course. Some people can live without their spouse being there all the time, and some people can't. In our case, it gave my wife some time to be at home without me underfoot. It's worse being married and alone than it is being single and alone. I really enjoy life the way it is. When I retire, I'm going down to Mexico and drink beer and fish and take up smoking again. . . ." His eyes flash, and he grins.

American flight engineer Max Neeland got married *because* he flies. "Eileen and I met on a blind date. One of the guys that I run with had been vacationing in the Caribbean and met Eileen down there. He told me that he and his wife thought she was real special. About three weeks later, when I ended up with a Virgin Islands trip on my schedule, I called my friend. He insisted that we were perfect for each other, and he called Eileen and set up the introduction. We both almost backed out at the last minute. She told me later that she liked the sound of my voice on the phone. Once we began seeing each other seriously and became engaged, her friends were constantly giving her a hard time about marrying a pilot. I guess it just proves that we really do have a bad image, probably second only to sailors."

"I have a tendency to try and establish a relationship if I'm going to be flying to a place like New York for months on end," says Ted Goff, talking about layover time. "If you're going to spend a lot of time there, you'd like to find somebody. How do you find somebody like that? Well, jeez, I don't know, department stores—you know—clerks. I see somebody I'm interested in, and I ask her out. This month I've been flying Sacramento the first night, Chicago the second night, Anchorage the third night. That's not a particularly good trip. How do you find somebody in Anchorage? That's a problem. Actually, there's a couple of girls I would like to date up there, but I've never run into the occasion where I can ask them out properly. . . . You go in and out of the airport at Fairbanks enough, and pretty soon you recognize quite a few of the employees and you say, 'Hey, little girl, you wanna get a Coca-Cola?' "

Goff says he remembers the old days, when layovers were less a chance to rest between trips than an excuse to have a good time. "You carried a bottle in your suitcase, and when you got where you were going, you partied. I don't think that stuff happens much anymore. The way we fly now, the pilots' and flight attendants' sequences are always different. Booze used to be a big deal. Everybody used to drink, back in the old days—twenty years, fifteen years ago. I don't know when the transition happened, but we don't drink anymore. You don't get guys going out partying and drinking all night long. Back then, whenever you got someplace, you'd have a long layover, and everybody'd just have a big party.

"Now drugs, I don't know anybody that does drugs anymore. There are guys I think maybe did some marijuana, but I don't know anybody that does cocaine or even marijuana now—even the flight attendants. I'm maybe a little naive about stuff like that, and I'm sure there's maybe a lot of coke around—but I don't know anybody that does it. Given the percentage of the general population, there's got to be some, huh?"

Partially due to the image Max Neeland and Ted Goff allude to, the specter of alcohol and substance abuse looms large in the aviation industry. Not surprisingly, NTSB accident reports always include a section on the health of personnel involved and notation as to whether their performance was in any way impaired by alcohol or by illegal or prescription drugs. Bob Scott defends the industry on this subject. "First of all, we *have* a drug-free cockpit. We don't have problems with that. We don't have an alcohol problem either. However, we are a cross section, and believe me, we have people who have an alcohol problem. But they don't get in the cockpit. If they don't turn themselves in, we will. It's as simple as that."

"Alcohol is a problem," says Craig Donlevy solemnly, "because it affects performance. In other jobs you can function and be under the influence. We honestly haven't run into drugs yet, but we all know it's coming. Because the new generation of pilots coming along have been into drugs. Pilots have enough money to buy designer drugs, and I don't know why frankly more of them aren't into it. Drugs are harder to detect; it will be a whole new learning curve for all of us. And, yes, I think they're more dangerous than alcohol in the cockpit from the little I know about it.

"We've tried studying about it and gone to seminars and things like that, and I still know precious little. . . . The only control we have on alcoholism at the moment is liver enzymes, but before it gets to liver enzymes, we catch them. So maybe that's the answer right there. If a guy was abusing cocaine, before it affected his job performance, we'd know about it. At least that's my great hope. I think coke happens so much faster, especially if you're into crack. Crack is right now. Last week I wasn't and this week I am. I suppose that sounds naive as hell. I think we're going to have to grope our way along and develop a strategy and a plan just like we have done with alcoholism."

The strategy relative to alcoholism that Donlevy alludes to has become a model for the aviation industry. The program and the need for it are something with which Bud McKenzie is intimately familiar. McKenzie has been a pilot for United Airlines for almost thirty years. He enjoys his job and has a comfortable bachelor's lifestyle. He owns a small but well-furnished home, a vintage Jaguar that he is restoring, and a four-wheel-drive truck. He has plenty of time to spend hiking, skiing, and walking on the beaches he likes so much. McKenzie almost lost it, however, because for over half the time he has flown for United, Bud McKenzie was a practicing alcoholic.

"In the service," says McKenzie, "it was drink and fly, fly and drink. It was exactly like Yaeger said—the whole scene. Historically it goes back to a tremendous mystique from World War II and the fighter pilot. That kind of flying is a high-energy, constant go-go kind of operation, and you have to have a respectable amount of ego, especially when you're new. So when Yaeger talks about riding motorcycles in the desert when you're blitzed, I've been through experiences like that.

"In later years there were times when I absolutely had no memory of being drunk, because of the blackouts. Generally the business of feeling good was the target, the old 'let's have a couple of drinks and relax.' Which was the way it was for many, many years. . . . Blackouts can happen to people in cars; they can happen to people walking down the street; they can happen anytime.

"What does that say for somebody who's a drinking alcoholic and flying? It seems there's a lot of potential for a person being on duty in a blackout. We've had that happen to people. The one case I can think of—this guy is now retired medically—but years ago he described himself as having done a checklist in a blackout on a flight to Los Angeles from the East, and he woke up or came out of it with the checklist in his hand. He had no memory of what had happened before that, although apparently he had operated on a completely normal basis during the flight. The captain didn't know. In another incident the pilot who showed up in Vegas some years ago, who walked into the office ready to fly, must have been in a blackout. Somebody got to him before he got on the airplane.

"The state of aviation and alcoholism is really in a preventive mode right now in terms of identifying people who need help and helping them, although it can be tricky. The individual is usually totally deluded about the reality of his or her situation. So what we in the employee assistance field do—and we do very effectively—is we listen for specific kinds of comments, and we pay attention to how people operate. Everything, from personal appearance—the condition of a person's uniform, for example—to their driving record, which is a good parameter.

"There's no procedure for automatically screening pilots who have drunk-driving convictions. However, there are some guidelines from the National Council on Alcoholism. For example, if you've been arrested once for drunk driving, and it's an isolated case—you're coming home from a party and you have 0.12 points of alcohol in your blood—and you're clear for five years, the chances are you'll probably never do it again; you've learned your lesson. But in most of the cases where a person gets arrested for drunk driving, they're arrested again within a year.

"Years ago before there was anything like employee assistance programs [EAP] or any alcoholism or chemical dependency treatment facilities, if a commercial pilot showed up for duty while under the influence, it was automatic that he was fired. There was no appeal whatsoever. So the attitude toward that has changed, and I think that's good. The old attitude drove people underground. In my case, it was one of those things where I would drink too much on the airplane dead-heading home after a flight. Finally one night someone saw me get off the employee tram; I slipped. After that, they began putting two and two together; then they looked up my record and found the two DUIs. With the support of an employee assistance representative, I checked myself into a detox facility, and it became my business to get sober."

How does a pilot who is a practicing alcoholic regulate his or her drinking so as to never show up drunk? McKenzie ponders that thought a moment. "It's tough to do," he replies matter-of-factly. "The way we talk about it in AA, it's the hardest job we've ever had. When I used to set two clocks to wake up in the morning, I did it for a reason. Not just because I thought the hotel wouldn't give me a wake-up call. I was afraid I was going to oversleep because I was drinking too much the night before. I usually drank by myself. At home I drank with my wife; we drank a lot together. That's not to excuse my drinking at all.

"Generally on out-of-town trips I drank in bars, very often by myself, or I'd buy a six-pack of beer and take it back to the hotel room. It was a series of continual efforts to feel better and avoid dealing with what was going on inside me. I drank because I didn't know how to deal with myself, how to interact at a comfortable, normal level, as most people do. I needed to be propelled into a sense of being comfortable by drinking.

"I managed somehow. I never connected things up. I never connected why it was I felt so fatigued, for example. I remember one schedule in particular. We'd get up at two A.M. in Hartford and we'd go to Chicago, and then we'd go to San Francisco, and then dead-head home, so by the time I got home, it was four o'clock in the afternoon, San Francisco time. I'd go to the gym; I'd get in the sauna. I'd do all sorts of things to try to ward off this fatigue. It was incredible. In the beginning, drinking may help you sleep, but later on, as you do more and more of it, it keeps you awake. Four hours after you have a couple of beers, or six beers, or whatever you have, your body's going to tell you, 'I need more.' I also think part of the fatigue that I felt came from a sense of guilt, a sense of doing something that wasn't right, not operating within the twenty-four-hour rule, which is what we had at that time. All sorts of excuses come up in that area. You try to convince yourself by using rational-izations like, 'Other people never pay attention to it' or 'Besides, it's ridiculous.' Which of course it was, for normal drinkers."

Currently FAA regulations prohibit a pilot from drinking within an eight-hour window before the scheduled departure of a trip. Previously the limit had been set at twenty-four hours. Among pilot folklore the story circulates that the FAA regulation was changed because an FAA inspector and a pilot who had been drinking together the night before caught each other within the FAA window when the inspector showed up for a check ride with the pilot the next day. The FAA limits are minimums; each airline is free to set its own standards. American Airlines continues to maintain a twenty-four-hour rule, although American pilots concede it's probably the most frequently broken regulation in the company. United thinks twelve hours is safer than eight.

"Why does the FAA say only eight hours?" asks Bob Scott, with a sigh. "Who knows why the FAA does anything. But again you have to remember that they're dealing with minimum standards. Some people dissipate alcohol faster, so we felt that twenty-four hours would take care of everybody. Maybe within eight hours some people are still going to be drunk as a skunk, while with others, it's gone. Generally I'm suspicious of whether a guy can hold his liquor and eight hours later get onto a plane and fly the thing full of five hundred passengers. I personally don't think so. Twelve hours?

Maybe, but I personally feel it should be twenty-four. As far as I'm concerned, the public's impression that twenty-four hours is the rule is pretty well respected by pilots and by other people who know them. Their friends don't say, 'Naw, go ahead and have a drink.'"

What is the goal of prohibiting people from drinking during a certain amount of time before they fly? "I think mainly their judgment and their skills," says Bud McKenzie. "The speed with which they can absorb quick radio transmissions and things like that. If they need to act quickly, they may not be able to; they may be a little bit slow. As far as the physiological affects of alcohol on flying are concerned, the first thing that happens is that the person who's drinking would rather be someplace else. Even if they're not actually under the influence, they may feel uncomfortable either emotionally or perhaps mentally. They might be feeling bad because they've got a hangover. Those kinds of things, or a combination of those things, will probably serve to make a person apprehensive and wanting to be someplace else—what I call edgy. And flying an airplane and wanting to be someplace else is not a good combination. In fact that's a good parameter for picking out a person who may be a candidate for our program. You can feel that kind of tension."

"My feeling about alcoholics," says Craig Donlevy, speaking about how his company's employee assistance program identifies alcoholic pilots who are still drinking and flying, "is that less than fifty percent come to us. That's not something that an alcoholic does, anyhow. He thinks, 'I don't have a problem. Why are you talking to me about this? I don't have a problem. I can stop drinking any time I want to. If I had a problem I'd come to you, but I don't have a problem.' We don't necessarily have to wait for the whole mosaic to reveal itself in order to identify a person as a possible alcoholic. The EAP committee, which is composed of two pilot representatives, someone from management, and a full-time employee assistance person as well as the company doctor, will consider a number of different factors and come to a consensus on a need for professional evaluation if the person comes to our attention either through our efforts or by identifying himself, which happens—although only once in a great while.

"With alcoholism we don't act on a single source, and we don't act quickly, because we know if there's something really there, we're going to continue to hear about it. The same thing can be said about psychological problems. At first it may be that you hear that a guy is eccentric, and then maybe the stories get worse and worse and worse. But we've got some good people to help us with this. We've got a staff psychiatrist that works with us in Denver who's very helpful. He does the evaluations for us; he lets us know in a level-headed, commonsense way what's going on with an individual who may be having problems and what maybe we can do to help them.

"We've got EAP reps scattered around all nine domiciles, which is good, because they listen to people. Sometimes people just want to come in and vent. You can see it on their faces; it's like, 'Please, will somebody just listen?' But if it goes beyond that, they have the capability of referring them to good, qualified people. I think our EAP reps have a good rapport with most employees. Unfortunately, they don't with the pilots, except for alcohol, because again it's not macho for a man to come in and admit he has a problem he can't handle. And that's too bad, because it's hard to fix a problem yourself. So I just don't think we're attuned enough to *all* the problems in the pilot group as we should be.

"It's somewhat difficult to define behavior that we look for that might be a symptom of a problem. I know it may seem funny that a couple of guys would be talking about something like that, but a change of behavior in a person is a major thing. And because we don't have in-house management watching this group of employees all the time, I think we have to rely on others to tell us these sorts of things. The problem is that nine times out of ten there is no major problem, and often you get desensitized, with the result that the person that's really hurting out there finally just goes underground, and we never know about him or her.

"Ideally our employee assistance group really ought to focus beyond alcohol, so that we can identify more people with problems. I'm constantly concerned, and we're constantly trying to remind ourselves that we're not just an alcohol program; we're a program that takes care of people generally. We have gotten so good with the alcoholism that we've become susceptible to tunnel vision. But I'm concerned, as we get better and better in the alcohol program, that the rest of the problems end up falling by the wayside, and our efforts aren't as holistic as maybe they should be."

Bud McKenzie considers the effects of the problems Donlevy brings up. "In terms of the challenges in aviation, I would rank alcoholism among pilots number three as a serious threat to air safety," he says carefully. "The first is overall human factors. That's always your number one liability. Because we're all exposed to liabilities of human factors, that is negative performance or poor performance on the part of any given person on the ground or in the air. That encompasses a lot of people. The number two liability is air traffic control, specifically the problem of midair collisions. And then I would say alcoholism and drug misuse or abuse among pilots would be probably number three.

"Based on what the national average is in our overall population, the latest I heard is that nine to ten people out of every one hundred in any cross section of our population are alcoholic. So if you translate those numbers to the airlines, it seems to fit that there are some pilots out there who still need to be identified. They may not be flying and drinking at the same time. They may be drinking and their life may be controlled by booze when they're off-duty, but what we want to do is prevent them getting to the job while under the influence, either directly or indirectly.

"There are still some airlines that are dragging their feet. There are still some other industries that are dragging their feet, some in which the executive office is filled with alcoholics. But time will take care of that."

• • •

In January 1993, as part of an action to reduce its work force by twenty-eight hundred people, United Airlines terminated its nine full-time employee assistant representatives and their immediate staffs.

CHAPTER 9

Crew Interaction

In twenty-eight years it's never happened to me that things have gotten so tense in the cockpit that people ended up shouting at each other. In a few instances, I've witnessed or experienced some low levels of tension. I have, however, heard people talk about incidents like one in which a second officer, who decided he'd had enough of this captain, asked him to step outside when the airplane landed.

—BUD McKENZIE, United Airlines
DC-10 captain

A

heavy Great Lakes storm blanketed the dingy airport buildings with snow and dampened the sound of traffic; the air hung cold and damp. Because of the wind, visibility was poor, and the snowblowers had been called out to clear the runways. At O'Hare International Airport, airplanes of all types were stacked up on the taxiways, their auxillary power units running to keep hot air flowing to the cabins. High-tension cross-chatter filled the airwaves between the planes and ground control. Pressed by scheduling demands, pilots badgered controllers for information. Air traffic control had shut down the airport, however, until the runways could be cleared and visibility increased.

Even under these conditions, some of the people gathered at the Westin Hotel, close to the Chicago airport, given the chance, would have opted to be out there in the cockpit of one of the delayed planes. Being battered by weather and with a load of anxious passengers would have been easier to take than sitting in an overheated conference room at seven-forty-five in the morning.

The small room was packed, and a low murmur greeted latecomers, a combination of the rustle of self-conscious voices making small talk, papers being shuffled, and cups and saucers clinked together in the familiar ritual of early morning coffee. The mood was strained. Unsure of themselves, some of the participants were anxious about what lay ahead. Some had arrived prepared; others felt off-balance because they hadn't done the assigned "homework." Some were present because they were required to be, even though they were theoretically opposed to what they thought would be expected of them.

At eight o'clock sharp, Capt. John Staitsman walked purposefully down the center aisle between the tables. He was a solid-looking man, tall and with a heavy build, dressed in a conservative black-and-white checked sports coat, well-pressed gray slacks, and matching gray tie and pocket handkerchief. The latecomers and hard-core coffee drinkers moved to take their seats. Another man in a well-cut brown suit followed Staitsman and then walked around the room distributing papers and urging people to get settled.

From behind a podium in the front of the room, John Staitsman began his remarks. "The airline industry has known for many years now that mechanical failures have pretty much been designed out of airplanes. That doesn't mean we never have a mechanical problem, but that generally our airplanes fly and will continue to fly. Why then do we have accidents? We have accidents because crews faced with a problem diagnose it incorrectly or make the wrong decision about what to do about it. The Eastern L-1011 in the Everglades is a classic example of a crew that concentrated on the twenty-nine-cent light bulb while the autopilot kicked off, and the airplane descended into the swamp. Or take our own accident in Portland in '78—the plane that ran out of fuel because, in essence, the captain was waiting for the flight attendants to finish preparing the cabin for what he thought was going to be an emergency landing. Well, he got his emergency landing all right, because they ran out of gas."

Staitsman paused to allow his remarks time to be absorbed. There was a faint buzz in the room; people shifted position, fiddled with the pencils set out in front of them. Most kept their gaze focused straight ahead on the podium where Staitsman continued his remarks. "And yet we know the copilot and engineer in that plane obviously realized the fuel state was something less than ideal. They mentioned this to the captain in a very tentative way. They really never got his attention, and he never really made a decision. He just let the fuel run out." Staitsman paused and looked at the sea of faces before him. There was little reaction from the room.

"So how do you address all of this? There's conjecture that the copilot and the engineer were waiting for the captain to save them, as he always had. They probably didn't want to say too much because of the type of person they perceived him to be, right or wrong. They might have thought he'd bite their heads off. Maybe they thought they might upset him. What they didn't think about was the probable outcome of the events in which they were participating. What if they *had* challenged the captain? In reality, probably the worst thing that could happen to them—or you—in a case like that would be an audience in front of the chief pilot or perhaps counseling. But look at the other side of it. The worst thing that could happen is you're dead. *And* you take a bunch of people with you."

It was an uncomfortable thought. The room rustled again; people shifted in their chairs, reshuffled papers, fiddled with spoons and coffee cups. Staitsman smiled brightly. "So if you look at it in that light, you'll say, 'Well, maybe this is worth a shot.' What we had in this situation is a two-pronged problem—the captain not listening and the crew not being able to get out what they wanted to say to him. You can't change a person's way of doing things; I can't change your way of doing things. But I can change *mine*. This is not a program to make everybody do the same thing. The idea here is to help you see how you react in different situations and show you some strategies for avoiding these types of confrontations. The whole idea is to aid you in making decisions and taking action in a crisis situation by understanding not only who *you* are and what you do, but also the other people involved."

Pilots in a classroom talking attitude adjustment and new-age sensitivity training? Yes, and more. Cockpit management programs designed to inspire better coordination among flight crews, streamline cockpit procedures, and minimize pilot-induced error have become more common in the aviation industry. As human factors experts have warned about the liabilities of automation, and as cockpit tapes have revealed lapses in communication between crew members in vital situations, the major carriers have been forced to deal with a subject to which they had previously given little attention: human nature.

To many it might seem that this realization is long overdue; that it's taken far too long to overcome the image of the take-charge, self-reliant aviator battling all adversity to bring his aircraft safely home. One pilot/one decision may have worked forty years ago when airplanes were slower and much less automated and the copilot was considered an apprentice rather than an integral member of the flight crew. But today, in this complex age of aviation, it cannot be assumed that each man or woman who walks through the cockpit door will have the right mix of flying and management skills needed to make things work. While pilots agree that they must put aside personal distractions in order to concentrate on their work, unfortunately few have either the training or skills to be able to do so effectively.

A variety of factors makes this difficult for pilots. As Craig Donlevy has noted, pilots as a group tend to be reticent about discussing their personal problems and may themselves be out of touch with what is bothering them. Pilots have high expectations for themselves and tend to expect the same of others. John Staitsman, who enjoys telling stories from his cockpit resource management seminars, also mentions that, because pilots are trained to interface with complex machinery rather than people and to be independent and act on their own, they tend to be fairly rigid and have a somewhat mechanistic view of human nature. Bill Fredericks has suggested that it is part of the pilot mind-set not to suffer fools lightly and that to believe fervently in one's personal abilities and capacity to make decisions in tight situations. And as other observers have noted, and pilots have corroborated, flying requires a strong ego, which, in a position of authority, can result in unilateral communication, from the person in charge *down* to the subordinates. Trained to respect procedure and the importance of routine, some pilots are also short on adaptability skills.

It seems likely, therefore, that when it comes to what the psychologists call interpersonal relationships, pilots are at a disadvantage. In addition, changes in commercial aviation in the last decade or so have complicated cockpit relationships—what pilots see as more demanding flight schedules; hassles about salary and compensation; calls to activism through strikes and other labor actions; challenges associated with learning new, technology-driven airplanes; women in the cockpit; younger, less-experienced crews; and mergers of pilot groups because of a takeover or buyout. Dealing with such upheaval can be difficult for people who prefer things to be predictable and routine.

John Staitsman left his job as a line pilot to join his company's cockpit management program. He has become knowledgeable not only about the variables that affect his own pilot group but about the problems of other carriers and what is being done in aviation and other industries to increase employee efficiency and reduce error. "Of course there are altercations in the cockpit," says Staitsman, as he attempts to explain the need for the type of program he has helped develop. "We had a captain who knew he had a problem with interpersonal behavior; he was just an abrasive person. Actually his actions weren't nearly as bad as he came across, but he came across bad. And he just didn't realize it a lot of times. He'd catch himself, but often too late. One day as they were taxiing out for takeoff, he said something very curt to the second officer and something very rude to the copilot. They got clearance for takeoff, but the copilot told the tower, 'Negative, we're going to pull off to the side.'

"The captain asked him what he was doing, and the copilot said, 'We're going to pull over, we're going to park this thing, and we're going to talk.' So the captain pulled the plane over, probably thinking that he'd never been talked to that way by a crew member.

The copilot asked, 'Do you realize what you've done in the last forty-five or fifty seconds? You've chewed out the engineer for something that is absolutely uncalled for. You just misunderstood what he said. You insulted me, and that's inexcusable. We've got to resolve this because I'm not a part of your crew right now, and I don't think he is either.'

"The captain thought a moment and admitted, 'You're right. Nobody ever said that to me before. You're absolutely right. I shouldn't have done that. I'm sorry.' After that, he actually started seeing a psychiatrist to help him in his interpersonal relationships. He told me the psychiatrist told him, number one, that he is such a perfectionist that he expects everybody else to do things exactly the way he does it. Number two, he doesn't tell people how he wants things done. He waits until they do it the wrong way three or four times and then blows up, rather than telling them what he wants in the first place. He'd sit there and steam and stew and get upset. His adrenaline would go up and his blood pressure would go up and then, when they'd do it wrong for the fourth or fifth time, he'd explode and only *then* tell them how he wanted things done.

"This guy told me that what the psychiatrist said was probably one of the best things anybody ever did for him. He said, 'Now when somebody does something I don't want them to do, or that I don't like, I tell them I'd really appreciate it if they did it this or that way. It's amazing how much better I get along with people.'"

"If you don't get along with the flight engineer," says Ted Goff, "there's not much harm done there, but if you don't get along with the captain, you're going to have some problems. It's not so much disputes, it's lack of communication in all areas—in flying, in assisting you—whatever. If you don't get along with this guy you're sitting next to, you're just going to be pissed off at him the whole damn time instead of paying attention to business."

"The important thing is the interaction of the crew in an emergency situation," says Bud McKenzie, "when you have not been trained specifically for all you're dealing with. You can't possibly be trained for everything; you can only train for elements of a given situation. But when you're facing a lot of unknown things as a crew, that's what really brings out how well you are performing from a human factors standpoint. What also brings it out is operating on a very, very long trip or an overnight trip, where everyone is tired and you're operating on your reserve energy—every bit of fiber that you have—to get you there safely.

"There is a great deal of concern among the airlines about attitudes toward the captain's authority, including the captains themselves, specifically a fear of erosion of that authority, either because other crew members aren't respectful or because the captain has not used his authority in a responsible way. The business about team players can work both ways. The only people I've seen who have gotten into trouble with captains or other crew members are those who for some reason don't want to be part of a team or don't realize it's important to be part of a team. I think that's a profile situation rather than human nature, because you have some people who are perpetual fighter pilots. And that's not how we operate."

"The morale in the cockpit is so important," says Joyce Kennedy. "People don't realize the morale in the cockpit's going to make the difference between missing something on a checklist or not, for example. It can really make a difference if there's an emergency. I flew for a three-day trip last month with a guy who so was so pissed off. He made the trip miserable. His attitude and morale were just so low that he was like spring-loaded. He was ticked at the company over the fuel situation; he was ticked about flight times. I did not think this guy should be flying. He was a nervous wreck. He was doing his job, but he was mad. And I could see how his anger was affecting him. I could see how anger could affect any two pilots that have differences of opinions."

Kennedy attributes some of the strain she speaks about to adjustments required in the Northwest–Republic merger. Similarly, Pete Browner thinks changes in management philosophy under Texas Air affected pilot performance at Eastern Airlines. "Pilots are pretty good stress managers in the cockpit," says Browner. "We're taught through training and through the simulators, through years of experience flying the airplane, how to handle that thing probably in the worst of conditions and with lots of nasty stuff. I don't know that we manage stress too well out of the cockpit. I think when a pilot doesn't feel or isn't sure that he has some control over his destiny, he doesn't like it very well. He feels very uncomfortable with it. And I think this is where a lot of the guys are having trouble.

"As a result of the appearance of this new and induced stress at Eastern—for lack of a better word, we'll call it *stress*—after we saw this absolute unheard of change in management philosophy, and we saw what it was doing to the pilots, ALPA commissioned a study. Because you don't want pilots in the cockpit preoccupied with problems at home and the problems of whether or not the company is going to be there tomorrow. It's much nicer that they devote their complete attention to flying the airplane. . . . One of the wives called up deeply concerned about her husband because he would come home from a three-day trip and lock himself in his room for a whole day. Wouldn't speak to anybody—not the kids, not his wife, no one. The man needs help, and we got it for him. *We'll* take care of the guys who the pressure's getting too heavy for."

"It was the FAA's Allan McArtor," says John Staitsman, "who said that pilots don't kill people, crews kill people. That's usually what it is. It's how a crew works together or fails to do so that causes problems. A single pilot might be able to let a problem go and fly the airplane and get it on the ground just fine. But as soon as you have crews, they start to talk about things; everyone gets involved; they get out the books and go through checklists and then everybody ignores the real mission, which is to keep the airplane in the air and get it down."

Staitsman puts a historical perspective on the development of programs that acknowledge the human component in the cockpit. "[In the seventies] the airplanes were getting better and better and better, to the point that up around sixty to seventy-five percent of accidents and incidents had nothing to do with mechanics, in that the airplane flew and would have continued to fly. It was the crew trying to solve the problem that crashed, even though the airplane was airworthy. Up until the seventies, there wasn't any training about chain of command. Most captains would tell the rest of the crew that they should speak up if they saw anything they didn't like. But there was no real language for this, and it was easy enough to do unless you were in a tight situation. Because it was a very informal thing and not structured, we could go through dozens and dozens of accidents, all of which involved a failure of the crew to talk about what the problem was." Staitsman pauses and recounts accidents that he thinks were caused by these conditions. "Like the TWA accident at Roundhill, Virginia. The airplane was given clearance to descend and was cleared for the approach, and the crew made the assumption that they could now descend to the minimum altitude, as opposed to following altitudes on the chart or questioning the directions. As I recall, the voice recorder indicated that someone did question that the terrain altitude on the chart didn't seem to fit with what they'd been given. But it was kind of dismissed out of hand, and they hit the hill. The United cargo plane is another case of nobody flying the airplane." (Staitsman is referring to the incident

Bill Fredericks described, in which a cargo plane flew into a Utah mountain.)

Aside from crew coordination and communication problems, there is also the troubling issue of what might or might not be bothering a pilot on any given day, and the role of other crew members under such circumstances. Staitsman explains, "If you show up with a cold today and you're not feeling well and you should have called in sick but you didn't, you might just kind of drop out of the loop. Your kid just got a speeding ticket, your wife is ill, you've got an IRS audit on Wednesday, and you might fly that whole trip as just kind of a cipher. Your mind is going through all of these things. You're not a bad person; you're not a bad pilot, but today on this trip, there are stresses upon you that make you not really involved.

"It's important for the other crew members to see this. They are supposed to take up the slack in such a situation—make the decisions for someone who's not with it—but most importantly, they're supposed to try to shake him out of it. That's one of the most important skills we try to teach—being able to face people and ask if everything's okay; to say something to the individual who's acting funny like, 'You're not the guy I knew; you're not with it.' And for the other person to respond, 'You know, you're right. I'm going to call the crew desk at the next stop and get off.' Or 'I'm going to put that behind me. I didn't realize that it was affecting my work that much, and I'm going to get on with it.'

"It's not an easy thing to do. Or the tougher one is maybe I got a tax audit and my wife is sick and my kid just got a traffic ticket and instead of being complacent and out of it, I'm furious. I'm in my own little world where I'm going to do what I want to do, and it doesn't matter the help that the crew tries to give me. The tough thing is for my copilot or engineer to say, 'Do you realize what you're doing to the rest of us? You're just cutting us out.' That's a tough thing to do and a very difficult thing to say."

"The idea is not that you're challenging the captain's authority," says Bud McKenzie, speaking about what he's learned in cockpit resource training and with the insights gained from his work in the airline's employee assistance program. "But it's important that the ultimate decision, whatever the situation, reflect the input of other crew members, regardless of the experience level, because on any given day we can all, even highly trained people, react very differently to the very same situation. In other words, the captain does have the final authority, and he does have the role of the decision maker, but the process that leads up to the making of that decision is critical. You have to have a lot of give-and-take, back-and-forth communication. That's a thing that I'm very big on, communication.

"I can tell very quickly even before we leave the flight office and certainly within a few minutes in the airplane how a fellow is going to operate on the basis of his attitude. That's something that comes with experience. I tend to give somebody who is not participating something to do if that's what I think he needs. I have a preference personally to look for anything that's positive and bring that out and try to avoid any kind of negativity within the situation. I'm a little unique in that respect in that in a comparable situation on the ground, I probably wouldn't be as tolerant. It's a necessary professional attitude in terms of looking at the priorities that affect the operation at the moment and dealing with them that way. In other words, bringing everyone's area of focus, including my own, back to where it should be—on flying the airplane.

"Teamwork—that's one of the words I usually use if I get a new crew member. I'll chat with him and the other crew members for about a minute—that's all it takes—just to give him a general idea of how we operate. Not how *I* operate; it's a *we* situation. I tell everyone to remember they're part of the team. Each person can save an airplane as well as anyone else, and it's important that each person participate and speak up. No one person in the cockpit knows more than the three of us put together.

"I had a new second officer on the DC-10 when I first started. He was a little bit edgy, and he told me he was new on the airplane, and I said, 'Congratulations, so am I.' I just turned to him and told him—the copilot was listening—I said, 'Remember, you're part of this team, and it's important that you participate and speak up. Because I'll have the comfort of knowing that you're participating. And you'll have the comfort of knowing that I receive input from you.' So those are my personal preferences in terms of establishing an attitude or a philosophy for people who have not worked with me before. And it seems to work pretty well."

In describing his profession, Brad Prescott talks about pilots always being in a take-charge mode, especially captains. Prescott's image implies a multidimensional individual, someone who has the scope and interpersonal skills as well as the talent and intelligence to be a leader. Unfortunately, this ideal combination of characteristics is not always present in those individuals who choose to be pilots. In fact, one aspect of pilots' limitations is their sometimes-restricted world view.

"Pilots aren't politically attuned," says Stan Page. "Pilots think that right is right and wrong is wrong and all of those things. Motherhood and apple pie. Only when it comes to them on a personal level do they get involved or try to understand the problem."

Craig Donlevy thinks of it another way. "A pilot's image isn't as important to him as it should be," says Donlevy. "Although I really think in the last ten years things have gotten better. They don't look as klutzy; you don't see so much the stripes and the plaids together. The half glasses are still standard—see, they're practical. There are a lot of little social things that pilots in general are not trained about, etiquette, just being polite. It's like they learned all their etiquette in the Old Oak Club. 'Pass her over here; have another beer.' That's the era. We changed our brown uniforms to blue years ago, and we've got one guy here who still wears his old brown uniform pants when he's not on duty. He comes in here in the flight office like that. Guys still have their old uniform shirts. Give me a break. I don't even paint in mine. But it shows the technician in them. They're real practical people with real practical solutions. The shirt fits, it's still usable, it covers him up, and nobody will notice. The sad part of it is everybody notices, and nobody says anything. If somebody said something, that would be the end of it."

"We have our choices of three different uniform fabrics," laughs young American Airlines flight engineer Max Neeland, "and this is another good one that tells a little about the mentality of pilots. You can either get a polyester, a typical worsted wool suit fabric, or what they call a tropical wool blend, which is a very lightweight wool. From a distance, they all appear about the same. They're the same color. The polyester's about $100 cheaper, and surprisingly, a lot of the guys have the polyester. You can tell because they have a shine about them. It's the same blue, but the polyester sort of glistens.

"The typical pilot outfit on a layover is his uniform shoes, his uniform pants, and the worst polyester knit shirt, about two sizes too small. Thank heaven we have to wear uniforms, though, because if guys were allowed to choose what they wanted to wear to work it would be embarrassing. You really see it when you go back to the flight academy in Dallas where we get our check rides and our training. I sit there in the cafeteria and watch the guys file in, and it's unbelievable, it's truly unbelievable. Where they find those polyester pants and shirts and the ties. Maybe it gets back down to the fact that some of them came from small towns and never really developed much of a sense of what was classy."

"Pilots are not secure unless they're in their own environment," says Donlevy, "and their environment is not necessarily inside the airplane; it's inside the cockpit. I don't see that pilots in general treat flight attendants the way they should, for example. Most of them won't even call them flight attendants. The call them "stews." And the male flight attendants don't appreciate it when pilots say, 'The girls in the back.' That hurts. That hurts them a lot. I'm learning slowly to change my vocabulary, and I am as sensitive as anybody.

"And if you sit a pilot down and try to talk to him about it, he doesn't even know that he's being insensitive. He really doesn't. Flight attendants will be civil, but they're biting their tongues. I've watched it; it's like watching a train wreck. And once it's done, it's done. Flight attendants don't necessarily respect pilots. Period. How would you like it if we'd just met, literally just met, how would you like it if I pinched your butt? Absolutely, they still do that. They just don't know how to act in public. Sometimes I just want to shake them.

"Is that a potential safety problem? Only if we won't get the early call that something's going on in the back. That's what worries me. When the problem is still small and certainly not insurmountable by the flight attendants, they may not let the pilot know in a timely fashion. A very small fire, for instance—I want to know right away so we can get it out, whereas they may not think about telling me. If pilots don't establish the rapport of being somebody that really cares about what's going on in the back, and if we don't keep reinforcing that as a group, this kind of attitude is going to continue.

"And it doesn't take very many like that and the reputation starts to precede itself. You can tell immediately; somebody like Bud McKenzie comes in and says to a flight attendant, 'How are you today?' and tries to be civil; I honestly see this happening to Bud. He comes in to the flight attendant briefing, and here's this flight attendant who's got this glare in her eyes, and her fists are up because of the last crew she flew with. And Bud says, 'How are you? The flight's going to be this long and that sort of thing.' And she says 'Okay,' and that's about it. And Bud thinks, 'Okay, if that's the way it is,' and he goes into the cockpit. It's built up, not just from the last flight; it's built up from flight after flight after flight."

Donlevy's remarks about pilots and flight attendants suggest the potential for similar male-female problems in cockpit relations. "I think," says Max Neeland, "the image people have of pilots is based on the fact that the bulk of the early commercial flyers were from a military background. They carried with them the kind of an attitude that was bred in the military, especially at the enlisted-man level, where you have a couple of thousand guys based somewhere relatively isolated and out of touch with the normal social situations. What happened is they developed a different attitude about dealing with women.

"As a result, on the airlines it's very common to see in the military bunch a kind of social ineptness, an inability to deal with women on an equal basis. And that brings to mind a picture of those guys cooped up on an aircraft carrier or on a South Sea island. Their talk is centered around sex and what they're going to do on their next leave. The mentality just mushrooms; it gets blown out of proportion, and it sticks with them for the remainder of their lives. I think the younger group has grown up in an atmosphere with a much more liberated attitude toward women than what these guys have. The older guys, they're heavy chauvinist and don't treat women with a lot of respect. And most of them don't have a clue about what it's like to be in a comfortable social situation with women."

"As a group, pilots are rednecks," says Donlevy. "You're dealing with an all-male world in which, until very recently, females weren't allowed. And many pilots still tend to have that macho attitude that leads them to think, albeit a bit defensively, that a woman can't do this job. But it's interesting that although they may be philosophically or theoretically opposed to the idea of women flying airplanes, they seem to be able to make exceptions on a one-to-one basis. If you ask them, 'In general, what do you think about women flying?' they'll tell you, 'Oh, I don't like them, but so-and-so, *she's* okay.'"

"You have to realize a lot of men pilots don't have respect for women as professionals," says Ann Alexander. "They think of women as someone they pick up in a bar or their wife or their children. They've never really worked with a woman before, unless it was as a station agent or a flight attendant. My experience, however, is that at every airline that I've worked for, almost everybody has treated me as a professional, as somebody who knows her job.

"I know I have flown with men who do not like women pilots; I know because I've heard it through the grapevine. I happened to overhear one of the guys I flew with talking to another pilot after our trip. The other guy said, 'Oh, you had a woman pilot; that must have been a real joy.' And the captain said, 'Actually it went real well. I would never have believed it, but it went real well.'

"I've only once come across a really bad, prejudiced attitude, flying with someone that I will probably never fly with ever again. He was one of these guys who couldn't understand why I was hired and all of his friends were still walking the streets. I found out later he was like that to all the copilots; he just used the gender as an excuse to see how much he could intimidate me. Every time I did something in the cockpit, he'd double-check it. It got to a point where I just said, 'Hey, I'm really sorry. I can't seem to do anything right here, can I?' And I might have walked off the airplane if we'd been at the gate.

"He eventually wrote a letter on me. I was still on probation, and as it turned out I never saw the letter. I guess the chief pilot called in about four other captains that I'd flown with. And when one of the guys who I will be forever thankful for found out about it, that I was just this close to getting fired, he called up a couple of the people that he knew that I'd flown with and said, 'You'd better go in and talk to the chief pilot right away.' It was a horrible feeling, some of the things that were said.

"What I learned from that is how I will *not* be as a captain. When I make captain, I will make sure that if I have a problem with someone, I will sit down and talk with them about it, and if we can't figure it out between the two of us after we've talked about it, then I might write a letter.

"I think it's up to the woman to have the right attitude to begin with. If you go into the cockpit with the attitude of, 'They're going to have to like me whether they like it or not, and I don't want you to swear in here, and I don't appreciate off-color jokes, and you say one thing against women and you're going to get popped in the mouth,' then you're asking for trouble. I always give the man the benefit of the doubt. Maybe he doesn't care whether you're a man or a woman. Or maybe it's just such a new experience for him that it takes him a few days to get used to it. I think mostly they are judging me on an individual basis about my piloting ability, because I have heard a couple of comments like, 'Boy, she is really a good stick,' or 'Nice gal, good pilot, nice gal.'"

Like Alexander, Lisa Johnson has encountered a mixture of intolerance and understanding from male pilots with whom she has flown. "When I went to introduce myself at the beginning of the month, this captain shook my hand and squeezed it as hard as he could possibly squeeze it, and he said, 'I'm going to do everything I can to make sure that you are fired before your probationary year. Women should not be flying.' I knew I just had to be strong. I had to be quiet, and I had to do my job and try not to say a word in the airplane. But I didn't really know how to handle all the rest of the stuff he was giving me, so I went into the office and talked to my flight manager, who was maybe ten years older than I am but just a wonderful guy. He told me, 'You're doing everything just fine. The biggest thing is, don't cry. Don't get upset, don't yell back. Just sit back, be as quiet as you can. Do your job. Let's just get you through your probation year without any problems.'

"We have these big plastic cards that the engineer writes the takeoff and landing information on for the guys up front. One day the captain threw it back at me because he wanted different information on it, and he hit me with it. The copilot almost got out of his seat at one stop and hit him. I said, 'Oh God, Jim, please don't do this; it's just going to make everything worse.' Jim couldn't stand it, however, and he went in the office and told them that this guy was driving us both nuts.

"So what they did is they took me off the next trip and they put a check engineer on. And the check engineer wound up writing the captain up because of all of these things he did wrong flying-wise. Meanwhile, the captain wrote a letter to the office about what he thought I was doing wrong and how women should not be flying. And they called him in and they said, 'We have these two letters. Now, we can process them both, and go through interviews, and discuss the whole situation with each of you, or we can trash them both.' And they trashed them both. I never knew this until my probationary year was up."

Joyce Kennedy took her biggest beating as a corporate pilot. "The chief pilot told me, 'Your ass is mine now.' These were his exact words my first day on the job. And all I'm thinking is, 'Jet time, jet time.' My clothes weren't appropriate, my boots weren't appropriate. My car wasn't appropriate. I had a '65 Mustang. They all had 'Vettes. I had to take everybody out for breakfast before a trip, and for the first two weeks I didn't realize I couldn't put that on my expense report. I had to carry everybody's bags. I had to put down the right sugarless chewing gum on their console on the left side. I didn't think it was for real."

From behind the desk in his office, John Staitsman continues his explanation of the evolution of cockpit resource management programs. "In the midseventies, they knew the problem existed, but they didn't really have the facts and the data and hadn't done the research. United had something I think called a *command course,* the gist of which was a course for captains on how to lead. But just like any project without a real goal or any guidance, it just sort of fell apart. And then the Portland accident occurred, and the NTSB recommended, among other things, that airlines should have assertiveness training for crew members." Staitsman is referring to the 1978 crash of a United DC-8 on approach to Portland airport. There was what looked like a problem with the landing gear, and the crew circled for an hour while they tried to deal with the emergency, and the flight attendants prepared the passengers for landing. They circled too long, however, and when the captain finally decided it was time to land, the engines had run out of fuel. According to the NTSB report, the cause of the accident was the captain's failure to properly monitor the aircraft's fuel and to heed his crew member's advice. But, as Staitsman suggests, there was more to it than that. The NTSB also cited the failure of the 2 crew members to communicate their concerns to the captain. The crash of the plane six miles from the airport resulted in the death of 8 passengers, the flight engineer, and a flight attendant and serious injuries to 21 passengers and 2 crew members.

"You can hear on the voice recorder from that accident that it was obvious that the copilot and the engineer were not comfortable with what was going on," says Staitsman, "but they really didn't get it out in such a way that they got a response from the captain. We did a training tape of that incident that combines the tower tapes with a little video. I must have seen that thing five or six times, and every time that airplane makes that last turn away from the airport, my heart just sinks. Because you just know that this time when you watch the tape, the guy's going to pull it out of the bag. But he never does; he always makes that last turn away from Portland. And the adrenaline starts to pump, and you say, 'Oh God, why did he do that?'

"The ideal captain will get as much information as he can get. The ideal crew will give as much information as they can give. They then resolve whatever conflict exists, because if you have an idea and I have an idea about how to do something, we have conflict. It doesn't mean that you're going to punch me out or vice versa. But when we have two different ideas of how to do something, what we have by definition is conflict. Now, how do we resolve that? We resolve it in the time available by getting some more information.

"The crews find that when they begin to talk about something, it brings up something they read in their manual or something they had in their last performance check, and they say, 'Yeah, I know how this works.' If they hadn't talked about it, it's unlikely that it would ever have come up. So they resolve the conflict, the captain makes the decision, and then if they have time they should critique that decision.

"I know that in the years since I've been doing this, I've had several occasions where I felt like I was diving off this high board. You take a deep breath before you say the words, and then you turn to the guy next to you and say, 'Do you realize what you're doing?' And when he asks you what you mean, you say, 'Well, do you realize that you jumped all over that flight attendant for nothing? She was right and you were wrong.' And then you sit back and say to yourself, 'Please, I hope this works.'

"In that particular incident, the guy said, 'You know, you're right. You're absolutely right.' And he picked up the intercom and called her up and apologized. That was not an easy thing for me to do. I'm sure it wasn't an easy thing for him to call her up and apologize. But I know that I'm never going to be in jeopardy of being a mutinous crew member as long as I have my facts together. It's ridiculous to think that a pilot is going to get on an airplane every time he or she flies a trip and not be affected by the things that are going on in their life."

Has the FAA caught up with the fact that this is a substantial problem? "Yeah," says Staitsman, "but the problem is whether they will go as far as they should with this. We have excellent support from the FAA and the NTSB. . . . And I will freely give away stuff. We're trying to save lives here. This is not the kind of thing where you hoard your information.

"But I think what's going to happen is that the FAA is going to come up with a proposal that all airlines have a program like this. Because what's going to happen is the airlines—not United, not American, not Delta, well, maybe Delta—they're going to do the minimum they can get away with. I hope they come up with a program that's good enough, and that it's not a one-day lecture. Because those things don't work. They just don't have the impact of sitting there going through one of these seminars like we do here."

•   •   •

The fifty-nine men and one woman in the Chicago hotel had gotten off to a slow start; John Staitsman introduced the exercise by explaining his own experience. "I lost entire sight of the objective of the exercise," he began, looking out at the roomful of serious faces in front of him. "I resolved to do well for my team, and I just pommeled the poor other guy. The idea of the exercise is to work with the other person in order to reach the right answer. That should be obvious, right?" A vague murmur of agreement rose from the group. Staitsman waited for the sound to subside and then said, "Not to me, it wasn't. My idea was to go out and *show* the other guy. The best answer was of no consequence to me. Winning was. We get into that with our spouses, we get into that with our friends. We get into that between ethnic groups, between political groups—you name it. It doesn't matter what the facts are; the real facts are I don't like you and I'm going to win. I may not even know who you are. I don't know whether I like you or not, but I'm still going to win. I'm going to win because I want *you* to lose. That's the point I'm bringing out. When you get involved in these win-lose things, even if I don't particularly want to win, I sure don't want *you* to win.

"My experience with this was one of the most life-changing things I've gone through. I was the most dumfounded person in the world to realize that I had fallen into this trap *and* to realize that I might be doing the same thing in the airplane."

Having concluded his introductory remarks, Staitsman went on to provide the group with a hypothetical situation similar to what might happen on an actual flight. The exercise was organized so each table of participants would be considered a team, or crew, each with an elected leader who would argue its position with his or her counterpart from another table. The two leaders would be required to bargain to achieve a solution to the given problem. Their score would be tallied, and if they failed to reach agreement, both teams would be scored zero for their efforts.

After some deliberation, the first pair of seminar participants rose to report that they had managed to agree on a solution to the problem; the second team, a man and woman, did the same. However, the third pair, two middle-aged pilots with similar backgrounds flying international routes, indicated they had not been able to agree. When Staitsman asked for their conclusion, the younger of the two answered, "Well, sir, we don't have an answer yet." The older man nodded his agreement.

"Then you get a zero, two zeros, one for each of you," said Staitsman with a flourish.

"But you can't do that," snapped the older man.

"Too bad," said Staitsman. "I just did it. You're out of time. If you'll notice, there're two zeros up there."

"All we need is a couple more seconds," argued the younger.

"You ran out of time," Staitsman repeated, adding, "You knew how long you had to do this, and you knew you had to give me a decision of some kind on this. But you don't have it, you ran out of gas."

There was silence in the room as the three men stared at each other. Finally the younger man spoke. "Well, it's really not important." The remark was just what John Staitsman had been waiting for. "Why didn't you reach a decision, then? If it means nothing to you, why didn't you let the other guy make the decision? Why didn't you say, 'Go ahead, make whatever decision you want, and I'll go along with it?'"

The younger man didn't answer, but the older man made a futile attempt at defense. "You can't do this," he said harshly.

"I can't?" blinked Staitsman. "Just watch me," and with that he took a piece of chalk and double-underlined the two zeros already up on the board. Furious now, the younger man glared back, "I couldn't do it because *he* kept saying no to everything I said." As he spoke, he pointed accusingly at his partner. The other man responded angrily, "That's not true. It's you, you're the one who screwed it up." The younger man stood up, threw his pencil on the table, looked straight at his partner, and said, "I've known you for twenty years now, and you know what? I never realized you were such an asshole." Both men stopped, looked at each other, and then at John Staitsman. The room was hushed as the rest of the participants stared. "Ah," said Staitsman, watching the reaction of the other pilots, "I can see the wheels turning." He went on to briefly explain to the two men what they had done, after which they returned to their tables, chastened. The remaining pairs gave their scores, and finally the group broke for dinner.

After they had eaten, one of the men raised his hand to comment. "I don't know how many of us I'm speaking for," he began, "but I think some of us feel that we could do a lot better on these exercises if we had more time." A murmur of agreement followed from the others. Encouraged, he continued, "And if the seminar days were shorter, we could be more alert. His remarks brought more agreement. Somewhere in the back of the room someone clapped briefly.

John Staitsman thanked him for his suggestion and watched the man, hero for a moment, sit back down in his chair. "Anyone else feel that way?" Staitsman asked. A few participants showed their hands, not as brave now that they were singled out. "Good," he answered quickly, as if he had been lying in wait for someone to ask that very question. "The seminar days are long intentionally, for two reasons. One, it keeps you out of schedule for less time, and the other is related to what we want to do in this seminar. There's no question that as you get tired, your tolerance drops, along with some of your defenses. Everyone wants to come in here and be a great guy. You don't want to step on anybody's toes. You would die before you insulted somebody. You've done a lot, you've answered questions, you've written papers, and you're getting tired and maybe getting a little crabby. But what's it going to be like in the airplane?

"I had a guy last time—somebody told him that they thought he was wrong about something, and he shot back at them, 'What do you mean, I'm wrong? This is right, take it or leave it.' Now he would never have done that in the beginning, but he was tired and cranky, and what he wanted was to go to bed. In the airplane it's the same way. When we get complaints that it's a long day, I always think, 'Yeah, so? It's fourteen hours to Hong Kong.'

"We all know the toughest part of any flight is the approach and landing. Research tells us that the traces for pulse rate and blood pressure and respiration rate are down—relatively normal—during the cruise part of the flight, but the lower that airplane gets, the higher these things go and the wilder they get. So here you are, you've flown for fourteen hours, on the wrong side of the clock, in stale air with a guy that doesn't smell good, eating airline food, drinking too much coffee. But none of that matters, because now you have to perform, even though it's at the wrong end of that whole thing.

"Those poor guys flying to Hong Kong, I'm sure they would really rather be in bed than flying this approach into Hong Kong with the mountains around after a fourteen-hour flight. Of course they would. They'd be stupid if they said, 'Hey, man, this is living. I love this. Bring on the rain. Crank up that crosswind.' I really doubt they say that. In fact what they do is before the descent they get up, have an apple, walk around, do a couple of exercises, get the blood flowing again, so they're ready to shoot that approach that's coming up in twenty minutes or half an hour.

"But here we are in a hotel room in Chicago, where you have three decent meals a day. You get a chance to get up and walk around once in a while, and you're not cramped in that thing with bad air and a guy that smells bad and all that. And you're going to tell me you've had a long day. You tell me, 'We could do better work, we could learn more, if we had more rest.' Part of what we're trying to teach here is that you have to perform sometimes in conditions that really aren't what you want. Part of this is so you'll learn something about how you operate when you get tired, when you get cranky."

Satisfied he had made his point, Staitsman finished and took a few questions from the floor as he prepared for the next exercise. At a table toward the back of the room, two men sat talking. The first looked fairly bright and alert, the other tired and annoyed. The second man had taken his glasses off and put them on the table; with his right hand he ran his fingers back and forth through his hair. The two men had been on the same team throughout the day and both had been active contributors to the discussion and had a positive influence on their groups. However, the second man had become strangely quiet as the evening wore on. He was now sitting straight in his chair, his back tense, staring across the room. For ten minutes the other man watched him carefully, trying to analyze what his friend's body language meant.

"Who are you looking at?" he asked, as he followed the direction of the other's gaze.

"See that clown over there in the corner?" the tired man answered. "I don't know his name, but he's really getting to me."

"Why is that?"

"He's got a big mouth and he doesn't say anything. He just talks a lot." The tired man put his glasses back on as if to get a better look at the offender.

"Oh, really?" his friend answered patiently. "Just take your eyes off him."

"I can't," the man responded impatiently. "He gives me tight jaws."

Bud McKenzie, laughed. But he knew what his friend meant. "Well, at least he's not in the cockpit," he thought to himself as he patted his buddy on the back. Beyond them the exercises continued. Outside, the wind was quiet, and it had stopped snowing.

EPILOGUE

On August 9, 1990, Frank Lorenzo resigned his position as chairman of the board of Texas Air Corporation. In doing so, he signed a noncompete clause that restrained him from working in the airline business for seven years. On January, 18, 1991, Pete Browner lost his job at Eastern Airlines. After six years of Texas International management, the airline that had been known as a pilots' airline and an aviation institution finally succumbed to a long succession of pressures it was unable to overcome. In March 1991, Midway Airlines, one of the most successful of the deregulation niche carriers, filed for chapter eleven protection. On February 23, 1991, America West, a similar airline serving the West Coast, had done the same. On November 7, 1991, unable to meet its obligations, Midway ceased operations.

In August of that same year, USAir, thought to be one of the more stable of the conglomerate airlines since deregulation, announced that its profits were down and that it was suffering from diminution in its cash flow, prompting analysts to predict that it may only be a matter of time until USAir, too, bites the dust. And in November 1991, Pan American planes based in Europe took off and headed for home for the last time.

During that same period, Stephen Wolf, chairman of UAL, the parent company of United Airlines, explained to the press that the major reason the company's quarter earnings were down was because United competes on many of its routes with airlines that are operating under chapter eleven bankruptcy protection. They lower their fares, said Wolf, in order to get people on the planes so they can keep flying. In order to compete, United, although healthy, has to do the same. It doesn't make for a good bottom line.

Pete Browner was recently presented with a citation from the Air Line Pilots Association president acknowledging his twenty years of safety work on behalf of the union. Today, Browner is currently working as a full-time aviation safety consultant, a far cry from the cockpit. Hank Barnes and Bob Scott have each retired from flying. Barnes is pursuing an interest in working with inner city youth, and Scott is still involved in aviation safety issues. Craig Donlevy is still working his magic in the employee assistance field, and John Staitsman is enthusiastically training pilots. Jim Kennedy is now flying out of Boston instead of Detroit. Joyce is still on leave. Lisa Johnson and her family recently moved into a larger house in Brentwood west of Los Angeles. Ted Goff is still flying and still wooing the ladies. Stan Page continues to keep a watchful eye on Continental management.

Having survived the PSA–USAir merger, Ann Alexander has cause to worry again about the future of her adopted carrier, USAir. Sandra Luft continues to hold her own at Continental. Max Neeland is still looking forward to the newest technology, and Dick Riley is another year closer to having to fly the heavy equipment. Indefatigable Bill Fredericks is still worrying about fatigue, and Rex Chamberlain continues to be concerned about flight crews and automation. Greg Scott is now a copilot on the DC-10 and has flown with Bud McKenzie. McKenzie has recently upgraded to captain on the Boeing 747-400. Jason Young has married; he and his wife are expecting a child, and he supplements his B-scale salary teaching flying. Brad Prescott decided to stay in the Los Angeles area where he is based and bought a house in Fawnskin in the local mountains.

In its January 11, 1993, issue, *Aviation Week*, an industry trade publication, reported that commercial aviation has lost over four billion dollars in the last two years. In February 1993, the "MacNeil/ Lehrer NewsHour" on PBS described the industry as losing more money in the last few years than it has made in profit since its inception.

In February 1993, Frank Lorenzo, the man whose name has become synonymous with deregulation, announced that the restrictions had been lifted on the 1990 noncompete clause barring him from commercial aviation and that he would soon be back in the commercial airline business.

And so much has changed and nothing has changed. Many of the fundamental issues remain to be addressed.

"We're just a case study," says Ted Goff. "The personal

motivation and greed of people who run the airlines today. . . . They seem to stress that more than building a country like our forefathers did. It's a game, and the government wants to let them play it. And people buy tickets. What can you do?"

"We'll talk with anyone who may be an avenue to get the information out," says Bob Scott, who now and again serves as an unofficial pilot spokesperson. "We can see things that need to be straightened out. And we are frustrated by the inaction of the FAA, our own companies, and people that are standing in the way of our motherhood—safety. I think if people realized what we're trying to say, if they get the message, they will help us effect the changes that we see are needed."

Perhaps their words, well-spoken here, will help.

ABBREVIATIONS

ALPA Air Line Pilots Association
ATC Air Traffic Control
CAB Civilian Aeronautics Board
DME Distance Measuring Device
FAA Federal Aviation Administration
FAR Federal Aviation Regulation
IFR Instrument Flight Rules
ILS Instrument Landing System
INS Inertial Navigation System
MEL Minimum Equipment List
MMEL Master Minimum Equipment List
NASA National Aeronautics and Space Administration
NTSB National Transportation Safety Board
TCA Terminal Control Area
VFR Visual Flight Rules
VOR Very High Frequency Omni-Range Radio

BIBLIOGRAPHY

The following list of sources is by no means exhaustive. It is meant as an introduction for the casual reader and a place to begin for the more serious investigator.

AVIATION HISTORY

Berstein, Aaron. 1990. *Grounded: Frank Lorenzo and the destruction of Eastern Airlines.* New York: Simon and Schuster.

Caves, Richard E. 1962. *Air transport and its regulators.* Cambridge: Harvard University Press.

Competition in the airlines: What is the public interest? A round table held on July 12, 1977. Washington: American Enterprise Institute for Public Policy.

Hopkins, George E. 1971. *The airline pilots: A study in elite unionization.* Cambridge: Harvard University Press.

_____. 1982. *Flying the line: The first half century of the Air Line Pilots Association.* Washington: Air Lines Pilots Association.

Jordan, William A. 1970. *Airline regulation in America: Effects and imperfections.* Baltimore: Johns Hopkins Press.

Meyer, John L., and Oster, Clinton V., with Clippinger, Marni. 1984. *Deregulation and the new airline entrepreneurs.* Cambridge: MIT Press.

Morrison, Steven A., and Winston, Clifford. 1986. *The economic effects of airline deregulation.* Washington: Brookings Institute.

Newhouse, John. 1982. *The sporty game.* New York: Knopf.

Sampson, Anthony. 1984. *Empires of the sky: The politics, contests and cartels of world airlines.* New York: Random House.

Solberg, Carl. 1979. *Conquest of the skies: A history of commercial aviation in America.* Boston: Little, Brown and Co.

Sterling, Robert J. 1974. *Maverick: The story of Robert Six and Continental Airlines.* New York: Doubleday.

_____. 1980. *From captain to the colonel: An informal history of Eastern*

Airlines. New York: Dial Press.

Whitehouse, Arch. 1971. *The sky's the limit: A history of the U.S. airlines.* New York: Macmillian.

Whitnak, David R. 1966. *Safer skyways: Federal control of aviation 1926–1966.* Ames: Iowa State University Press.

DEREGULATION

Bock, Gordon. 1987. Is this any way to run an airline? *Time.* Nov. 23: 55–65.

Dallos, Robert. 1987a. Pan Am has history of being first. *Los Angeles Times.* Dec. 11: IV-4.

_____. 1987b. New linkups in the sky. *Los Angeles Times.* Dec. 27: IV-1.

_____. 1988. Pilot power. *Los Angeles Times.* May 29: IV-1.

Dallos, Robert, and Lichtblau, Eric. 1988. Lorenzo buckles his belt for Texas Air bumpy ride. *Los Angeles Times.* April 25: I-1.

Dempsey, Paul Stephen. 1991. The disaster of airline deregulation. *Wall Street Journal.* May 9: A-15.

Dubin, Reggi Ann. 1988. Fixing the system. *American Way.* Aug. 1: 68–73.

Easterbrook, George. 1987. Lorenzo braves the air waves. *New York Times Magazine.* Nov. 29: 17–19.

Egan, Timothy. 1991. Air traffic controllers fight stress and savor it. *New York Times.* Feb. 10: 14.

Ellis, James E., and Schine, Eric. 1990. On a wing and a prayer at McDonnell Douglas. *Business Week.* July 30: 23.

Englade, Kenneth F. 1988. Better managers in the friendly skies. *Across the Board.* June: 37–45.

Fotos, Christopher. 1990. Labor relations putting U.S. airlines at crossroads. *Aviation Week and Space Technology.* Dec. 24: 56–57.

Gibney, Frank, Jr. 1988. Southwest's friendly skies. *Newsweek.* May 30: 49.

Hunt, Morton. 1987. Was man meant to fly? *New York Times Magazine.* Nov. 1: 42–43.

Jenkins, Holman, Jr. 1987. Coffee, tea or crisis. *The Washington Times—Insight.* Oct. 26: 8–17.

Kelly, Kevin, and Zeller, Wendy. 1991. Dogfight: United and American battle for global supremacy. *Business Week.* Jan. 21: 54–62.

Kelly, Kevin, Rothman, Andrea, and Payne, Seth. 1992. The seatbelt sign flashes for KLM and Northwest. *Business Week.* Nov. 30: 80.

Kolcum, Edward H. 1991. Airline mainstay Eastern stops flying after 62 years. *Aviation Week and Space Technology.* Jan. 28: 64–66.

Lohr, Steve. 1991. War and recession speed up the airlines' flights to oblivion. *New York Times.* Feb. 17: E-5.

Ott, James. 1990. New trend toward partnerships reshaping world airline industry. *Aviation Week and Space Technology.* Dec. 24: 55–56.

_____. 1993. Massive airline losses force draconian cuts. *Aviation Week and Space Technology.* Jan. 11: 30–31.

Shifrin, Carole, A. 1991. British Aviation Agency urges end to rule limiting airlines at Heathrow. *Aviation Week and Space Technology.* Jan. 28: 66–68.

Stockton, William. 1988. Trouble in the cockpit: The airlines tackle pilot error. *New York Times Magazine.* Mar. 27: 39–41.

Uchitelle, Louis. 1991. Off course: What happened to America's airlines? *New York Times Magazine.* Sept. 1: 12–17.

TECHNOLOGY AND AIR SAFETY

Air Force Studies Board—National Research Council. 1982. *Automation in combat aircraft.* Washington, D.C.: National Academy Press.

Belian, J. R., Rosenblatt, L. S., Hetherington, N. W., et al. 1972. Human performance in the aviation environment. NASA Contract NAS2–6657.

Bergeron, H. P. 1981. Single pilot IFR autopilot complexity/benefit tradeoff study. *Journal of Aircraft.* 18: 705–706.

Boehm-David, D. A., Curry, R. E., Wiener, E. L., and Harrison, R. L. 1983. Human factors of flight deck automation: Report on a NASA-industry workshop. *Ergonomics.* 26: 953–961.

Coates, G. D., Brown, B. R., and Morgan, B. B. 1974. Interactions of circadian rhythm with the effects of continuous work on sleep II. *Proc. 18th Annual Meeting Human Factors Society,* Huntsville, Alabama.

Connor, T. M., and Hamilton, C. W. 1980. Evaluation of safety programs with respect to causes of air carrier accidents, ASP-80-1. Columbus, Ohio: Battelle Columbus Laboratories.

Edwards, E. 1977. Automation in civil transport aircraft. *Applied Ergonomics.* 8: 194–198.

Fenz, W. D., and Craig, J. G. 1972. Autonomic arousal and performance during sixty hours of sleep deprivation. *Percep. Motor Skills.* 34: 543–553.

Foushee, H. C. 1984. Dyads and triads at 35,000 feet: Factors affecting group process and aircrew performance. *American Psychologist.* 39: 885–893.

Friedman, J., Globus, G., Huntley, A., et al. 1977. Performance and mood changes during and after gradual sleep reduction. *Psychophysiology.* 14: 246–250.

Gannett, J. R. 1982. The pilot and the flight management system. In

Behavioral Objectives in Aviation Automated Systems Symposium. Warrendale, Penn.: Society of Automotive Engineers.

Gartner, W. B., and Murphy, M. R. 1976. Pilot workload and fatigue: A critical survey of concepts and assessment techniques. (NASA Tech. Note TN D-8365.) Moffett Field, Calif.: NASA-Ames Research Center.

Hamilton, P., Wilkinson, R. T., and Edwards, R. S. 1972. A study of four days partial sleep deprivation. In *Aspects of Human Efficiency: Diurnal Rhythm and Loss of Sleep,* edited by W. P. Colquhoun. London: English Universities Press.

Hartman, B. O., Strom, W. F., Vanderveen, J. E., et al. 1974. Operational aspects of variations in alertness. NATO Advisory Group for Aerospace Research and Development, AGARD AG-189.

Holley, D. C., Winget, C. M., DeRoshia, C. M., et al. 1981. Effects of circadian rhythm phase alternation on physiological and psychological variables: Implications to pilot performance. (NASA Tech. Memo. 81277.)

Hopkins, H. 1983. Over-dependence on automatics: The black box one man band. *International Journal of Air Safety.* 1: 343–348.

Howland, D., and Wiener, E. L. 1963. The system monitor. In *Vigilance: A Symposium,* edited by D. Bucker and J. J. McGrath. New York: McGraw-Hill.

Hurst, R., and Hurst, L. eds. 1982. *Pilot error: The human factors.* New York: Jason Aronson.

Johnson, L. C., and MacLeod, W. L. 1973. Sleep and awake behavior during gradual sleep reduction. *Percep. Motor Skills.* 36: 87–97.

Lyman, E. G., and Orlady, H. W. 1981. Fatigue and associated performance decrements in air transport operations. (NASA CR 166167.) Moffett Field, Calif.: NASA-Ames Research Center.

Mackie, R. R. ed. 1977. *Vigilance: Theory, Operational Performance and Physiological Correlates.* New York: Plenum.

Mullaney, D. J., Johnson, L. C., Naitoh, P., et al. 1977. Sleep during and after gradual sleep reduction. *Psychophysiology.* 14: 237–244.

National Transportation Safety Board. 1979(a). Aircraft Accident Report: Pacific Southwest Airlines, Inc., B-727, N533PS and Gibbs Flight Center, Inc., Cessna 172, N7711G, San Diego, California, September 25, 1978.

_____. 1979(b). Aircraft Accident Report: United Airlines, Inc., McDonnell Douglas, DC-8-61, N8082U, Portland, Oregon, December 28, 1978.

_____. 1979(c). Aircraft Accident Report: American Airlines, Inc., DC-10-10, N110AA, Chicago-O'Hare International Airport, Chicago, Illinois, May 25, 1979.

_____. 1982. Aircraft Accident Report: Air Florida, Inc., Boeing 737-222, N62AF Collision with 14th Street Bridge, Near Washington National Airport, Washington, D.C., January 13, 1982.

_____. 1986. Aircraft Accident Report: Delta Air Lines, Inc., Lockheed L-1011-385-1, N&26DA, Dallas/Fort Worth International Airport, August 2, 1985.

_____. 1987. Aircraft Accident Report: Collision of Aeronaves de Mexico, S.A. McDonnell Douglas DC-9-32, XA-JEd and Piper, PA-28181 N481F, Cerritos, California, August 31, 1986.

_____. 1988(a). Aircraft Accident Report: Northwest Airlines, Inc. McDonnell Douglas DC-9-82, N312RC, Detroit Metropolitan Wayne County Airport, Romulus, Michigan, August 16, 1987.

_____. 1988(b). Aircraft Accident Report: Continental Airlines, Inc., Flight 1713, McDonnell Douglas DC-9-14, N626TX, Stapleton International Airport, Denver, Colorado, November 15, 1987.

_____. 1990(a). Aircraft Accident Report: United Airlines Flight 811, Boeing 747-122, N4713U, Honolulu, Hawaii, February 24, 1989.

_____. 1990(b). Aircraft Accident Report. United Airlines Flight 232. McDonnell Douglas DC-10-10, Sioux Gateway Airport, Sioux City, Iowa, July 19, 1989.

Price, W. J., and Holley, D. C. 1982. Sleep loss and the crash of flight 182. *Jour. of Hum. Ergology.* Suppl: 291–301.

Taub, J. M., and Berger, R. J. 1969. Extended sleep and performance: The Rip Van Winkle effect. *Psychon. Science.* 16: 204–205.

_____. 1973. Performance and mood following variations in the length and timing of sleep. *Psychophysiology.* 10: 559–570.

_____. 1976(a). Altered sleep duration and sleep period time displacements: Effects on performance in habitual long sleepers. *Physiological Behavior.* 16: 177–184.

_____. 1976(b). Effects of acute sleep patterns alteration depend upon sleep duration. *Physiolo. Psychol.* 4: 412–420.

Taub, J. M., Globus, G. G., Phoebus, E., and Drury, R. 1971. Extended sleep and performance. *Nature.* 223: 663–664.

Warm, J. ed. 1984. *Sustained attention in human performance.* London: Wiley.

Wegmann, Hans M., Conrad, Bernhard, and Klein, Karl E. 1983. Flight, flight duty, and rest times: A comparison between the regulations of different countries. *Aviation, Space and Environmental Medicine.* March: 212–217.

Wiener, Earl L. 1985. Beyond the sterile cockpit. *Human Factors.* 1: 75–90.

_____. 1989. Human factors of advanced technology ('glass cockpit') transport aircraft. National Aeronautics and Space Administration.

Wiener, Earl L., and Nagle, David C. eds. 1980. *Human factors in aviation.* New York: Academic Press.

Wilkinson, R. T. 1969(a). Effects of up to 60 hours' sleep deprivation on different types of work. *Ergonomics.* 7: 175–182.

_____. 1969(b). Sleep deprivation: Performance tests for partial and selective sleep deprivation. *Prog. Clin. Psychol.* 8: 28–43.

Wilkinson, R. T., Edwards, R. S., and Haines, E. 1969. Performance following a night of reduced sleep. *Pyschonom. Science.* 5: 471–472.

FAA AND AIR TRAFFIC CONTROL

Billings, C. E., Grayson, R., Hecht, W., and Curry, R. E. A. 1980. Study of near midair collisions in U.S. airspace. NASA Aviation Safety Reporting System: eleventh quarterly report. (NASA Tech. Memo. 81225.) Moffett Field, Calif.: NASA-Ames Research Center.

Billings, C. E., Lauber, J. K., Funkjhouser, H., Lyman, G., and Huff, E. M. 1976. NASA Aviation Safety Reporting System, quarterly report 76-1. (NASA Tech. Memo. TM X-3445.) Moffett Field, Calif.: NASA-Ames Research Center.

Dutch Aircraft Accident Inquiry Board. 1979. Verdict of aircraft accident inquiry board regarding the accident at Los Rodeos Airport, Tenerife, Spain. The Hague: Dutch Government.

Gravat, J. 1978. Transfer of information: Not a fair exchange. *Air Line Pilot.* Feb.: 6–8.

Hart, S. G., and Loomis, L. L. 1980. Evaluation of the potential format and content of a cockpit display of traffic information. *Human Factors.* 22: 591–604.

Klass, P. J. 1979. Collision avoidance plan views diverge. *Aviation Week and Space Technology.* July 23: 70.

_____. 1980. PATCO, FAA debate ATC system safety. *Aviation Week and Space Technology.* Jan. 7: 27.

Kreifeldt, J. G. 1980. Cockpit displayed information and distributed management in air traffic control. *Human Factors.* 26: 671–691.

Morgan, L. 1970. Collision avoidance from the captain's chair. *Flying.* Jan.: 70–73.

National Transportation Safety Board. 1978. Annual Review of aircraft accident data. Washington: NTSB, Report No. NTSB-ARG-78-2, Nov. 16.

Senne, K. 1977. What happened to IPC? They renamed it ATARS. *Journal of Air Traffic Control.* July–Sept.: 12–15.

Spanish Ministry of Transport and Communication. 1978. Report of collision between PAA B-747 and KLM B-747 at Tenerife, March 27, 1977. Translation published in *Aviation Week and Space Technology.* Nov. 20 and 27.

Wiener, E. L. 1977. Controlled flight into terrain accidents: System-induced errors. *Human Factors.* 19: 171–181.

_____. 1980. Midair collisions: The accidents, the systems, and the realpolitik. *Human Factors.* 22(5): 521–533.

Zeller, A. F. 1972. Human error in the seventies. *Aerospace Medicine.* May: 492–497.